Food Justice Now!

Food Justice Now!

Deepening the Roots of Social Struggle

Joshua Sbicca

University of Minnesota Press
Minneapolis
London

Portions of chapter 2 were previously published in "These Bars Can't Hold Us Back: Plowing Incarcerated Geographies with Restorative Food Justice," *Antipode* 48 (2016): 1359–79; reprinted with permission from John Wiley and Sons. Portions of chapter 4 were previously published in "Farming While Confronting the Other: The Production and Maintenance of Boundaries in the Borderlands," *Journal of Rural Studies* 39 (2015): 1–10; reprinted with permission from Elsevier.

Published by the University of Minnesota Press
111 Third Avenue South, Suite 290
Minneapolis, MN 55401-2520
http://www.upress.umn.edu

The University of Minnesota is an equal-opportunity educator and employer.

Library of Congress Cataloging-in-Publication Data
Names: Sbicca, Joshua, author.
Title: Food justice now! : deepening the roots of social struggle / Joshua
    Sbicca.
Description: Minneapolis, MN : University of Minnesota Press, [2018] |
    Includes bibliographical references and index. |
Identifiers: LCCN 2018001588 (print) | ISBN 978-1-5179-0400-5 (hc) |
    ISBN 978-1-5179-0401-2 (pb)
Subjects: LCSH: Nutrition policy–United States. | Social justice–United
    States.
Classification: LCC TX360.U6 S25 2018 (print) | DDC 363.8/5610973–dc23
LC record available at https://lccn.loc.gov/2018001588

For Jen and Enzo

History is not the past. It is the stories we tell about the past. *How* we tell these stories—triumphantly or self-critically, metaphysically or dialectically—has a lot to do with whether we cut short or advance our evolution as human beings.

—GRACE LEE BOGGS, *THE NEXT AMERICAN REVOLUTION*

Contents

Food as Social Justice Politics

Creative efforts to rearticulate the conditions that produce inequities in the food system and what it means to practice food justice abound. Amid entrenched social antagonisms, expressed in the guise of social movements confronting neoliberal capitalism and institutional racism, the food justice movement is mobilized similarly in opposition. The difference? It uses food as a tool for social justice. This positions the movement to intervene in many conjunctures in the ongoing dialectic between food and social change.[1] Activists are aware of the challenges of bridging food justice to an array of social problems that reflect unique constellations of power and structural conditions. Yet, instead of activists seeing this diversity as a barrier, it is the inspiration for tirelessly reimagining how to increase human flourishing in the face of widespread social suffering. Over the course of five years of research, I followed this dialectical process in major California cities. What I found surprised me. The major problems confronting activists committed to food justice revolved around mass incarceration, labor exploitation, and immigration. These appear disparate upon initial inquiry, but in the eyes of activists, they are an opportunity, albeit not always realized, to use the social justice commitments that motivate food justice to radically deepen the democratic potential of food politics. In the pages that follow, I argue that food justice is the sine qua non that connects activists across a range of interests and stretches the frontiers of food politics precisely because of the resonance of food justice in broader social struggles.[2]

I first began to understand the radical potential of the food justice movement and its importance to the dialectical expansion of food politics during a hot and dry summer day in June 2012. I was building a permaculture-designed edible landscape alongside formerly incarcerated people in the small backyard of a Berkeley, California, home. This was one of hundreds of gardens built over a six-year period by an Oakland food justice organization called Planting Justice, most of which were built by formerly incarcerated people paid a living wage. During this installation, four black men who were recently released from San Quentin State Prison, one other white man, and I broke up and removed concrete, installed irrigation, assembled raised vegetable beds, spread fresh soil and mulch, and planted an assortment of fruits and vegetables. After breaking for burritos, our staple lunch that summer, we removed debris found while transforming this yard from an underutilized space into a food oasis and swept up loose soil and cardboard. We then packed up the big, blue biodiesel work truck and rumbled down the road displaying the organization's motto on a large magnet adhered to the tailgate: "Grow Food, Grow Jobs, Grow Community." My time in Oakland taught me a lot about the devastating impacts of mass incarceration on working-class black communities and about the difficulties of the prisoner reentry process. I also learned that political work across ethnoracial and class boundaries must be deliberate and sensitive to the needs of those facing systematic forms of oppression.[3] In this case, urban agriculture imagined through the lens of food justice generated a capacity to disrupt the prison pipeline.

To continue my fieldwork to learn about urban food politics in California, I left Oakland after two months to return to my home city, a place that had changed greatly since I was a child decades prior. I started farming in San Diego along the U.S.–Mexico border with a group of organic farming and local food activists and observed different strategies to distribute the food we grew to local well-to-do foodies and low-income people. I wrestled daily with the complexities of farming in an ecosystem bisected by a militarized border representing a history of boundary production, colonialism, and racial resentment. But I also found that some organic farming and local food activists hoped for the elimination of borders and a deeper embeddedness within the local ecosystem. One day, a farmer named Titus and his Rottweiler led me around the unplanted backfields of Wild Willow Farm to show me where the farm was going to expand into an area with fertile soils previously farmed by others. While explaining the prior use of the land, he also pointed out the coyote trails, which were visible because of their distinct scat, and the shallow, eroded beds of dried-up rivulets etched into the landscape. Shifting from a natural history to a social history of the space, Titus started talking about the movement of people and shared that earlier in the morning, Border Patrol agents in their cars and helicopters were chasing down border crossers: "There are many immigrant trails that run through this landscape. People have been using them for a long time; it's like the Underground Railroad." Active solidarity with those escaping slavery allowed the Underground Railroad to thrive, which set in motion future movements that fought for freedom and equality. In another way, the borderlands presented a choice of whether or how to support immigrants, such as those who end up as farmworkers in San Diego.

After five months of building gardens and farming, I moved to Los Angeles to intern with United Food and Commercial Workers (UFCW) Local 770, a hardscrabble labor union representing over thirty thousand workers. I was interested in the labor politics of the grocery retail and meatpacking industries. As an intern in the Organizing Department, I was absorbed into the planning, strategizing, campaigning, rallying, and protesting that are labor union mainstays. In this contentious environment, the union put me to use calling community partners, finding new allies in the food movement to support Black Friday strikes against Walmart, and engaging in the sticky politics of representing cannabis dispensary workers. I found that labor organizing in Los Angeles required building bridges with working-class communities of color and immigrants; first- and second-generation Latinx workers in particular make up ever-larger numbers of the labor force, especially in low-wage jobs in the food system.[4] Knowing that the labor movement could not continue to be "male, pale, and stale," UFCW 770 diversified its leadership over time.[5] Almost everyone in the Organizing Department spoke Spanish, and issues formerly peripheral to the union, such as food insecurity, were vital to building labor power. Through strategic partnerships with food justice activists and labor organizers, UFCW 770 has helped shift the conversation over food security from supply-side to demand-side solutions. As an organizer named Ann told me, "When we are talking about food justice issues . . . we can't organize up here and not tie it to, 'How do you put your food on your table?'" Their answer is that racial and economic justice are prerequisites for food justice.

As these initial anecdotes of food politics suggest, different social antagonisms structure how and whether people practice food justice. They also have practical implications for identifying how food justice ties into furthering other social justice movements. Witnessing many organizational strategies and hearing people's creative analyses left me with the distinct impression that our imagination of food politics is too narrow. Alas, I found three uniquely promising arenas for movement building: carceral politics, labor politics, and immigration politics. Each arena offers new ways to think about pressing political conjunctures as well as the political uses of food to advance social equity. Until fairly recently, food justice activists have remained within the food movement without strategically broadening their food politics to work across movement boundaries.[6] Expanding our view of food justice requires decoupling food justice from the overly simplistic idea that food itself is the site of struggle.[7] Food politics that first identify the root causes of problems and then work to tackle these problems will *then* transform people's relationship with food. My book chronicles a diversity of approaches, challenges, and opportunities associated with such a political project.

Food Justice Foundations

In many respects, the current development of food justice reflects the environmental justice movement's insistence that environmental inequalities are not ultimately about the environment but about how structural inequalities harm people as they relate to the environment.[8] Similarly, food justice is primarily concerned with oppression and inequity in the food system. Food demarcates the focus of struggle. In the first major scholarly look at what is now commonly referred to as the food justice movement, Robert Gottlieb and Anupama Joshi characterize the movement's vision as "ensuring that the benefits and risks of where, what, and how food is grown and produced, transported and distributed, and accessed and eaten are shared fairly."[9] Although a useful starting point to ascertain how people experience food injustices, and therefore open enough to account for various food justice practices, Gottlieb and Joshi's book does not offer an analysis that captures the specific structural drivers of food injustices. There is less explicit attention to colonialism, capitalism, and institutional racism.

Partially in response, Alison Alkon and Julian Agyeman use a critical race framework to contend, "Communities of color are beginning to engage in *food justice* activism in order to provide food for themselves while imagining new ecological and social relationships."[10] Their vision of this new social movement "recognizes the agrifood system as a racial project and problematizes the influence of race and class on the production, distribution, and consumption of food."[11] Yet the food system is more than a racial project; it reproduces and reflects the conditions of neoliberal capitalism and patriarchy.[12] This is where Kirsten Valentine Cadieux and Rachel Slocum draw on a wider set of political practices to synthesize four ways that food justice activism intervenes in structural inequalities. They conclude that transforming the food system requires the following:

1. Acknowledging and confronting historical, collective social trauma and persistent race, gender, and class inequalities
2. Designing exchange mechanisms that build communal reliance and control
3. Creating innovative ways to control, use, share, own, manage, and conceive of land, and ecologies in general, that place them outside the speculative market and the rationale of extraction
4. Pursuing labor relations that guarantee a minimum income and are neither alienating nor dependent on (unpaid) social reproduction by women.[13]

This vision opens the possibility for diagnosing many forms of oppression that influence and are the target of food justice activism.

Debates over what counts as food justice expose different emphases and therefore the political stakes. This is important because the radical hopes for the food justice movement do not always reflect actual food justice activism in the United States and Canada. Food justice organizations tend to focus on increasing access to healthy, affordable, and culturally appropriate food, many through empowerment strategies to get low-income communities of color involved with urban agriculture. Those with radical political ideologies and programs seeking to transform the food system are the exception or are unrecognized.[14] To bridge this gap through praxis requires seeing that food justice activism does not take place in a food system vacuum free from other social forces. Perhaps more to the point, clarifying the relationship between economic, political, and social contexts and food justice struggles can help identify cross-movement linkages. From an analytical perspective, food justice activists and scholars tend to share the conviction that it is necessary to eradicate oppression in the food system. This is the basis upon which to examine and theorize the possibilities for integrating the insights and strategies of different social justice struggles.

Food Justice Now! asks several key questions about the development, practice, and potential of food justice–oriented food politics. First, what are some of the historical antecedents to the food justice wing of the food movement? When considering that food justice is at core a critique of and call to eliminate structural inequalities in the food system, many previous social justice movements have influenced contemporary articulations of food justice. This social movement spillover effect roots food justice in the past while opening new possibilities going forward.[15] Relatedly, how do activists interpret contemporary conjunctures through food? Neoliberal capitalism, postsettler colonial conditions, and institutional racism intersect in complex ways to produce interrelated social problems. Many food justice activists evaluate their work through the resulting problems to deduce a strategic course of action. Third, what economic, political, and social alternatives can a dialectical analysis of food justice help interpret and imagine? Approaching food justice in this way is useful precisely because food justice struggles transform many relations of subordination into sites of antagonistic food politics aimed at eliminating oppression. Last, can an expansive notion and practice of food justice create a diverse political platform that inspires new social struggles? The future of the food justice movement requires reading food justice activism against the heterogeneity of contemporary conjunctures. Responding strategically to address these contexts strengthens the political position of food justice. Food justice activists are therefore in the unique position to adapt ideologically and push the food movement to expand in new directions.

Food Justice Futures: Recovering History and the Terrain of the Conjunctural

In 2010, organizers at Planting Justice articulated their theory of social change and approach to food justice. They used the metaphor "compost the empire" to inspire the belief that oppression never lasts because it produces conditions that people resist and use to build more equitable societies. Empire, understood as the modes of capitalism, imperialism, and institutional racism that oppress and stratify social groups, is not totalizing. Instead, it is an ongoing process open to recognizing the commonality of oppression across different crises. As opposed to reducing crises to universals of "class" or "race," the variegation of empire creates opportunities to advance social equity through recognizing, reimagining, and reassembling the particular. While oppression is ubiquitous, how it manifests allows for unique interventions. For Planting Justice, the analysis leads to engaging in food politics that reclaim farming, gardening, and eating to intervene in mass incarceration to advance economic and racial justice. Their paper reads in part,

> By emphasizing the "systems" approach to our food justice work, we make visible the limitations of many contemporary food-related movements in North America. These movements have emerged over the past 40 years to change the way we eat and produce food in the Global North. Many of these movements, however, have been led and maintained by white, male or other privileged subjects that prioritize only certain moments in the agrifood system itself. This has led to the obfuscation of many struggles and concerns pertaining to workers, people of color, women, and the land. By emphasizing the agrifood systems approach to organizing our movements we hope to reveal the many spaces within the agrifood system that remain unaddressed by dominant food movement agendas. In this effort, we will locate struggles for food justice from below, from communities of color, particularly native (women's) struggles, and how they dismantle multiple oppressions through intervening at each stage of the agrifood system.[16]

These insights dialectically link oppression, resistance, and food justice. In doing so, they elevate what the eminent historian Howard Zinn referred to as "people's history." This recovery of alternative narratives and radical trajectories identifies unrecognized crises and hence sites of social struggle. Oppression may be common throughout the food system, but particular relations of subordination set the stage for distinct forms of resistance and reimagining how to advance food justice.[17]

The theory of social change I develop throughout each chapter begins with a similar premise. There are many conjunctures, each a potential terrain to resolve antagonistic social relations in favor of oppressed groups. Antonio Gramsci's conjunctural analysis is particularly useful in this regard. While imprisoned by Benito Mussolini's fascist government for his revolutionary work with the Communist Party of Italy, he wrote, "A crisis occurs, sometimes lasting for decades. This exceptional duration means that incurable structural contradictions have revealed themselves . . . and that, despite this, the political forces which are struggling to conserve and defend the existing structure itself are making every effort to cure them, within certain limits, and to overcome them."[18] These crises, such as mass incarceration, the militarization of borders, and the exploitation of immigrant workers, "form the terrain of the 'conjunctural.'"[19] Oppositional forces organize on these terrains to establish new social relations. They are the immediate problems that help activists interpret structural conditions. From the vantage point of food justice, while the goal is to advance equity in the food system, this requires identifying and expanding political opportunities. In the same passage, Gramsci contended that "in the immediate, it [opposition] is developed in a series of ideological, religious, philosophical, political, and juridical polemics, whose concreteness can be estimated by the extent to which they are convincing, and shift the previously existing disposition of social forces."[20] This book is at once a dialectical synthesis of the generative power of historical and social forces that propel the development of food justice and constitutive of the dialectical process of discovering new opportunities to transform food politics. Instead of seeing oppression and resistance in isolation, this theory of social change places them in a dialectical relationship.

The first step in this conjunctural analysis is to trace the lineage of food justice. While the collection of historical narratives in this book is not exhaustive, I suggest they teach us that the stories the food justice movement tells itself partially determine the kind of food politics imagined as possible. There is a long social movement history of activism that uses food and hunger to push for progressive social change. In the mid-1600s, groups like the True Levellers called for the overthrow of the English monarchy and sought to abolish private property in order to create small agrarian communes for the poor and dispossessed.[21] This group later became known as the Diggers, a group of Protestant radicals who built colonies and farmed on common land in order to advocate for self-determination and to resist enclosure. A little more than fifty years later, as urban industrial capitalism accelerated in England, there began a series of food riots by those resisting the commodification of basic staples and the subsequent increase in prices. These riots took place over a one hundred–year period, as rioters demanded a return to traditional modes of exchange and a removal of elites from the realm of food production.[22] Then, during British colonialism in India, Mohandas Gandhi led the famous Salt March to the coastal village of Dandi to produce salt without paying tax. This was an act of self-determination on the part of the independence movement to confront the British monopoly of a common staple.

There are also examples of similar food politics in the United States. Indigenous tribes have sought to recover cultural foodways disrupted during the initial genocidal colonial era when white settlers forced them onto reservations, thus creating dependency on food rationed by the government.[23] Such endeavors include regaining access to ancestral hunting, fishing, and gathering grounds, planting indigenous plant varieties for nutrition or medicinal purposes, and engaging in farming practices that strengthen cultural heritage. In urban and rural communities alike, food has figured prominently in debates over poverty.[24] As part of the late civil rights movement, the Poor People's Campaign linked racial justice to economic justice. Activists produced reports, pushed politicians to hold hearings, and camped out in front of the Department of Agriculture to condemn the callousness of food and farm policy to the needs of poor communities of color and poor whites.[25] Their demands included free food stamps and school lunches, which ultimately led to federal antihunger and nutrition assistance programs.[26] Hunger and food access have also been important to a politics of survival and black liberation.[27] Black Panther Party chapters throughout the country developed the Free Breakfast for Children Program to feed children before going to school, to create a space for political education, and to point out the failures of the American government to support black people. In Philadelphia, an all-black anarcho-primitivist group called MOVE lived communally, committed to armed resistance against racism and police brutality, grew much of their own food, ate mainly a raw vegan diet, and advocated animal rights. The police considered the members of MOVE to be so subversive that they bombed their commune in 1985, killing many of the members and imprisoning others.[28]

Yet when we think of food justice, these histories are obscured or lost. Even those books and articles that draw historical parallels and attempt to trace the use of the term *food justice* overlook the fact that food security was not a simple end, nor was it the only connection between the words *food* and *justice*.[29] Throughout the 1980s, there were many charitable and religious organizations working on a range of social justice issues, one of which was hunger. Antihunger activists tied their food politics to poverty, war and peace, and the link between paying for expensive foreign policy and cutting domestic social welfare. Beginning in 1982 in Chicago, a group called Food Justice Programs engaged in community organizing and hunger relief work and published a newsletter called *Food Justice*. In addition to eaters, the history of food justice includes workers. In rural communities of color, there is the notable focus on farmworkers. If you consider political organizing on farms in California, there is a long history of tying together notions of food *and* justice. In 1984, the United Farm Workers started a magazine called *Food and Justice*. Labor organizers used this medium to publicize the history of multiracial farmworker organizing, the struggles of farmworkers against pesticides and unfair labor practices, and ongoing boycotts.[30] This magazine was a cultural tool that fostered the solidarity of supporters with frontline accounts of the farmworker movement.

Even some of the early visionary statements on food justice remain buried. In 2008, a multiracial group of twenty-two people from eleven states and sovereign Native American lands came together for a six-day retreat convened by the Center for Whole Communities at Knoll Farm in Waitsfield, Vermont. Claiming that food justice is a movement "rooted in historical struggle" and building on "social movements of the past and present," the group engaged in a collective visioning process to develop principles and approaches.[31] The group's resulting manifesto, *Food Justice: A People's Movement Whose Time Is Now,* acknowledges diversity as a strength and a means to oppose oppression and to work toward liberation.[32] In covering many topics, ranging from the opposition to the racist criminalization of immigrants and capitalist violence against workers to the sacredness of food and the need for ecologically resilient and sustainable food systems, the manifesto argues for a systems-level analysis and a leaderful food justice movement. Although it advocates for alternative and equitable food enterprises, it emphasizes the need to help shift "the structure of ownership" to support "an equal distribution of resources." Furthermore, it reveals an anti-neoliberal agenda that repeatedly politicizes food and acknowledges the positive power of the state: "We are seeking political power to bring about policy change and to hold those in power accountable to our social change agenda." The manifesto is an ideological artifact that integrates decades of radical left thought to set a foundation for the continued expansion of food justice.

I begin with these examples to assert the analytical and strategic advantage of a dialectical understanding of food justice. From an activ-

ist perspective, articulations of radical food politics advance the dialectical work of discovering how to intervene in the problems activists face on
the ground. Attention to the rich history of what we might call food justice work pushes beyond the current myopic focus on food. Although
this is perhaps counterintuitive given the obvious centrality of food to
bringing together those who want to solve problems in the food system,
this preoccupation often overlooks the internal economic, political, and
social conditions that produce relations of subordination in the food
system and broader society. Ironically, the emphasis on trying to increase
local food availability often misses the local ways in which corporate
concentration manifests itself beyond the preponderance of fast-food
chains, big-box retailers, and what activists and scholars have referred to
as "food from nowhere."[33] Overlooked are the ways race, ethnicity, class,
gender, and the state intersect with corporate power to produce an array
of inequities. This includes how redlining, capital divestment, and white
flight produce food insecurity, or what some refer to as "food apartheid";
the exploitation of the working class, women, and people of color in food
service; and the fetishizing of "ethnic" food that overlooks how institutionalized discrimination has disrupted cultural foodways.[34] It is important for scholars to operate from a theory of social change that is relevant
to the food justice movement to navigate the practical implications of
these related histories and narratives.

Dialectical Humanism and Social Movement–Relevant Theories of Social Change

The dialectical relations between grassroots struggle and a host of social
forces represent what David Meyer and Sidney Tarrow have called a
"social movement society."[35] Social movements are a key factor in social
change; they are the social and historical antithesis to various manifesta-
tions of the status quo. At present, crisis seems to be the status quo, with
some of the biggest crises affecting the food system, which in turn rally
many social movements. Neoliberal political and economic restructuring
after the Great Recession, ethnoracial conflicts, and ecological feedback
loops between climate change and a range of socioecological disruptions
produce the conditions under which food justice emerges as a hopeful
alternative. Food justice activism alone is incapable of solving these crises.
However, it offers some grassroots-generated paths at a time when there is
widespread engagement with prefigurative politics and participation in

democratic social movements.[36] As food justice continues to intersect with many of these endeavors, it is part of the dialectical motion of social change in the food system and wider society.

For the purposes of understanding the transformative potential of food justice as an idea and practice, dialectics offers a useful method of inquiry. Dialectics builds on the ideas of Karl Marx. Although Marx never used the term, other radical thinkers developed dialectical materialism to explain human action and the hope for social transformation, namely, how society would transition out of capitalism to communism.[37] While capitalism as an economic system consists of many social actors organized differentially around their relationship to capital, a historical process that Marx sought to understand relationally, it is not the only system around which social life is organized, nor is it the only system open to a dialectical analysis. Some Marxists might cry foul for divorcing dialectics from a strict class-based approach to political economy. Yet from the perspective of many relational methods of inquiry, Marxists have refined a very useful method.[38] The relationship that different peoples of color and women have to capitalism varies.[39] Black women in the United States, for instance, have been in a weaker economic position not because of something inherent in their personhood that is exploitable by capitalists. Rather, white men have institutionalized laws that elevate their social position, benefit economically from the history of slavery and patriarchy, and tend to be the capitalists who work to maintain this state of affairs.[40] The individual and localized experiences of these relations motivate specific forms of movement building. Any analysis that overlooks these internal political and social conditions is therefore inadequate for understanding distinct dialectical relationships and appropriate strategies for intervention.[41]

Reflecting a position that is common among post-Marxists, French sociologist Henri Lefebvre wrote in reference to the contingent relationships between economic, political, and social conditions and social struggle, "No expression of dialectical materialism can be definitive, but, instead of being incompatible and conflicting with each other, it may perhaps be possible for these expressions to be integrated into an open totality, perpetually in the process of being transcended, precisely in so far as they will be expressing the solutions to the problems facing concrete man."[42] But it is not just that social life is open to change and is constantly evolving as different social forces compete for hegemonic dominance. People's embeddedness in *relations* of subordination means that human agency is enduring at the individual and collective levels.[43]

Dialectical humanism, as developed by James and Grace Lee Boggs, pushes these debates from the perspective of activist scholars who approach dialectics from an experiential and heterodox reading of crises. The Boggses spent most of their lives in Detroit organizing for economic, racial, and environmental justice. They infused this work with an evolving social movement–relevant theory of social change. In *Revolution and Evolution in the Twentieth Century*, the Boggses analyzed revolutions in Russia, China, Guinea Bissau, Vietnam, and the United States to argue that contextualized social analysis is central to developing the thinking required for future revolutions. They drew on Hegel to advance a dialectical method of thinking that focuses on the internal causes of social problems that perpetuate conflict and prevent the solutions necessary to actualize humanity's potential. This method aims to develop revolutionary ideology to inform revolutionary politics. The Boggses reasoned that to produce "a new unity," ideological and political struggle is required to resolve the contradiction: "But this new unity is only temporary, since within it a new duality or a new contradiction between the actual and the potential is emerging, creating the basis for further struggle towards a still higher form of existence."[44] Translated to the case at hand, social inequalities obstruct the actualization of food justice and set the conditions for a range of social struggles that strive for food justice. This leads to new analyses that inform strategies to resolve the contradictions with innovative food politics. Beginning with the premise that the nature of social struggle in democracies like the United States represents a dialectical process of contestation and the construction of new hegemonies, food politics can lead to closures that produce the antagonism necessary for radicalizing democracy.

Dialectical humanism as praxis prioritizes actions that work toward human flourishing and views the revolutionary process to resolve previous contradictions that obstruct this flourishing as a series of contested ideological, economic, political, and social conditions. Tracing these conditions is the first step to develop an understanding of various conjunctures to inform future action. While revolution often connotes closure, either in its common usage (e.g., *The* American Revolution; *The* Bolshevik Revolution) or in romanticizing past revolutions (e.g., the proletarians overthrew the bourgeois capitalists), dialectics suggests otherwise. There are ongoing social struggles to alter the hegemonic circumstances that perpetuate oppression in all its unique entanglements.

In the pages ahead, I develop a *food justice dialectics* that asks how food justice activism as a process seeks to address an array of conjunctures, and how research into these processes helps reproduce oppositional yearnings.[45] In fusing the theoretical with the practical with the intent of informing contemporary food justice struggles, this book is a work of public sociology. Michael Burawoy, who increased the space for public engagement in his 2004 American Sociological Association (ASA) Presidential Address, later contended that we need a "political imagination," capable of what another former ASA president, Eric Olin Wright, refers to as "envisioning real utopias."[46] It is insufficient to merely point out why there are problems in the food system. As Marx famously remarked, "The philosophers have only interpreted the world in various ways; the point is to change it."[47]

A food justice dialectics can inspire a radical political imagination and a set of strategies within the contemporary postpolitical era.[48] Grounding this era is the notion that there is no alternative to capitalism.[49] The postpolitical logic also buoys the color-blind logic of racial neoliberalism by ignoring the political origins of institutional racism and affirming that any ethnoracial inequities are the result of an individual's inability to get ahead within a meritocratic society.[50] Social life is no more than individual market-based decisions, and political institutions engage in technocratic governance to manufacture consensus around a set of practices amenable to private interests.[51] The belief that we have reached the end of history has colonized politics.[52] Liberal democracy, a representative form of government based on elections charged with protecting individual liberties within free-market economies, is the penultimate form of social organization. Based on a logic of personal responsibility or at best a kind of charitable humanitarianism, government functions as a bureaucratic management tool that disciplines the realm of politics to its formalized rules and regulations. If you have a problem, go to the polls or buy something different. The personal problem supersedes the universal problem it represents. In C. Wright Mills's terms, the postpolitical thwarts the politicization of "personal troubles" into "public issues."[53]

These conditions, while hegemonic, are a site for democratic struggle.[54] The postpolitical does not foreclose on other kinds of politics, although it represents a power imbalance between forces that benefit from these conditions. Although there are pressures to bend the practice of food justice to these logics, there are many counterhegemonic forms of food politics that push back. Sometimes they are confrontational. Sometimes they are prefigurative. Regardless, food justice strives to universalize the problem and establish new hegemonies predicated on human rights and social justice. Referring to demand-based social movements and political activities (e.g., food justice now!), Slavoj Žižek notes, "The situation becomes politicized when a particular demand starts to function as a metaphoric condensation of the global opposition against Them, those in power, so that the protest is no longer just about that demand, but about the universal dimension that resonates in that particular demand."[55] Herein lies the power of food justice. It is a demand that *expands* the field of political struggle by reminding society of the structural inequalities that only political struggle for food justice (e.g., racial justice) can eliminate.

Much like a Gramscian conjunctural analysis identifies crises as entry points into determining universal demands, the Boggses' dialectical humanism encourages social movements to address and abolish the fundamental injustices that divide people.[56] Identifying the contours of the neoliberal counterrevolution to the social movements of the 1960s, they concluded that while capitalist development in the United States had largely succeeded in integrating a wide cross section of society, it had focused on technological overdevelopment at the cost of social and political underdevelopment. The role of new social movements was to rise to these historical conditions by refining their methods of struggle to revolutionize people's relationship to material needs by improving social relations and increasing political engagement. Instead of seeing the end of history, James and Grace Lee Boggs offer a way to identify the plurality of political spaces to participate in democratic struggle. Their method is therefore open to emergent political practices that reduce the prevalence of social antagonism at different points in the matrix of oppression.[57] Food justice activism is part of the dialectical process to uplift and build bridges across the diversity of our humanity. It includes protest politics to reform the food system as well as strategies to revolutionize our everyday cultural practices and create alternatives to transform dominant systems, say, through an autonomous, immigrant-run community garden. This is very much in line with Grace Lee Boggs's assertion, "Fighting on the side of Humanity against the Empire of Money, we need to go beyond opposition, beyond rebellion, beyond resistance, beyond civic insurrection. We don't want to be like them. We don't want to become the 'political class,' to change presidents, switch governments. We want and need to create the alternative world that is now both possible and necessary. We want and need to exercise power, not take it."[58] Although it is important to assert power to change the food system, not every effort is capable of transforming power imbalances. While strategic interventions into problems in the food system abound, there are also different political imaginations that inform these social struggles. Dialectical humanism helps to identify the forms of food politics that can advance social justice and build collective power to advance the interests of the food movement in the face of difficult odds.

(Food) Justice for All

When many popular food writers cover food-related activism, they tend to focus most on those aspects of the food system that appear to have a simple solution.[59] The attention is often on pesticides in farming, E. coli on our spinach, antibiotics in our chickens, waste lagoons from factory farms, the prevalence of obesity, the experience of hunger, and so on. These are largely tangible and have an apparent solution: do more or less of something to increase or reduce the pervasiveness of the problem. Yet, as many critical food scholars have shown, colonialism, neoliberal global capitalism, and institutional racism produce the conditions behind such problems. The root conditions become apparent when we consider the social relations between those making decisions about how to grow, process, and sell food and those carrying out, responding to, or disproportionately experiencing the negative outcomes of those decisions. In short, there are inequities. The solution lies in pursuing social justice.

But what does it mean to pursue social justice to achieve equitable outcomes or even liberation? As some environmental justice and food justice scholars contend, we need to look at justice in terms of recognition, process, procedure, and outcome and how these mutually constitute one another.[60] For example, there is a deep commitment by many food justice activists to ensure the recognition of indigenous communities and communities of color historically marginalized in the food system. In practice, this might mean recognizing the need for indigenous peoples' access to ancestral fishing and hunting grounds as a form of cultural reproduction and food sovereignty. But it is insufficient to recognize the culturally specific experiences and needs of groups. It is also important to ensure that an equitable process includes the voices *and* methods of historically marginalized groups. In cities with food policy councils, for example, citizens need to be cognizant of the many stakeholders involved, but especially those normally excluded from the process. Groups like farmworkers and dishwashers, who in a city like San Diego overwhelmingly come from Latinx communities, are rarely included in discussions about how to improve the food system. Relatedly, procedures need to be in place or developed that ensure that the rights of people are respected and upheld. Take labor rights. While workers may have a right to a safe workplace or collective bargaining, in practice it is difficult for nonunionized meatpackers who speak another language and lack economic resources to access the procedures that guarantee these rights. Although vital, it is hard to imagine equitable distribution of material resources, such as healthy food, without mechanisms that empower oppressed groups. Determining that there is inequity in outcomes such as wages, land, or food security is important, but also requires an appreciation of the social processes that produce such outcomes in order to decide how best to respond.

My focus on conjunctures leads me to conclude that the politics of food justice can expand with respect to a wider field of social inequities. This begins with first elevating social justice demands, which broadens the predominant emphasis on environmental sustainability within most local food politics in the United States. Specifically, food justice includes all ideas and practices that strive to eliminate oppression and challenge the structural drivers of all inequities within and beyond the food system. Food justice also advocates for the right to healthy food that is produced justly, recognizes diverse cultural foodways and historical traumas, and promotes equitable distribution of resources, democratic participation, and control over food systems. In brief, food justice includes not only social struggles often outside the purview of the food movement but also justice in terms of recognition, process, procedure, and outcome.

Food Justice Now! argues for the advantage of a dialectical mode of inquiry into institutional practices and food politics to evaluate the degree to which activism in different contexts ameliorates inequities. In Oakland, food justice organizers use food to advance economic and racial justice for formerly incarcerated people. In Los Angeles and San Diego, labor organizers and local food activists see food justice in relation to reforming or creating alternatives to the food system, but how they engage with the problems of labor, immigration, and social boundaries varies. I grapple with the lessons offered by these cases to provide suggestions on how to build a food movement that prioritizes food justice. This requires positioning these cases within a history of social movements that mobilized food and envisioned the food system as a space to advance social justice. Furthermore, these cases provide empirical evidence to base recommendations for dissolving some of the boundaries of the food movement to build collective power across social movements committed to social justice. Food justice deepens movement building and broadens food politics to new terrains of social struggle.

Book Organization

In chapter 1, "Inequality and Resistance: The Legacy of Food and Justice Movements," I develop the argument that structural inequalities shape social movement struggles. Within the food system, the prevalence of class and ethnoracial disparities illustrates that conjunctures like food insecurity and the exploitation of food-chain workers stem from problems like institutional racism and corporate concentration in capitalist economies. I begin with historical lessons from the agrarian populist movement of the late 1800s to contextualize a discussion of the proliferation of social movements that have emerged since the 1960s in response. Most notably for the case studies in Oakland, San Diego, and Los Angeles, these include the organic farming, farmworker and food labor, and black power movements. Despite the unique conjunctures that informed their terrains of social struggle, these social movements shared a commitment to social justice. This dialectical observation suggests the importance of dialectical evaluation. How can the lessons of the past inform opportunities for intervention? Consider the desirability, viability, and achievability of a social movement's goals. In other words, it is imperative to dissect the legacy of these social movements with reference to the relations of subordination that they sought to transform. The case studies teach that the food movement continues to grapple with these relations and that food justice activists can learn from the past to inform current possible resolutions.

In chapter 2, "Opposing the Carceral State: Food-Based Prisoner Reentry Activism," I investigate how the current system of mass incarceration entrenches racial inequities in Oakland and informs the fusion of social justice–oriented carceral and food politics. Before, during, and after people enter prison, they experience a range of structural barriers and institutional biases that make it difficult to break out of the prison pipeline. Chapter 2 chronicles the responses of food justice and restorative justice networks in Oakland to inequities experienced by prisoners and formerly incarcerated people. The resulting cross-movement collaborations develop not only socially just alternatives with reentry work that reduces recidivism through permaculture-informed urban agriculture initiatives but also political campaigns that target political elites. Activists committed to prison reform and abolition, restorative justice, permaculture, and economic justice expand the parameters of food justice. This *restorative food justice* of healing and mutual aid produces living-wage jobs, reimagines relationships to food and land, opens new policy paths, and creates spaces to overcome the historical trauma of mass incarceration.

I discuss strategic responses to a food system that undervalues food work and exploits food-chain workers in chapter 3, "Taking Back the Economy: Fair Labor Relations and Food Worker Advocacy." One of the multifaceted requirements for food justice is economic justice. This entails creating new forms of meaningful and equitable food work and advancing the interests of food-chain workers with greater labor protections and rights. While initiatives in San Diego are revaluing food work with noncommodified forms of labor that prioritize the social and ecological values of organic farming, labor and food justice movements in Los Angeles are exemplary of a food politics that focuses on labor justice for food-chain workers. In contrast to those who claim that food work is exceptionally difficult to remunerate fairly, I show how reimagining food justice is a prefigurative act to re-create wage labor relations and a reform effort to engage politically with food-chain workers to improve their livelihoods. Moreover, labor conjunctures are so entrenched that food justice activists should be wary of sacrificing quality jobs for access to healthy food. Instead, food justice can be a means to engage in a demand-side analysis and confrontational food politics.

Whether or not activists confront the inequities faced by immigrant food-chain workers in the United States, this ongoing reality in California abuts whiteness and privilege in the food movement. Chapter 4, "Immigration Food Fights: Challenging Borders and Bridging Social Boundaries," considers these dynamics. Chapter 4 begins on the U.S.–Mexico border. It looks at how largely white organic farming and local food activists in San Diego experience, understand, and attempt to think beyond the production and maintenance of social boundaries between themselves and migrant farmworkers. I investigate the tensions between maintaining an "us" in the food movement and a "them" needed to keep the food system running. This informs the prospects of a food politics that is capable of overcoming ethnoracial and citizenship boundaries. I then compare how labor organizers in Los Angeles navigate the economic conditions in grocery retail and meatpacking as they strive to represent immigrants and second-generation workers. The ethnoracial and class makeup of food workers pushes labor organizers to challenge the race-to-the-bottom practices of food corporations. Last, I offer an example from Oakland of how food justice organizers can stand with immigrant rights movements, and how the opportunity is urgent and seemingly everywhere.

In chapter 5, "Radicalizing Food Politics: Collective Power, Diversity, and Solidarity," I synthesize the lessons of chapters 1 through 4 to suggest that food politics is a practice of dissensus that is most potent when informed by social movement history and a commitment to food justice. By reimagining the historical roots of food justice, foregrounding food justice as an idea to combat oppression in all its guises, and devising both prefigurative and confrontational strategies that use food to advance social justice, the food movement can become relevant to far more people. Through a survey of strategic considerations relevant to my cases and beyond, I contend that building collective power with a diversity of strategies and solidarity across social boundaries can help achieve greater equity in the food system. Food justice offers hope for achieving a more radical and plural democracy because it universalizes social struggles around a commitment to equity while respecting the need for strategic breadth to address distinct problems.

I conclude the book, in "Notes on the Future of Food Justice," by putting my main arguments and ideas in conversation with a pressing dialectical development: the revanchist politics embodied by Donald Trump and the Republican Party. At the same time, the dialectical openness of food justice creates a political opportunity to join with other social movements to engage on many conjunctural terrains. Some parts of the food movement are already working beyond movement boundaries, with food justice offering the clearest means by which to mobilize alongside forces for economic, racial, climate, and environmental justice. Instead of seeing movement building as a zero-sum game, the food movement is beginning to consider the need to challenge deeper power relations and networks to advance social justice. One of the initiatives I chronicle is the emergence of discussion and organizing for a national food policy. To achieve this might require first fighting for a national food strategy. I bring together these different political urges with the critical role that food justice will need to play to offer a compelling vision to mobilize people beyond simple resistance to revanchist reactions. Therefore, a *food justice* national strategy might begin the process of institutionalizing a commitment to social justice in the food system by mandating federal agencies to reform previous laws and devise new ones.

1

Inequality and Resistance

The Legacy of Food and Justice Movements

Structural inequalities drive many problems in the food system. Thinking counterfactually we might ask, "What would happen if everyone could afford and access healthy food?" or "What would the lives of food workers be like if they all received living wages and free health care?" There would be higher levels of human flourishing. Yet, as of now, not everyone has the same life opportunities. Patricia Allen, a sociologist who has long studied food and agriculture, outlines the current predicament thusly: "It is clear that our food system does not meet the fundamental criteria of social justice such as freedom from want, freedom from oppression, and access to equal opportunity."[1]

A focus on inequality throws contemporary racial neoliberalism into relief. Neoliberalization is an ongoing social, political, and economic process premised on valorizing individuality and reducing society to capitalist exchange. The institutional corollary is the rollback of social welfare and the rollout of the privatization of public goods and initiatives that control, criminalize, and discipline the poor, working classes, and people of color.[2] For example, neoliberal narratives overlook how hunger results from labor exploitation and poverty and justify policies to remove social safety nets in the name of meritocracy and individual responsibility. Color blindness mutually constitutes this process as a racial project to undermine the victories of the civil rights movement.[3] The narratives of color-blind racism, along with related policy imperatives, neutralize debates about racial inequality and prevent solutions to race-related social problems.[4] Some of the major frames reinforce neoliberal narratives, like "But everyone has the same opportunity." There is also a naturalization of racial stratification where people assume "things are just the way they are" and "we all prefer to be with our own kind." These two perspectives then justify blaming indigenous communities and marginalized communities of color for their social disadvantage and minimizing their experience of racism. Common deflections include "They are interested in other things" or "It's better now than in the past."[5]

The stakes in the debate over why we have inequality and how to solve the problem are high. Consider three stark examples that influence the food politics discussed in this book: income and wealth distribution, immigration, and racism in the criminal justice system. In the United States, top incomes have surged, and the top 0.1 percent holds 22 percent of wealth compared with a low of 7 percent in 1978.[6] Over two million undocumented immigrants have been deported from the United States since 2008, which carries harsh legal consequences and contributes to a private immigrant detention complex that houses about half of the thirty thousand people held in detention facilities every day.[7] Police shootings of unarmed people of color are excessive and reflect a racialized system of mass incarceration where people of color face longer sentences and account for 60 percent of all prisoners.[8] In response to these conditions, groups with less institutional power to determine the rules governing their lives have found ways to create alternatives and seek structural reforms. Since the Great Recession, public outrage has been palpable and has spilled over into the practice of food justice. The Occupy Wall Street movement erupted on the streets of hundreds of cities throughout the United States and called attention to collusion between economic and political elites, while the demand for a $15 minimum wage by the Fight for Fifteen movement followed in its wake. The DREAMers, a social movement driven by undocumented youth, used civil disobedience, community organizing, and lobbying to force President Obama to pass the Deferred Action for Childhood Arrivals in 2012 and to push back against immigrant deportation and detention and the dehumanizing "illegal" narrative. The Black Lives Matter movement spread rapidly after the high-profile murders of black people at the hands of white police officers, inspiring widespread protest and organizing that are resisting anti-blackness and color-blind racism and are demanding criminal justice reform.

Like the movements mentioned above, historically, the largest left-wing social movements in the United States were fundamentally concerned with some structural inequality.[9] This stems from the historical legacy of the institutionalized power of Protestant white men over indigenous groups, African slaves, many waves of immigrants, and women. Added to these social conditions is a dominionism that placed humans above nonhuman species, which justified the exploitation of natural resources and those who historically acted as their stewards. The advantages afforded to those at the top of the socioecological hierarchy were accumulated through the plunder of land, the exploitation of labor, and the legal codification of white supremacy and patriarchy. This history reverberates today through a dialectical process of social struggle that has eliminated some of the most oppressive conditions, only to set in motion new forms of prefiguration and resistance.

Given that the promise of democracy is unrealized, each set of dialectical conditions fosters political commitments. Social movement scholars have often differentiated between "old" social movements and "new" social movements to distinguish eras of mass mobilization in the United States and Europe and their associated strategies and targets.[10] This refers to the historical differences between "old" left mobilization around working-class desires to overthrow or make reforms to capitalism to "new" left mobilization in opposition to racism, sexism, homophobia, and the degradation of the environment. Despite the heterogeneity of targets, these social movements meet the political criteria outlined by political philosophers Ernesto Laclau and Chantal Mouffe of engaging "in a type of action whose objective is the transformation of a social relation which constructs a subject in a relationship of subordination."[11] In the case of old social movements like the industrial workers movement, large blocs of working people resisted structural inequalities in factories and demanded the redistribution of resources and the right to equitably participate in political and social life.[12] In the case of new social movements like the environmental justice movement, poor, black, Latinx, and indigenous communities have mobilized to reduce their disparate exposure to urban, industrial, and chemical hazards and sought to create healthy environments for all people.[13] These and other oppositional social forces consider their inequitable disadvantages as problematic. Their response is to deploy democratic discourses, such as equality, to show that relations of subordination are oppressive and need eradication.

In the pantheon of social movements, what makes the food movement a unique force for social change? Social movements are "a loose collectivity acting with some degree of organization, temporal continuity, and reliance on noninstitutional forms of action to promote or resist change in the group, society, or world order of which it is a part."[14] In its current manifestation, the food movement encompasses a wide cross section of interests and concerns aimed at reforming and transforming the food system. After all, the food system entails more than a produce-distribute-process-sell supply chain. It reproduces relations of subordination. In response, the food movement engages in food politics that include, but are not limited to, agroecology, antihunger, food safety, food security, food sovereignty, food-chain workers, genetic engineering, local food, land access, nutrition and health, permaculture, sustainable farming, urban agriculture, vegetarianism, and veganism. Topically, the food movement is diverse. Substantively, it takes on greater significance in the history of social justice movements in the United States when activists act on food justice principles with food politics that confront inequality within and beyond food systems. The distinction of food politics infused with food justice is the diversity, and therefore the degree to which activists operate outside different "institutional or organizational channels" to eliminate oppression.

With the previous description in mind, it is necessary to see food politics as much more than the kind of "alternative" initiatives ascribed to the food movement. Scholarly and activist debates over the past two decades have framed food politics around whether they create alternatives to the conventional food system. These include initiatives promoting organic agriculture, supporting small farmers, developing direct-to-consumer markets, and expanding urban agriculture.[15] While many scholars have analyzed alternatives when they fail to take into consideration issues of social equity and justice, they have paid less attention to how food politics are always in flux. Food politics reflect who participates and where they participate. For instance, the reasons why a white college student versus a refugee family from Guatemala engages in urban agriculture are likely different. What food can accomplish for each group is distinct. Based on one's social position, the motivations and the outcomes of participation vary. The white college student may be concerned about corporate control of the food system, and so she wants to assert her agency by growing her own food, while the Guatemalan family may experience economic and social marginalization, and so they grow food to supplement their income and maintain their cultural foodways.

Measured in terms of the increase in organic food production, farmers markets, urban agriculture, and the spread of food policy councils, there is a shift in how people value food and their willingness to join together to change the food system.[16] Yet, for many years, the center of this shift has reflected a consumer politics interested in shorter food supply chains, food quality, dietary health, and the environment.[17] Left out of much of the public enthusiasm and scholarly literature is an appreciation of the different and often competing forms of food politics. Especially important is the question of whether certain forms of food politics recognize and confront inequities. There is a wing of the food movement whose secessionist food politics focus on the needs of farmers, environmental sustainability, and eating good food. It uses the market to increase the connection between producers and consumers, often through "buy local" and "get to know your farmer" initiatives.[18] This wing has its prefigurative vanguard, say, in those who develop land cooperatives to expand organic or permaculture farming practices, as well as its neoliberal contingent whose members only vote with their forks. The wing of the food movement whose food politics are instead confrontational seek structural changes in the conventional food system, emphasize policy and the governing authority of the state, and prioritize economic and racial justice for eaters *and* workers.[19] Members of this wing run the gamut from those who start nonprofits to politicize food and intervene in structural inequalities to grassroots community-based groups who engage in direct action to feed people or reclaim land for local food production.

While food movement coalitions form and dissolve regularly, which reveals a degree of ideological flexibility to work across differences, leveraging coalitions into a sustained power bloc that prioritizes food justice at a national level remains unrealized. Will corporate agribusiness co-opt the food movement as marketers and economists figure out how to make sustainability and health key to a disciplined consumer subject? Are consumer politics capable of developing alternatives that operate outside the grasp of corporate agribusiness and reach across stratified sectors of society? There are also questions about the potential of confrontational politics that target structural inequalities. Will food politics evolve due to the increased involvement of those committed to food justice? Might an expansion of food justice to include the concerns of other social movement allies strengthen food politics? Or perhaps there will be one wing of the food movement that gets institutionalized like the mainstream environmental movement, and another environmental justice–like grassroots wing that is committed to equity and social justice.

For food justice activists, the future relevance of the food movement rests on its ability to create more than alternatives; it must embrace confrontational politics, just like those historic left-wing social movements that fought against structural inequalities.[20] In order to understand how food justice informs the development of food politics and to evaluate its transformational capacity, a dialectical analysis compares the root causes of inequity and the kinds of movement building that tie food to specific social problems and power dynamics. Attention to historical problems in the food system shows that previous social movements set the groundwork for certain food justice strategies to expand the current vision of food politics. Looking back in time helps project what might be possible going forward.

Structural Roots of Food System Inequalities

The sociologist Eric Olin Wright offers a valuable framework to evaluate social alternatives to institutions that perpetuate oppression and inequity, namely, whether they "would eliminate, or at least significantly mitigate, the harms and injustices identified in the diagnosis and critique."[21] One way to determine how social justice commitments can expand food politics is to link problems in the food system to their economic, political, and social roots. This relationship helps to illuminate how the analyses and strategies of relevant social movements historically motivate the contemporary practice of food justice.[22] Driving this dialectic is the generative relationship between inequality and the problem-solving ethic of food justice activism. Strategically speaking, such an examination can account for whether emergent food justice goals are, in Wright's language, "desirable," "viable," and "achievable." The first step is to diagnose and critique the most salient social forces driving an identified problem.

The production of food in the United States includes a history of oppression, dating from the plantation economy of the South to the expansion and settlement of the West reliant on subsequent waves of Chinese, Japanese, and Latinx immigrant agricultural labor. Farmworkers are historically at the social margins, but so too are workers in meatpacking and food-processing facilities. As the muckraker Upton Sinclair famously wrote, "Here is a population, low-class and mostly foreign, hanging always on the verge of starvation and dependent for its opportunities of life upon the whim of men every bit as brutal and unscrupulous as the old-time slave drivers; under such circumstances, immorality is exactly as inevitable, and as prevalent, as it is under the system of chattel slavery."[23] The mistreatment of workers also takes place in food retail. For example, restaurant workers "behind the kitchen door" experience poor pay, racial and gender discrimination, few benefits, and low job security.[24] There are currently over twenty million workers in the food system, most earning low or poverty wages and more likely than workers in other industries to be receiving social welfare such as food stamps.[25] In particular, people of color and women are more likely to earn lower wages and hold fewer management opportunities than their white and male counterparts.[26] These food-chain jobs are in some of the most dangerous industries in the United States, especially farming and food processing, which are overwhelmingly performed by a Latinx and undocumented workforce.[27]

There are also many structural problems at the point of consumption. Traditional foodways have been lost or disrupted, many communities lack access to healthy food, and these same communities have been inundated with local food initiatives that tend to benefit white people more than people of color.[28] As public health reformers are quick to point out, low-income, black, and Latinx communities are most likely to suffer from diet-related diseases such as obesity. Perhaps one of the unintended consequences of ensuing interventions is an overly deterministic view of who is more likely to be "fat." The social stigma emanates from a public and many health-care professionals who blame individuals for making "bad" eating choices.[29] Such stigmatization, coupled with social constructions equating thinness and beauty, obfuscate the structural forces of capitalism and neoliberal policies that produce these health problems.[30] After World War II, fast-food corporations proliferated rapidly and were quick to lobby political elites to avoid any policies that might educate the consumer on the nutritional quality of their food.[31] While consumers can now access an incredible variety of food, access to the highest-quality food remains stratified along class, gender, and racial lines. In cities such as Oakland, as white people moved to the suburbs and set up racial covenants, and redlining in neighborhoods with large black populations prevented economic development, disinvestment in food retail in black neighborhoods reduced access to healthy food options.[32] These trends reflect the capitalist political economy of the food system and institutionally racist development patterns, which produce cheap food at the cost of equity and human health.[33]

Problems furthermore proliferate in the food system in terms of the domination of nature. While this is important insofar as humans harm nonhuman species, it also reveals something about contemporary social relations. Murray Bookchin argues that "*all ecological problems are social problems,*" because "dominating nature *stems* from the domination of human by human [due to] . . . institutionalized systems of coercion, command, and obedience."[34] The fact of social hierarchy suggests that those with greater environmental privilege can protect themselves from the environmental problems they are most responsible for creating.[35] As the environmental justice movement has clearly shown, those marginalized by race, ethnicity, nationality, class, and gender disproportionately experience environmental problems. This is similarly the case at all stages in the food system.[36]

Industrialization of the food system in the United States perpetuates peak oil, peak phosphorus, virtual water, pesticide toxicity, dead zones, genetically modified organisms, biofuels, and global warming.[37] For example, pesticide dependency leads to the contamination of fresh water supplies, the death of domestic animals, degradation of fisheries, and collapse of vital bee colonies, which grows worse as pests become more resistant and necessitate greater pesticide application.[38] Agriculture and food corporations profit not only from environmental degradation *but upon the exploited labor that the system relies.*[39] To reiterate, humans dominate each other as a prerequisite to dominating nature. Low-paid precarious labor is the shaky foundation the food system is built on to deliver cheap (i.e., environmentally destructive) food. Such problems are rooted historically in the expansion of capitalism and urbanization, which set off a series of ecological rifts alienating humans from each other and from the natural environment.[40] As rapidly industrializing economies force farmers into cities, leaving agricultural livelihoods for factory jobs to fuel a growing consumer economy, the soil nutrient cycle collapses; food waste is often not reintegrated back into soils, and because more food has to be exported to cities, fertilizers are imported from elsewhere.[41] One of the best examples illustrating this process is the Dust Bowl. Intensive industrial farming methods depleted soil nutrients to feed a rapidly increasing urban population and various war efforts, which simultaneously led to topsoil erosion. Humans dominating each other in the form of the expanding power of capitalists over wage laborers and the violence of war drove agricultural practices that compromised ecological integrity.[42] Consumption of more food nutrients in the cities (and trenches) exceeded what was recycled back into the soil on farms. Entire grassland ecosystems in the Great Plains were devastated, in turn contributing to the displacement of over half a million poor people.[43]

Conjunctures in the food system originate from colonialism, capitalism, and institutional racism and continue to refract their problems through the human need for sustenance. Together, the current production, consumption, and ecological conjunctures set the terrain of social struggle. The forces of opposition, in this case, the food movement, are responding in many ways. While each conjuncture suggests unique responses—there are obvious differences between preventing labor exploitation and environmental degradation—a common ideological, political, and semantic vantage point displays unified opposition. As the history of those strands of food politics most germane to my cases suggests, food justice holds the potential to be that unifying force.

Social Movement Legacies and the Evolution of Food Politics

The food movement has started to prioritize addressing structural inequalities in the food system. On Food Day 2015, the Los Angeles Food Policy Council, in conjunction with the Equity Summit hosted by a nationally recognized nonprofit called PolicyLink, decided on the theme "Food Equity in Action." The renowned Angela Glover Blackwell gave a keynote in which she advocated, "Equity is a superior growth model." She meant this not just in terms of economic justice, but in the sense that an equity-focused food politics helps communities to bridge social boundaries such as race, while respecting the needs and traditions of each group. On the other side of the country, the Northeast Sustainable Agriculture Working Group held its annual conference in Saratoga Springs, New York, whose theme was "Putting MOVE in the Movement!" In addition to keynotes, there were workshops and discussion groups dedicated to what it means to build a food movement, antiracism in food movement activism, and food labor organizing. The description of the event linked the legacies of prior movements and social justice to the food movement: "Civil rights, labor, women's rights—the movements that transformed our world can give us insight on ways to accelerate food systems change. What can we learn from leaders past and present? How can we better organize our work, our networks, our message, our media? Learn and strategize with hundreds of attendees . . . as we work to build a movement and realize the change we want to see."[44] These food movement convergences recognize the diffusion of social movements over time and reflect how food justice can encompass a wide variety of social justice politics.

Social movements inform future mobilization in terms of the identification of problems and the discourses and strategies used by activists.[45] Three of the most influential social movements that reverberate in the food politics in my cases are the organic farming movement, the farm-worker and food worker movements, and the black power movement. With respect to a deeper historical timeline, the seminal agrarian populist movements offered frameworks for food and farming activists concerned with social inequalities. Most important, all these social movements aspired to widespread social change. Because they were embedded in larger structures of power and networks of support often well beyond their immediate loci of activity, their impacts still resonate. Yet most historical accounts of contemporary food politics only focus on those movements that influenced "alternative" food politics. In other words, the hippie, self-help, health food, and back-to-the-land movements, all of which were part of the counterculture movements in the 1960s and 1970s, serve as the historical foundation.[46] Yet this overlooks previous food- and farming-based social movements and fails to account for how other conjunctures and insurrectionary movements such as the black power movement would influence food justice activism.

Agrarian Populist Movements

The historical significance of agrarian populist movements in the United States rests in their symbolic value as pinnacles of grassroots democratic struggle. As such, they offer foundational lessons for the evolution of domestic food politics. The end of the Civil War left millions of black and white Americans, mostly farmers, marginalized economically and socially. Despite heroic efforts, many poor white Southerners were unable to pull themselves out of a crop lien system where merchants never paid for a year's cotton crop in excess of the debt accrued by the farmer for that season. During the 1870s, millions of white farming families migrated westward in hopes of finding cheap land and new opportunities (often at the expense of indigenous people). However, the economic reality was grim for those who settled out west and became increasingly worse throughout most rural communities. Landless tenant farmers increased, small landholders accrued larger debts, and peonage became widespread.[47] For many blacks who stayed in the South, there was similar populist outrage. While they directed some of this at building economic power through initiatives like farmers' cooperatives and exchanges, and boycotts of agricultural trusts, they also fought the rise of racist Jim Crow laws, and worked to increase political participation.[48] In turn, rumblings of revolt grew into the largest democratic mass movement in history, consisting of both blacks and whites and landed and landless people.

One of the main collective economic responses to the consolidation of land ownership, monopolization of the railroads, and tightening of financing was to create cooperative warehouses, grain elevators, and community-run exchanges.[49] Foremost among these endeavors was the National Farmers Alliance and Industrial Union, which set the organizational foundation for cooperative economic power and education on how the corporate state quashes participatory forms of democracy.[50] The populists also set up alternative social institutions such as newspapers and local schools, all the while making sure to increase rural scientific literacy and create agriculturally relevant programs within universities. At around the same time, there was the formation of the largest black agrarian organization in the country, the Colored Farmers' National Alliance and Co-Operative Union. This black populism devised similar mutual aid strategies, albeit under distinct conditions. Given widespread racial inequities, blacks also demanded an end to racially disparate practices such as the convict-lease system, which white planters used to prey on black men convicted of petty crimes by purchasing and exploiting this cheap labor pool.[51]

Although the populist revolt eventually withered because white Southern Democrats used violence, race-baiting, and fraud to cripple the movement, there are a few important legacies for contemporary food politics. First, cross-racial alliances developed both among farmers and between industrial workers and farmers.[52] Class solidarity was able to bring blacks and whites together even in the aftermath of the Civil War. This is not to suggest that white supremacists were absent from the movement, or that blacks, Chinese, and Jews faced no discrimination.[53] Race was a fatal wedge used to weaken agrarian populist movements in the face of left-wing populist factions agitating for more socialist and anti–big business policies. Second, women's political participation in populist organizations was important for mobilizing a fuller cross section of society, which provided a base of support for the passage of women's suffrage.[54] Third, in those places where the urban and rural poor built strong ties, the movement was successful, for example, electing their representatives in the People's Party or the Union Labor Party.[55] Fourth, agrarian populism proved mass movements can challenge the consolidation of land and the financial and legal infrastructure used to maintain elite capitalist power. Such movements, though, face stiff opposition and must find ways to leverage their resources and political opportunities. Nevertheless, using newfound influence to control the levers of political and economic power from below can reproduce such systems and all their flaws or require colluding with elites within these institutions to receive marginal personal gains or reforms while sacrificing structural transformations.[56] In brief, the mix of political organizing, empowering subordinated groups, and building bridges across social boundaries was central to one of the first historical examples of collective food politics in the United States.

The Organic Farming Movement

After World War II, there was a diffusion of chemicals into industrial agriculture, such as nitrate for bombs repurposed into the peacetime industry of nitrogen-fertilizer production.[57] In response, environmentalists were concerned with impacts on public health, which set off another major agrarian-based shift in the 1960s, but this time with the added support of an urban upwardly mobile consumer base.[58] The American public started to value sustainably managing natural resources. There was a growing recognition of the harmful environmental and social outcomes of scientific and industrial technology, and a desire among urbanites for closer communion with nature. In Rachel Carson's epochal *Silent Spring,* she wrote, "The earth's vegetation is part of a web of life in which there are intimate and essential relations between plants and animals. Sometimes we have no choice but to disturb these relationships, but we should do so thoughtfully, with full awareness that what we do may have consequences remote in time and place."[59] She was reflecting on how chemicals such as DDT—used during World War II to control typhus-carrying lice and malaria and then released to farmers as an insecticide to support industrial agriculture and to douse Mexicans entering the United States under the Bracero Program as farmworkers—were dangerous to all forms of life.

The sentiments, that the human and nonhuman environments are inseparable and that ethical questions imbricate survival questions, spread rapidly in the popular imagination and materialized in environmental social movements, lifestyle modifications, public policy, and economic practices.[60] In California, activism addressed a range of topics: land conservation, both for recreational and aesthetic reasons; healthy eating, which included nonprocessed "natural" foods and vegetarianism; pesticide reduction in the name of protecting farmworkers, animals, and eaters; organic gardening and small-scale farming; and back-to-the-land communes. Underlying many of these ideals was a distrust of industrial mass society pushed by government and business interests. The anti-capitalist countercultural currents of the 1960s and 1970s pushed the emerging organic farming movement to link its sustainable production methods to a range of social concerns.[61] For example, organic farming practices resisted the corporately controlled fertilizer and pesticide industries. These converging and interrelated countercultural practices have continued to diffuse into contemporary food politics.[62]

Chief among these contemporary shifts is the emergence of California's organic farming industry, which is the largest in the United States. California was the first state to have an organic labeling system, which California Certified Organic Farmers (CCOF) started in 1973. The founders of this certifying agency and trade association identified with the countercultural trends at the time. Many of them hoped organic agriculture would begin as an interstitial practice that eventually corroded the foundations of industrial agriculture. Toward such ends, CCOF devised standards to valorize organic produce and help people navigate the food consumer marketplace.[63] The idealism of CCOF and organic farming was short-lived, as other certification schemes and laws vied for legitimacy. Huge growers soon dominated the sector, which over time weakened organic standards and enforcement; perpetuated a lack of commitment to social standards; increased costs for small farmers, such as the price of land; and set up a pricing system that excludes many eaters. Now, there are also some activists and growers in the organic industry resisting labor regulations that protect farmworkers, which obstructs any kind of food politics broadly committed to economic justice.[64] The original populist appeal and agrarian ideal of organic agriculture now abut the industry's capitalist composition.[65] Although organic agriculture is ecologically and nutritionally superior and reduces harmful pesticide exposure for farmworkers, it falls short of an oppositional movement of small-family farms using agroecological practices that sells affordable produce and adequately pays farmworkers.

Since the 1980s, many organic farming activists have continued to move away from some of the founding radical ideals. The current organic craze has mutated into a consumer alternative to conventional food and forgone opposition to the economic and political structures upon which the food system relies.[66] Epitomizing this trend is Earthbound Farm, the largest grower of organic produce in the United States, most recognized for their packaged salads. Beginning on 2.5 acres in Carmel Valley, California, the company now boasts over fifty-three thousand acres under organic production, much of it contracted to a network of growers. Earthbound Farm sells its produce to over 75 percent of all American supermarkets. In 2012, the company had over $460 million in revenue and $75 million in earnings.[67] After the leveraged buyout specialists HM Capital Partners purchased a 70 percent controlling share in the company, HM Capital morphed into a new private equity firm, Kainos Capital, whose specialty is the food sector. White Wave, a division of the dairy giant Dean Foods, then bought Earthbound Farm for $600 million in 2013.[68] In addition to the influence of finance capital in the organic sector, multinational food corporations increasingly buy organic food–processing companies.[69] This consolidation includes major California organic companies. Examples include Kashi (Kellogg), Odwalla (Coca-Cola), Naked Juice (Pepsi), Muir Glen Organic (General Mills), Santa Cruz Organic (Smucker's), and Sweet Leaf Tea (Nestlé). In addition, organic and natural food retailers Whole Foods (Amazon) and Trader Joe's (Aldi) and distributors United Natural Foods and Tree of Life cornered most of their respective markets.[70]

The history of the organic farming movement in the United States illustrates that ideals do not always translate into expected outcomes. In this instance, the neoliberal logic of the prevailing political economy infiltrated the movement through initiatives like organic labeling.[71] Some proponents were concerned with this state of affairs, but the privileged social position of most others made it easier to let go of oppositional principles in the name of greater profit.[72] The history of the organic farming movement reveals that powerful corporations have capitalized on the new growth market in "green" products. Nevertheless, some of the same prefigurative politics that animated the original movement live on in those starting urban farms or community gardens, running small and midsized family farms, and leading organic advocacy organizations such as the Cornucopia Institute. What is less clear is the degree to which some activists integrate concerns with structural inequality with organic methods of food production. The legacy of the "market as movement" permeates how organic farmers create social boundaries between themselves and immigrant farmworkers.[73] This postpolitical tendency to prioritize market-based strategies can impede a confrontational food politics that fights for food justice. The trajectory of the organic farming movement suggests activists face historical choices of whether to adopt the structural analyses driving progressive movements or accept widespread neoliberal notions that ignore underlying inequalities.

Farmworker and Food Labor Movements

There is a long labor history in California of immigrant food-chain workers. Popular opinion often claims these workers are willing to work for less, work harder, and are more docile than the native-born population. Yet the historical record reveals ongoing labor struggles.[74] Not only do more people of color and immigrants work in the food system than whites do, they receive lower pay and fewer benefits, experience less upward mobility, face greater discrimination, and are exposed to more dangerous working conditions.[75] In response, farmworker and food labor movements have demanded society recognize the inherent human dignity of all workers. They have also fought to overcome subordination along the lines of race, ethnicity, nationality, gender, and class that are embedded in capitalist wage-labor relations. Given that a socially just food system is impossible without ending inequities, the history of farm and food worker resistance is essential to understanding the development of food justice–inspired food politics.

As the former labor organizer and sociologist Marshall Ganz has shown, there were three waves of farmworker organizing in California before the United Farm Workers (UFW) arose in the 1960s to carry out the most successful challenge to growers' power to date.[76] The first wave of organizing came about in the early 1900s by Japanese labor associations and the International Workers of the World (IWW), a radical labor union committed to organizing immigrants and other marginalized laborers. After the Chinese were prevented from immigrating in the late 1800s, there was a labor shortage, so the Japanese were encouraged into farm labor and by 1905 accounted for half of California's seasonal farm labor.[77] Because they could not own land, many Japanese farmworkers staged strikes to improve labor conditions, and when needed, they formed interethnic alliances with Mexicans and Filipinos to improve wages.[78] In the eyes of growers, farmworkers were a contingent and mobile labor force, so they would sometimes concede to workers' demands, but never with more than short-term contracts. One of the major IWW campaigns took off after building farmworker discontent in fields throughout California, so they targeted the single largest agricultural employer in the state, the Durst Brothers Hops Ranch in Wheatland, California. The housing conditions and pay were deplorable, with many workers laboring through dysentery and typhoid fever.[79] After Ralph Durst refused to improve pay, working, and living conditions, workers voted to strike. The following day, a riot ensued during an IWW organizer's speech after a deputy fired a gun, which protesters then wrestled away and used to kill him and the district attorney. In spite of the murder conviction of two Wobblies (common name for IWW members), the IWW inspired farmworkers to continue organizing throughout the state.[80] The IWW went on to win many workplace wage increases through wildcat strikes and established local union halls as free-speech spaces for migrant workers to build solidarity and organize around their interests.[81]

The next wave of organizing came during the 1930s and early 1940s. Due to sharp wage cuts and fewer farmworkers per acre of land, radical organizers, mainly from the Communist Party, Mexican and Filipino labor associations, and the American Federation of Labor (AFL) and the Congress of Industrial Organizations (CIO), stepped back into the fields.[82] Of particular importance was the Communist-aligned and Filipino-led Cannery, Agricultural, and Industrial Workers Union (CAIWU). Unlike most organizing efforts up to that point, there was little federal support for farmworkers. Although they successfully leveraged the National Industrial Recovery Act of 1933 to get the federal government to intervene in wage negotiations with growers, the intervention failed to generate the outcomes hoped for by farmworkers. Therefore, CAIWU staged some of the largest and most successful strikes to date. This era also saw the founding of unions in California's processing, packing, and distribution centers. Despite major territory and sector disputes between the AFL and CIO, the formation of the Longshoremen, Teamsters, and the United Cannery, Agricultural, Packing and Allied Workers of America created a new generation of unions representing food workers. Big labor union successes were modest, and oftentimes excluded Mexican and Filipino interests, who therefore formed their own labor associations to represent farmworkers as the newly formed industrial unions focused on organizing the growing urban labor force.[83]

Organizing continued throughout the 1940s and into the early 1950s due to the development of the first farmworker-only labor union, the AFL's National Farm Labor Union (NFLU). Unfortunately, the NFLU was largely unsuccessful in its boycott and strike efforts, and was not accountable to its Mexican and Filipino constituencies. Compared with the efforts of the IWW and CAIWU, which explicitly confronted racism and solidified their position as a greater ally, the NFLU failed to build the power necessary to take on growers. Moreover, because the AFL housed and funded this union, it was insulated from the demands and needs of farmworkers, which resulted in decisions that limited developing the cultural capital needed to organize Mexicans and Filipinos. The NFLU also did not quell the influence of a new bracero program. Growers outmaneuvered the NFLU by getting the Truman administration to increase the number of documented workers from Mexico, which applied downward pressure on wages and working conditions throughout the industry and prevented unionization of what was now an even larger workforce.[84]

The NFLU set the stage for the formation and future success of the UFW. Beginning in the 1960s, for the first time in the fields of California, labor organizers successfully linked demands for racial justice and economic justice to win major victories. The famous grape boycotts secured better wages, better working conditions, pesticide protections and bans, and most important, the power of labor contracts through collective bargaining.[85] Activists, the public, and scholars have overly focused on the exceptional nature of Cesar Chavez and Dolores Huerta as organizers and the once powerful UFW. Most important, however, is the fact that fifty years of organizing California's farmworkers paved the way for the successes of UFW. One of the culminating moments was the passage in 1975 of the landmark California Agricultural Labor Relations Act. The state passed this legislation to intervene in the historic struggle between growers, local political elites, and racist reactionary groups on one side and radical and liberal activists and labor unions and interethnic labor associations on the other side.

At around the same time that farmworkers were making gains, there was a wave of unionization in cities due to the efforts of the Retail Clerks International Union (RCIU). This resulted in major grocery retail chains such as A&P, Lucky Stores, and Safeway improving workers' pay and offering the union an opportunity to bargain for better working conditions. Much like many farmworker campaigns, the union adopted boycott and strike tactics. Because the grocery retail industry was not yet dominated by a handful of companies with the logistical capacity to absorb these actions and it could not be outsourced, grocery retail workers were advantageously positioned to make major gains. The major chains were 88 percent unionized by 1955, and membership in the RCIU grew from sixty thousand to five hundred thousand between 1944 and 1968.[86] These victories set the stage for workers and unions to fight to maintain their advantage over companies. As technological changes in the food system led to job losses, unions chose to consolidate. Most important for grocery retail, this meant a reduction in the number of butchers as more processed meats filled the shelves. These factors led to the Amalgamated Meat Cutters and Butcher Workmen of North America to merge with RCIU in 1979 to form the United Food and Commercial Workers International Union, becoming the largest union affiliated with the AFL-CIO.[87]

While workers in grocery retail made major gains, many fast-food establishments, restaurants, and big-box grocery retailers are still resolutely anti-union. Even in the fields, the gains of the UFW were short lived; organizing has dramatically declined, growers continue to exploit farmworkers, and an overwhelming majority of farmworkers remain nonunion with few other protections or advocates.[88] Because farm and food workers remain marginalized, the struggle for food justice is ongoing. Labor organizers have undertaken a wide range of strategies and tactics, many of which they borrowed or modified to fit the context. Yet they often face powerful social actors, such as politicians, business owners, or racist and nativist publics, as well as institutional conditions that shape the field of contention.

The Black Power Movement

On a march through Mississippi in 1966, in contrast to the chant of "Freedom Now" by activists associated with Martin Luther King Jr.'s Southern Christian Leadership Conference, the more radical Student Nonviolent Coordinating Committee led by Stokely Carmichael introduced the world to the slogan "Black Power."[89] Encapsulated in the difference between the two frames were strategic orientations to addressing institutional racism.

The demand for freedom centered on the need for legislative changes and protections. Although the call for black power did not always shunt the role of the state, it emphasized a black identity and consciousness promoting self-determination. For all the successes of the civil rights movement, black urbanites across the United States continued to experience racism in prisons, schools, and jobs and held little political power at local and state levels. Consequently, while the black power movement fought to reform local institutions, it also engaged in what the Black Panther Party (BPP) referred to as "survival pending revolution." Although the media caricatured the beret-wearing, gun-toting black radical who resisted police brutality, the movement consisted of many other participants and strategies, such as those who adopted African names and developed black-oriented groups within larger organizations such as universities and legislatures.[90] Survival meant supporting black community development on the way to dismantling racism. The goal was not strictly separatism, but empowerment.

The fusion of reform-based and autonomous political strategies coupled with the elevation of a distinctly black collective identity resonated in many cities with large black populations. In cities such as Chicago, Detroit, Los Angeles, Oakland, and New York, the BPP tapped into economically marginalized black residents who were frustrated with the failure of the liberal welfare state to lift blacks into the middle class.[91] Incidents around the same time, such as the assassination of Malcolm X early in 1965 and then the volatile police abuse of a black man months later in the Los Angeles neighborhood of Watts, were stark reminders of the racist conditions under which black urbanites lived. It was in this context that riots exploded in cities such as Chicago, New York, and Los Angeles, which highlighted the economic and social conditions undermining the welfare of black communities.[92] As Joshua Bloom and Waldo Martin put it, "The well-being of individual black bodies and the collective black community reflected the overall welfare of the larger black body politic. Improving the health status of blacks thus went hand in hand with improving their political, economic, and social status."[93]

The BPP improved the welfare of blacks by developing sixty-five different community programs between 1966 and 1982.[94] These included programs such as Benefit Counseling, Community Pantry, Employment Referral Service, Free Breakfast for Children, Free Busing to Prisons, Food Cooperative, Legal Aid and Education, Liberation Schools, Nutrition

Classes, and Youth Training and Development. These programs were the central work of the organization. Grounding their organizing was a Ten Point Program outlining the BPP's demands and beliefs. Black radicals explicitly understood that strategies for social reproduction responded to the hegemony of capitalism and institutional racism.[95] They developed these "survival programs" to build up the capacity of blacks to engage in revolutionary struggle. Their demands are directly relevant to contemporary food politics because food justice activists have adopted and modified them to fit other class, racial, and ethnic groups' needs.[96] These include the following:

1. We want freedom. We want power to determine the destiny of our Black and oppressed communities.
2. We want full employment for our people.
3. We want an end to the robbery by the capitalist of our Black and oppressed communities.
4. We want decent housing, fit for the shelter of human beings.
5. We want education for our people that exposes the true nature of this decadent American society. We want education that teaches us our true history and our role in the present-day society.
6. We want completely free health care for all Black and oppressed people.
7. We want an immediate end to police brutality and murder of Black people, other people of color, all oppressed people inside the United States.
8. We want an immediate end to all wars of aggression.
9. We want freedom for all Black and poor oppressed people now held in U.S. federal, state, county, city and military prisons and jails. We want trials by a jury of peers for all persons charged with so-called crimes under the laws of this country.
10. We want land, bread, housing, education, clothing, justice, peace and people's community control of modern technology.[97]

Although there are autonomous strands of food justice activism that build on this conjunctural analysis to develop solutions beyond the state, much of the activism *combines* prefigurative and confrontational strategies.[98] In the short term, food justice requires leveraging the state to ameliorate social problems, but long-term liberation is unlikely if it relies on an institution whose raison d'être is to accumulate and consolidate power.[99] This strategically overlaps with how the ideas and tactics of the black power movement set the foundation for contemporary struggles such as the Black Lives Matter, environmental justice, and prison abolitionist movements.

Tensions with the state permeate the political legacy of the black power movement. The historian William Van Deburg suggests there are two dominant ideological positions that informed strategy: pluralist and nationalist.[100] Although there was not always a clear distinction, the division illustrates differences between food justice politics that infiltrate and reform institutions and those that foster autonomy for certain racial and ethnic groups. On the one hand, there were activists and intellectuals who argued that blacks had to control land, which required entering and leading economic and political institutions, so blacks were in no way reliant on whites. To end de facto segregation in city halls, schools, and workplaces, community leaders needed to take over the bureaucratic apparatus responsible for administering daily needs. Greater representation was a prerequisite for the equitable distribution of resources. Black power activists coupled these strategies with developing black-run businesses that hired local black residents. Similarly, they advocated for community control of schools to improve the services offered to students and nurture students with culturally relevant education. These strategies relied on the belief that blacks needed to leverage their power to shape the institutions structuring black life. On the other hand, black nationalists eschewed the cultural, economic, and political establishment because it had failed blacks and did not appear to be improving in a post–civil rights era. The goal was to develop alternatives instead of trying to take over existing institutions; the only way to negotiate with whites was to control their own lives on their own institutional terms. Some thought this required black-only territories spread out across the country, while others believed there should be just one territory, either in the United States or somewhere in Africa. Compared with this territorial nationalism, revolutionary nationalists advocated for supporting African independence movements throughout the continent and engaging in revolutionary struggle to overthrow capitalist rule in the United States. This meant commitment to a socialist transformation led by the oppressed by any means necessary, including violence.

As with the other social movements discussed earlier, the black power movement faced political and social backlash. The covert operations of the Federal Bureau of Investigation's (FBI) Counterintelligence Program (COINTELPRO) had surveilled and infiltrated the civil rights movement for years, but ramped up its operations to discredit and disrupt the black radicals who came afterward, especially those with nationalist or revolutionary positions.[101] The state will adopt a counterinsurgency posture when it feels threatened. In the case of the BPP, which directly challenged the legitimacy of law enforcement, FBI director J. Edgar Hoover declared the BPP was "without question . . . the greatest threat to the internal security of the country."[102] Such assertions then justified actions that stoked violence against the BPP by "rival" groups, fostered internal dissension, and discouraged public support. The FBI was involved in a conspiracy to destroy the BPP. In Chicago, for example, this led to other tactics aimed at sabotaging the Free Breakfast for Children program, disrupting the distribution of their newspaper, and a COINTELPRO-backed police raid in 1969 on an apartment where the leaders Fred Hampton and Mark Clark were murdered.[103] FBI campaigns against the black power movement ultimately removed one of the few community-based bulwarks against the rising tide of racial neoliberalism that would economically ravage low-income black communities. These actions by the state reveal the levels to which political elites use their institutional power to suppress social movements that demand institutional transformation.

From Dialectical Observation to Dialectical Evaluation

In developing his "analysis of situations," Gramsci advanced a dialectical method of observing society to determine the possibilities for radical social change. In the *Prison Notebooks,* he wrote, "The most important observation to be made about any concrete analysis of the relations of force is the following: that such analyses cannot and must not be ends in themselves . . . but acquire significance only if they serve to justify a particular practical activity, or initiative of will."[104] While food politics can be observed and analyzed with reference to their historical significance, a further dialectical step of evaluation can identify opportunities for intervention.

We can evaluate each of the aforementioned movements' visions and politics in terms of their *desirability, viability,* and *achievability.*[105] The question of *desirability* takes place in the realm of utopian discussions of ideal institutions and abstract principles. Although discussions of desirable alternatives clarify ethical and moral principles, they lack a clear plan of action. For example, California's organic movement was predicated on the belief that a desirable world would be one in which corporately controlled industrial agriculture disappeared and would be replaced by an array of diversified small-scale farmers. Organic agriculture has not turned out in this way.[106] Failures raise the question of *viability*. Asking whether social alternatives are viable requires evaluating whether outcomes match the desires that led to the proposal. Unionizing and protecting farmworkers from pesticides, for example, used to be a radical proposal given the history of repression by racist growers and reactionary groups throughout the twentieth century.[107] There was no way for the Wobblies and Communists to know that what they thought was viable in the early 1900s would turn out to be achievable in the mid- to late 1900s with the rise of the United Farm Workers. Nevertheless, they imagined that another world was possible, one that would surmount the oppressive conditions they witnessed. Viability is historically and geographically contingent. Finally, there is the question of *achievability;* is a proposed transformation of existing institutions possible. Wright suggests that this "depends upon the extent to which it is possible to formulate coherent, compelling strategies which both help create the conditions for implementing alternatives in the future and have the potential to mobilize the necessary social forces to support the alternative when those conditions occur."[108] Interrogating what is possible considers relations of power, which requires determining the relative position of those seeking some transformative change. To take another case, one can evaluate the BPP's Ten-Point Program and point out the variability in its outcomes. While state repression thwarted the practical achievability of the whole program, the BPP still realized some semblance of self-determination over "land, bread, housing, education, [and] clothing" through their survival programs.[109]

Considering the food politics that have diffused into the practice of food justice helps to explain ideological and strategic differences. The range of political commitments and theories of social change run from the total rejection of capitalism and the state to the complete acceptance with some minor reforms. For those with a radical ideology of food justice that is critical of structural inequalities, there is greater support for strategies used in the farmworker, food labor, and black power movements.

Those with a "moralist" conception of food justice emphasize the goodness and rightness of creating alternatives, arguing that communities without access to local and organic food need to learn their value and accept help from others, which falls in line with much of the contemporary organic farming movement.[110] Social movement spillover also creates the opportunity to critique conceptions of food justice that are incapable of resisting and eliminating inequities. It avails scholars and activists alike with historical examples to imagine how to expand the conception and practice of food justice.

With hindsight, food justice activists can reflect on whether some of the abovementioned real utopian analyses and solutions are desirable. The short answer is yes. Food justice activists would like to see corporations lose their stranglehold over the food system, organic farming in its most ecologically sound methods predominate, food and farm workers thrive, and capitalism and institutional racism dismantled. While these are desirable ends, the process of getting there is riddled with questions regarding viability and achievability. The history of the struggles discussed in this chapter teaches that all social movements reflect specific conjunctures. A desire for an exact end abuts the conditions under which activists must navigate. While social change visions compel most activists, they need to focus in on the details of movement building. Food justice offers a vision for reevaluating certain strategies. It helps ask whether neoliberal initiatives reliant on consumer choice of organic food are going to lead to ending corporate control of the food system. It provides a way to look beyond the dominant narratives to consider how a vision for economic and racial equity requires intermediate and achievable ends, such as a federal policy mandating a $15 minimum wage and the right to collectively bargain. It helps tap into the history of social movements to learn that confronting institutional power is imperative to remake society.

The two movements reviewed here that were the largest threat to the economic and political order were the agrarian populist movement and the black power movement. These two movements adopted mutual aid and prefigurative strategies and simultaneously challenged elites and institutions in an endeavor to dismantle structural inequalities. Although also perceived as dangerous to the status quo, the organic farming movement focused most on creating alternatives to, while the farmworker and food labor movement worked on reforming labor practices within, the conventional food system. All these movements contributed ideas and

strategies that have influenced new generations of activists. As the food politics in each of my cases show, food justice is the conceptual container
capable of appropriating and reimagining these former movements for
the needs of today. Hence, I disagree with the overly pessimistic conclusions of Richard Walker, who writes in his history of California agriculture, "Looking back at California's triumphal march of agrarian capitalism, one catches a whiff of anarchism, socialism, and utopianism in the
air blowing out in the fields and packinghouses. . . . Yet none of these
alternative visions has come to pass. . . . Capitalism in the California
countryside has steamrolled the anarchist communist, the business populist, and the farmworker organizer with equal abandon. . . . That has
been the principal secret of its success."[111] While it is undoubtedly true
that many of these social movements did not reach their desirable ends,
there were moments of achievement.[112] Besides, the politics at the heart of
many of these movements live on, and with time, activists have rearticu-
lated what viable and achievable alternatives look like in the context of
actually existing neoliberal capitalism and institutional racism. I agree,
then, with the distinguished historian Robin D. G. Kelley, who argues,
"Unfortunately, too often our standards for evaluating social movements
pivot around whether or not they 'succeeded' in realizing their visions
rather than on the merits or power of the visions themselves. By such a
measure, virtually every radical movement failed because the basic power
relations it sought to change remain pretty much intact. And yet it is
precisely those alternative visions and dreams that inspire new generations to continue to struggle for change."[113] Such perspectives, including
those that reduce California's food politics to just another example of
neoliberalization, play into a narrative that oversimplifies food politics
and overlooks how food justice activism works across social boundaries to address structural inequalities.[114] They miss how ideas and activists go into abeyance and wait to reemerge, always in a new form, once a
political opportunity arises, a new collective identity is formed, enough
resources are captured to engage new campaigns, or a new threat sur-
faces.[115] This dialectical understanding accounts for relations of subordination beyond a single sector like the food system. Instead, it recognizes
the spirit of resistance passes down and morphs, in this case, to provide
inspiration that nurtures food justice politics.

2

Opposing the Carceral State

Food-Based Prisoner Reentry Activism

The H-Unit in San Quentin State Prison consists of five prefabricated warehouse units housing two hundred prisoners each. The men serving time in this medium-security division of the prison were convicted of lower-level crimes such as assault, burglary, and drug possession. A ten-foot-high chain-link fence topped with two more feet of spiraling razor wire surrounds the prison yard enclosing the prisoners, and three twenty-foot-high guard towers interspersed strategically around the yard monitor their every move. In the middle of these warehouses is a dirt field with a patch of grass struggling to survive these harsh conditions. Elsewhere is gray concrete, a basketball and volleyball court, and workout bars and benches.

Yet life bursts forth in two small segments of the yard. The hues of green and punctuated flashes of fuchsia, orange, purple, red, and yellow come from gardens run by the Insight Garden Program. This prison-based horticultural therapy program built the older of the two gardens in 2003 to help prisoners draw connections between nurturing plants, cooperation, and healing from the trauma of incarceration. The prisoners reflect the diversity of the flowers, herbs, and bushes in this 1,200-square-foot garden. California prisons are extremely racially segregated, so in this garden, as it is one of the only nonsegregated spaces in San Quentin, prisoners learn to relate across social boundaries. Complementing this time among the bees and in the soil are therapeutic sessions where prisoners collectively share their life experiences, struggles, and hopes for reentering their communities. In 2014, Planting Justice, a food justice organization based in Oakland, built another garden with the Insight Garden Program and the help of prisoners. After a five-year partnership with the Insight Garden Program, Planting Justice received permission to build four raised vegetable beds in a small corner of the yard. Although prisoners cannot eat the food grown in this garden, they gain vocational gardening and land-scaping training that some of them use once they leave prison; Planting Justice has hired and paid living wages to eighteen of these men to build edible landscapes and community gardens all over the San Francisco Bay Area.[1] None of the men have returned to prison.[2] By reimagining the restorative possibilities within the prison, this partnership revalues a discarded population upon reentry.

For decades, social reformers, health professionals, political organiz-ers, and social justice activists have devised horticultural strategies to ease the pain of prison and support formerly incarcerated people in reenter-ing their communities.[3] On one end of the spectrum, this has included a social control focus. Keep prisoners busy with growing food to prevent them from engaging in misconduct, and in the name of job training maxi-mize profit by exploiting their labor for little to no pay.[4] For these reasons, prison abolitionists and opponents to mass incarceration question the value of agricultural practices associated with carceral restrictions on free-dom. Indeed, even when social reformers claim the rehabilitative curative of gardening or the opportunity for skill development, the question is, where are prisoners heading toward? The same communities deprived of social investment and criminalized to manage the resulting poverty?

On the other end of the spectrum is a long history of gardens that have served as liberatory zones of freedom within prisons and offered horticultural opportunities that intervene to reduce recidivism and fos-ter community organizing around racial and economic justice.[5] While imprisoned for his revolutionary work against apartheid in South Africa, Nelson Mandela found solace in his garden. Reflecting on that time, he wrote in his autobiography, "A garden was one of the few things in prison that one could control. To plant a seed, watch it grow, to tend it and then harvest it, offered a simple but enduring satisfaction. The sense of being the custodian of this small patch of earth offered a small taste of freedom."[6] Combined with concrete economic opportunities and social support networks that link food production to successful reentry into free society, the bucolic ameliorative of a garden can become a liberatory social force.

To consider the meaning of food justice in relation to carceral con-junctures requires recognizing the reach of mass incarceration into the same urban communities where food justice activism predominates. These intersections present an opportunity to connect the production of racialized harms with creative solutions. As Ruth Gilmore reasons in her groundbreaking study of California's prison boom, "Prisons and other locally unwanted land uses accelerate the mortality of modestly educated working people of all kinds . . . and show how economic and environmental justice are central to antiracism."[7] Similarly, food justice is essential for advancing an anti-racist agenda. Practices such as urban agriculture can tackle racialized economic and political inequities associated with mass incarceration. If we only critique the fact that most urban agriculture initiatives fail to provide living-wage jobs or that not all prisoners want to work in the food system, we would miss the forms of mutual aid and healing that inspire social change.

Around the United States, food justice activism is deepening the connection between food and carceral politics. In 2015, after the eighth annual Growing Food and Justice for All Gathering, a Prisons and Food Working Group formed to develop a shared analysis and campaign agenda. In their position paper, they wrote,

> We call on those of us in the food movement to recognize the intersections between the exploitation of communities via the prison industrial complex and our food system; this recognition is essential to achieve our ultimate liberation. It is critical that we understand that the patterns of domination and exploitation that drive our prison and policing systems are inherently connected with the patterns of domination and exploitation that drive the inequities within our food system. We who believe in food justice, we who believe in food sovereignty must recognize the need for an abolition of all enslavement and exploitation in order to achieve real justice.

This urgency is shared broadly within food justice networks. As the violence of mass incarceration and police brutality continued to target black and Latinx communities only to fuel widespread urban rebellion and the Black Lives Matter movement, the crisis reached a tipping point at which other realms of social life, such as food, became related. In 2016, the blog *Civil Eats* published commentary from sixteen food justice leaders, which represented how their food politics have absorbed the carceral conjuncture.[8] Comments included reflections on the history of slavery and agriculture, the related forms of institutional racism perpetuating exploitation in prisons and throughout the food system, and the importance of a justice analysis and political action to end white supremacy and achieve liberation. What does acting at the intersection of food and carceral politics look like?

This chapter focuses on the politics of *restorative food justice*. I define this as a commitment to economic, racial, and restorative justice and permaculture, with mutual aid strategies that support formerly incarcerated people and their communities to heal from the trauma of mass incarceration and that advance policies to improve the reentry process. Engaging the carceral logic of confinement and social control opens the possibility for imagining a liberatory food politics. Central to making headway is an organizing commitment to inclusivity, leadership diversity, and organizational flexibility. In particular, Planting Justice prioritizes the experiences of those who have lived in heavily surveilled and policed spaces before, during, and after prison. Mass incarceration devastates working-class communities and communities of color by locking up and then exploiting the acquired bodies. This exacerbates poverty and segregation, disrupts families, quashes innovation, and pathologizes certain social groups. It also creates inequitable relationships to food by deepening food insecurity for families left behind and by poorly paying people to work in food-related prison industries. But Planting Justice organizers, especially those who were formerly incarcerated, respond to these carceral conjunctures with actions, critiques, and hopes that dialectically develop food justice and advance broader social justice goals shared by many social movements.

The Costs of Mass Incarceration and Police Power

The pervasive system of mass incarceration in the United States criminalizes and regulates the same working-class communities and communities of color disproportionately experiencing food inequities and other traumas.[9] This racialized system politicizes crime and exacerbates barriers to education, employment, food, housing, and political participation.[10] As a mode of social and spatial control, mass incarceration also intensifies preexisting class and ethnoracial inequities by targeting subordinated groups at each point in the prison pipeline: in criminalized neighborhoods, in prison, and upon reentry into the same neighborhoods.[11] Moreover, when citizens express outrage with mass demonstration and protest, law enforcement agencies and officers exact their monopoly on violence to quell popular democratic participation.[12] Combined, this potent mixture of state-sanctioned social control strategically incapacitates entire communities and social movements to maintain power.

Ethnoracial hierarchies in cities such as Oakland grew worse after California's prison boom, which accelerated in the 1980s with the War on Drugs, deindustrialization, and neoliberal counterrevolution.[13] As jobs disappeared and whites fled to the suburbs, the political class developed punitive methods to absorb the surplus labor pool. We now have a criminal justice system whose growth is predicated on targeting black and Latinx individuals. For example, they are disproportionately stopped, searched, and arrested and overly represented in Alameda County's prison population.[14] Although violent crime has fallen and property crime predominates, criminalizing poverty remains a preferred solution.[15] Politicians see fixing schools by adding teachers and restructuring curriculums to meet the needs of students, encouraging new business sectors to enter these communities, or rewriting laws to prevent discrimination in housing as less important. Nowhere is this more apparent than in spending priorities. Following longer-term trends, the adopted budget for 2013–2015 spent 42 percent of general funds, $194 million, on the Oakland Police Department, the largest single expenditure in the city's budget.[16] Despite accounting for a little less than 20 percent of the city's employees, the department receives one quarter of spent payroll dollars.[17]

Distrust of police and the criminal justice system in Oakland is widespread, yet it is racially stratified.[18] A survey found that black residents reported being half as likely as whites to have a positive interaction with police, and twice as likely to have an interaction initiated by police.[19] The same survey discovered that only 11 percent of those who had a negative experience with police reported it to the Citizens' Police Review Board or the Oakland Police Department's Internal Affairs Division. Residents are also dissatisfied with public safety expenditures and question whether spending extra tax dollars on law enforcement is the best use of that money.[20] After all, nine out of ten police officers are not Oakland residents, which pulls over $186 million a year in wages and retirement benefits out of the city.[21] Rank-and-file police officers also express concerns. Most think elected and department officials withhold adequate support, such as police equipment, and the residents of Oakland undervalue their work.[22]

Racialized power dynamics with the state not only frame citizens' overall interaction with law enforcement but also focus the attention of blacks and Latinx who bear the brunt of institutional racism and the resulting forms of bigotry and prejudice. The NAACP exposed that in Oakland there were forty-five police shootings between 2004 and 2008 and that thirty-seven blacks and no whites were victims. In 40 percent of the cases, police found no weapons. No police officers were ever charged. Oakland police officers operate in a culture of impunity, which reinforces poor behavior. For example, the police officers receiving the Oakland Police Department's top awards have been involved in more shootings and cases of brutality and misconduct than officers receiving lesser awards have.[23] Moreover, despite mechanisms to give civilians oversight of police officers, the city of Oakland has paid exorbitantly to settle police abuse cases. Between 1990 and 2014, Oakland and its private insurance carriers spent $74 million in settlements on 417 lawsuits accusing police of brutality, misconduct, and other civil rights violations.[24] Between 2001 and 2011 alone, the city paid out over $57 million in police abuse settlement claims and ran a $58 million deficit in 2011.[25] Three years later, the city was still running a $28 million deficit.[26] Instead of taking disciplinary action against police to halt organizationally sanctioned behavior, the state, and by extension the taxpaying citizen, pay for abusive behaviors.

Protesters have also experienced police abuse since the heyday of the Black Panther Party.[27] More recently, images of riot police marching on Occupy Oakland protesters; firing rubber bullets, bean bags, and tear gas canisters; and destroying the encampment are still fresh in the mind of Oakland's left-wing movements. A confluence of social movements, including prison abolition, criminal justice reform, and racial justice for Oscar Grant, the young black man killed by a white Bay Area Rapid Transit officer, joined for marches and teach-ins during Occupy Oakland. They manifested in the streets what a former Planting Justice board member believes is important for the success of social movements. "The surest way to get poor communication is to begin by talking about a specific strategy," Blaze argued. "Once there's a connection around your shared values and shared needs then it becomes a lot easier to sort of feel a sense of togetherness around choosing a specific strategy to learn how to move forward together." Occupy Oakland was a microcosm of the city's social movements, and the affinity group organization of Occupy allowed people with shared beliefs and needs to come together. A spirit of cooperation led to decisions to march in protest of public grievances, chief among them economic inequality and institutional racism in the criminal justice system. Speaking to these themes, Occupy Oakland renamed the site of its occupation across from Oakland City Hall, Oscar Grant Plaza. In response to the movement, the state met the protesters with violence. As a result, the city of Oakland has been embroiled in several federal civil rights–related lawsuits and has paid out over $7 million in settlement fees.[28]

The costs of an abusive police department stand in stark contrast to some recent cuts in public services. In 2012, Oakland cut $28 million from its general fund, which required job layoffs and a reduced service capacity for many departments.[29] Although threats to eliminate some public libraries never materialized, public school closures have proceeded apace, while the opening of charter schools has increased.[30] Coupled with reductions in state funding and a drop in enrollment partially attributed to gentrification, investment in keeping small neighborhood schools open has diminished. The economic outcomes are ethnically and racially disparate and apply downward pressure on formerly incarcerated people and black, Latinx, and working-class communities already suffering from high poverty, unemployment, and low wages.

While neoliberal economic reforms and institutionalized discrimination drive the harassment, abuse, roundup, and imprisonment of poor people and people of color, going to prison also *generates* inequality. Removing people from their communities disrupts local labor markets and possibilities for economic mobility, aggravates already-existing health problems due to stress and unreliable access to health care, ruptures family structures, furthers household disadvantage, and marginalizes former felons from civic life.[31] Moreover, when prisoners reenter their communities, they are subject to state surveillance. Most people currently under correctional control in the United States are not in prison, but are on probation and parole. In 2013, there were 6.89 million people under correctional control, 67 percent of whom were on probation and parole.[32] Furthermore, they experience social exclusion and stigma in terms of benefits, employment, and housing, and higher-than-average rates of post-traumatic stress disorder.[33] Even people who go through rehabilitative programs in prison or work with organizations and companies that support the reentry process still experience discriminatory laws and policies on the outside. The resulting challenges include learning to survive economically when faced with the requirement to disclose a criminal history, which can be grounds to reject an application. This complicates the emotional and social travails of reconnecting with family, especially for parents. Navigating the rules and regulations to overcome these challenges within the institutions responsible for perpetuating the stigma of incarceration is difficult for formerly incarcerated people and their allies. Because of the institutional momentum to incarcerate, law enforcement agencies lobbying for more tax dollars, widespread police abuse, and the shutting down of popular protest movements, finding strategies to intervene against these structural inequalities is no small feat.

Strategic Inclusivity, Leadership Diversity, and Organizational Flexibility

For the cofounders of Planting Justice, Gavin Raders and Haleh Zandi, previous social movement participation in the early 2000s informed the organizational structure and operation. Activism in the antiwar movement while in college taught them about global struggles against American imperialism, and their travels to places such as India taught them firsthand how people resisted corporate power. While canvassing for a nonprofit called Peace Action, they knocked on doors, made phone calls, and traveled to other states to fundraise and stir up support to end the wars in Iraq and Afghanistan. Burnout, however, was common because the organization lacked fair labor practices, such as adequate pay and democratic decision-making. Both Gavin and Haleh were frustrated that people who worked for organizations committed to social justice could not pay their bills and sustain this important work.

These experiences inspired a unique amalgamation of causes, strategies, and tactics. Of unique significance was canvassing hundreds of neighborhoods. Gavin recalled that "the regularity of the scene was sort of imprinting on me [because] . . . of space that wasn't being used to meet people's needs." He therefore concluded, "We need to do more organizing locally to have people working together and building community and creating tangible change in their communities." This epiphany solidified after Gavin spent time in a part of Kerala, India, where a community was contesting a Coca-Cola water-bottling plant that was stealing local water and offering low-wage jobs. In response, the community used traditional rainwater catchment systems and deepened public education during large protests and marches. "People just met their own needs and that was actually the most effective form of resistance," Gavin acknowledged.

After experiencing a model of organizing that paid people poorly as well as a social movement that combined both confrontational tactics and practices that fostered self-determination, Gavin was inspired to decipher how communities could reskill themselves to meet their own needs. So he undertook a permaculture design course for seven months. The founder of permaculture, Bill Mollison, defines this as "the conscious design and maintenance of agriculturally productive ecosystems which have the diversity, stability, and resilience of natural ecosystems. It is the harmonious integration of landscape and people providing their food, energy, shelter and other material and non-material needs in a sustainable way. . . . Permaculture design is a system of assembling conceptual, material, and strategic components in a pattern which functions to benefit all forms of life."[34] Gavin grew critical of how permaculture knowledge was privatized and widely inaccessible. While permaculture is a powerful concept and set of principles, the cost of a permaculture design course and its tendency to consist largely of white people reproduce some of the privileged attributes that underlie ecologically focused food politics.[35] Gavin's goal became to increase the access to and the relevance of permaculture for the socioeconomically diverse city of Oakland where he and Haleh lived.

Predating Planting Justice, they started a company called the Backyard Food Project that built edible landscapes. This tapped into the popularity of local food and gardening throughout the Bay Area.[36] But while there was a demand for landscape designs based on permaculture principles, Gavin and Haleh kept receiving correspondence by interested people who could not afford their services. Although Gavin and Haleh were improving their edible landscaping skills and still finding clients who could pay full cost, they felt compelled to come up with a better structure and started a nonprofit. They settled on a combination of community organizing and canvassing with a fee-for-service permaculture edible landscaping program that funded the work itself, created living-wage jobs and surplus money to invest in free or subsidized gardens. In the summer of 2008, they began Planting Justice.

Planting Justice's employment pool consists largely of people who grew up in working-class black and Latinx communities in the East Bay and/or spent time in prison. "I don't even think you can call it food justice without . . . creating economic opportunities within the food system for people who live in these urban communities that are most directly affected by food injustices," insisted Haleh. Given the economic disinvestment and criminalization of poor communities of color, there is a need for alternatives that empower people to care for themselves and their families, foster relationships and trust, and create more communal autonomy. These strategic priorities also deepen political commitments. Haleh offered an anecdote that speaks to how this can manifest while building edible landscapes: "One of our youth, his mom's been in prison because she wasn't documented and then he works alongside people who have been in prison because they're racially targeted in the streets. And so the kinds of alliances that kind of form . . . it's just really powerful and it's unique in terms of what can take place after that. Because they come from, you know, two different backgrounds, live in the same city, but now that they're aligned and working towards common goals, there's so much more that we can shift in our community by doing that." Further reflecting strategic commitments to break down social barriers and find commonalities around which to mobilize for food justice, Planting Justice has prioritized democratic organizational procedures. Haleh shared that in her experience nonprofits erected firewalls between board members and staff. "From the beginning, we really wanted to create an organization where that kind of hierarchy didn't exist and so we wanted to have anyone who wanted to be on staff, also be on the board of directors," reasoned Haleh.[37] In practice, about 50 percent of the board has consisted of staff members, including members of the constituencies they work with, such as high school graduates who went through Planting Justice programs, former San Quentin prisoners, and people working as community organizers on related issues. After asserting the need to reject the expectations imposed by the "non-profit industrial complex," Gabriel, a Latino former staff and board member, avowed, "We can give ourselves permission to challenge what we think is the most effective way of organizing."[38] Pointedly, the organization avoids clear demarcations of where food justice begins and ends. Gabriel elaborated: "People call it a movement of movements. . . . So, for me it is as much about alliances and coalition building as it is about honoring the lineage that your movements and social struggles have politicized you to get involved with the food justice movement. There is always coalition building within that." With different committees and programmatic branches that allow board members and staff experimental freedom and a consensus-based decision-making process, people can pursue projects that reflect their activist histories.[39] This structure allows for mobility throughout the organization and autonomy for each program. An open organizational structure that channels a diverse set of life experiences into collective action also creates the flexibility to link up with a range of social struggles.

Critical Interrogations of the Prison Pipeline

Planting Justice has worked with the Insight Garden Program since 2009 after seeing the founder, Beth Waitkus, give a conference talk in which she articulated a desire to start a vegetable garden inside the prison. Gavin recounted learning about this opportunity: "While we were volunteering at San Quentin State Prison [teaching food justice, permaculture, and urban farming,] we heard from all of the men how important this garden was for their emotional and spiritual well-being. However, we also heard that they weren't sure how they were going to incorporate this into their lives when they got out of prison and returned to their communities."[40] Biographical and organizational characteristics availed Planting Justice to respond. While the organization's leaders valued the

Figure 1. Planting Justice staff work with prisoners at San Quentin State Prison. Photograph by Kirk Crippens.

focus on horticultural therapy, they realized the unique prospect of offering skill development training that could tie into a reentry program. Most of the prisoners they worked with were people of color, and more than 90 percent of the formerly incarcerated staff members at Planting Justice have been black. Their experiences have shaped how the organization connects ethnoracial and economic inequities to reentry-related solutions. While the social context of a racialized system of mass incarceration shapes how the organization develops interventions, the experiences of formerly incarcerated staff at Planting Justice provide a tangible lived reality. Many staff reside in and reenter spaces where they are criminalized and racialized by the current carceral regime, spaces riddled with problems such as poverty and food inequities. The following sections outline the chief concerns, critiques, and analyses that inform the practices that emerge to resist oppression upon reentry.

Preincarceration

More important than the relationship between personal responsibility and crime are the racial and economic inequities embedded in criminalized neighborhoods.[41] Like many others, Barry, a middle-aged black man who suffered from drug addiction, had few opportunities where he grew up. He first told me about how his drug addiction resulted in incarceration: "Once you use drugs then you do a lot of procrastinating I'd say. Because you are on the substance you'll say, 'I wanna do this, I wanna change my ways.' You notice that it never pans out. You always find another reason to go back into the hole." He went on to note, however, that drug programs overlook how poverty perpetuates drug use: "If you don't have a place to stay, and you don't have a stable income, you are not going to be clean and sober on the streets." This leaves people with few options to escape, a reality that stems from the carceral power of politicians and law enforcement committed to confinement strategies in working-class black neighborhoods.[42] Barry suggested, "Some people don't mind being incarcerated . . . because they have no money, no transportation, they don't have no food and they don't have no house." He concluded his recollection with an affirmative Black Lives Matter movement frame that rejects the dehumanizing outcomes of racialized carceral strategies: "It is not just black lives that matter, it's brown lives, everybody that's being oppressed, actually."

Linda, who is Latina and a former probation officer and correctional case manager, recognized many of the same challenges identified by Barry: "The system is rigged against them. It is designed for them to fail. . . . It is really stressful out there." She arrived at these conclusions by recalling the stories of formerly incarcerated people: " 'Don't feel sorry for me; give me a job so I can feed my kids.' They don't need your sympathy. They don't need food stamps. Another thing I hear too is that people want a job they are proud of. . . . People want to make more money than they can hustling on the street." This anecdote suggests that pathologizing people for living in poverty ignores disinvestment in neighborhoods with large numbers of poor people and people of color. Linda contended, "It's really not so much about morality and bad people. . . . No, people need to survive."

In addition to economic disparity and criminalization, many of the formerly incarcerated men I interviewed spoke of the historical legacy of slavery that is reanimated through the mass incarceration of black people. Reflecting on the nature of this institutional racism, a middle-aged black man named Saul asserted, "I still don't believe that we have a fair shake. . . . I'm being punished for something I had nothing to do with, bruh. I wasn't around, whatever was happening in history four hundred years ago. That ain't have anything to do with me. . . . So for me to be penalized . . . not just me but all of us in general, as a whole, for us to be held back, held down, treated the way we have been treated, all these years, bruh? . . . We did nothing wrong to deserve the stigma, the treatment, and everything that we've been getting all these years." Committing crimes does not take place in a vacuum. The policing of black people is a continuation of the historical trauma of the plantation economy, made worse by the fact that neighborhoods with high arrest rates often lack public investment that would help people avoid entering prison to begin with. The experiences and stories related by people like Saul, Linda, and Barry challenge ascribing immorality into decisions to break the law. The prison pipeline begins in places that prevent people from being law-abiding because the state deems these places and the impoverished people who occupy them more worthy of punishment than of protection.[43]

Incarceration

The confinement of prison is only the formalized outcome of a larger system of mass incarceration. The men I spoke with all spent time in one of two places in San Quentin: H-Unit or the North Block. In both sections of San Quentin the conditions are difficult, not least because of overcrowding and the danger it poses for prisoners' health and safety.[44] San Quentin was built for three thousand prisoners, but at the time housed over five thousand prisoners.[45] This reflects a broader trend in California. Governor Arnold Schwarzenegger declared a state of emergency in 2006 because of the pressures associated with an all-time-high prisoner population. By 2011, conditions were still dire. The California Department of Corrections and Rehabilitation budget was at a record high of $9.6 billion, which translated to about $50,000 per inmate.[46] This set in motion events that culminated in a 2011 class action lawsuit that went all the way to the Supreme Court, where the overcrowding was deemed in violation of the Eighth Amendment's prohibition against "cruel and unusual punishment." Such rulings, however, remain a minor palliative.

Once incarcerated, prisoners experience further marginalization and sociospatial control. Strict prison rules and physical layout tightly regulate behavior, such as mealtimes, mandatory work shifts, breaks, whom one associates with, and whether one receives adequate or even any healthcare treatment.[47] On top of these conditions, California prisons offer few rehabilitation or mental health programs, and over 65 percent of prisoners return within three years.[48] Jamal, a young black man who was in San Quentin for robbery, surmised that these conditions perpetuate feelings of restriction and dispossession: "Well when you go to prison, it's a sensory deprivation camp . . . for however long that you're in there. So when you get out, you're back in the concrete jungle. . . . You still got that mentality of . . . 'I have to survive and I have to get this money, get this job.'"

A leading grievance about imprisonment is that prisons exploit prisoner labor. As stated in the Thirteenth Amendment, "Neither slavery nor involuntary servitude, *except as a punishment for crime whereof the party shall have been duly convicted*, shall exist within the United States, or any place subject to their jurisdiction" (emphasis added). Abolishing labor exploitation in prison is nearly impossible because the constitutional protection provided by this amendment makes it sacrosanct. Saul was particularly incisive about this state of affairs:

> Take prison . . . we call that modern-day slavery. And I say "we"
> because I just left there, and . . . they paid us crow. Some of the
> jobs that we do, they should get paid contractors, big money to do

that shit. They paid us peanuts. We had to do electrical jobs that you should be paying somebody at least thirteen, seventeen, twenty-seven dollars an hour. . . . You paying me seventy-five cents. Come on bruh! And then I'm working eight hours. Come on bruh! And that's just one job. . . . We make all the clothes, all the furniture, all the food. . . . They give us crumbs. . . . It's insulting. . . . Now when I say I don't want to do it you gonna write me up, and give me some more time in prison because I don't wanna work, basically, for nothing. . . . That's injustice inside the prison system!

This moral outrage is targeted at the institutional racism of mandated labor à la the plantation economy through which white supremacy solidified and upon which the United States built its global capitalist advantage. Said plainly, this labor exploitation is seen as racist.

These conditions of confinement also create opportunities for political engagement. Maurice Bell, a formerly incarcerated black man who works with Planting Justice, told the story of how he participated in a prison sit-down strike in 1996 to oppose California rescinding family-visitation rights for prisoners with life sentences. In an article written online, he recalled, "As a prisoner who was not a lifer and was getting family visits, I knew how important it was to receive family visits. . . . I felt compelled to participate in that sit-down as an act of solidarity. Even though the lifers did not get their family visits back, we still took a stand and said all in one voice, 'NO MORE!' "[49] These fleeting moments of empowerment respond to an oppressive prison system with acts of human agency and resilience that formerly incarcerated people can draw on upon reentry. Nevertheless, life after prison is inherently difficult.

Postincarceration

Key to the practice of restorative food justice is the response to the fact that most people currently under correctional control are on probation and parole.[50] Formerly incarcerated people often reenter the same criminalized communities, what the critical race scholar and human geographer Rashad Shabazz refers to as a "prison-like environment."[51] They face the same policing, surveillance, and poverty that put them in prison to begin with, only this time with the added pressure of a criminal record.[52]

Underlying the institutional marginalization of formerly incarcerated people is a culture of stigma. The ignominy of imprisonment is persistent. As Simone, a white community organizer, urban gardener, and reentry home provider, lamented, "They're lepers of our culture. . . . We scapegoat and they are the easiest targets." Maurice identifies how this stigma is racialized: "As long as I see people clutching their purse when they see me, or crossing the street to avoid me, I know that I'm looked at as a criminal because I'm black."[53] This ideological reflex that formerly incarcerated black men are "criminals" with no opportunity for restoration stems from decades of tough-on-crime rhetoric from politicians and police and a media echo chamber championing the imprisonment of working-class communities of color.[54] These narratives are reinforced by laws that sanction discrimination against formerly incarcerated people, which only intensifies stereotypes that justify the stigma.

I heard repeatedly of the constant threat or experience of poverty and alienation. Jamal told me, "The hardest thing is coming home. . . . We being shut out of jobs . . . or voting or housing or . . . food stamps or any of the myriad things that we shut out of by having a criminal offense." The daily drudgery of these economic struggles coupled with problems like post-traumatic stress disorder take their toll.[55] "Folks are coming back mentally disabled," explained Jamal. "It takes some time to trust people, it takes some time to get relationships with people. . . . Like on some real healing, you know, it takes time and a lot of the times folks don't got time because they trying to get their housing, they've got all of the other stuff that society tells us that we need and that's a necessity."

In the process of conducting some interviews, I witnessed how economic support from the state can be undermined by criminalizing people on parole, which perpetuates the subordination of people deemed "immoral" for committing a crime.[56] During a phone interview with Gene, a middle-aged black man, he was taking the bus to Contra Costa County Housing Authority to find a landlord who would not discriminate against someone with a criminal record. He had to hang up and call me back while he dealt with this. Once back on the bus, he informed, "I've been searching almost six months now for an apartment with a Section 8 voucher that will pay a landlord $1,200 a month for a one bedroom. That's the sort of thing to me that is broken." Gene went on to share, "I have a nine-year-old daughter, but I have a court order to see her a couple days in the week. I don't have a place to bring her; I don't have a lot of money. . . .

I'm working just to pay child support, man." In true Kafkaesque fashion, the formerly incarcerated navigate a state that offers support that can be undermined with discriminatory practices or other state mandates. Constant surveillance of parolees can also thwart the desire to participate in publicly visible activism to reform the reentry process. To reject the carceral logic superimposed on black communities, a logic that relies on a steady supply of black bodies to send to prison, can be risky. Referring to the conflict between being on parole and engaging in advocacy with Planting Justice, Saul detailed, "It's really actually hard for me to get out there and protest and get involved with a lot of things that they're doing out in the community. . . . Say I'm publicly speaking, I run into a policeman or woman who's gonna grab me up . . . they can send me to jail. . . . I don't have time for that, man." Moreover, employers might closely monitor the performance of someone convicted of a felony. Gene used to advocate for more community-based services money for reentry work, but he felt once he had a job, he had to limit this advocacy: "I'm in my probation period [at work], so I can't be running back and forth between this and that like I was." Therefore, the healing and mutual aid network described in the following section become vital during reentry.

Critical Connections and Food-Based Interventions

On a sunny afternoon in Oakland, I sat down on the stoop of a house Gabriel was renting with friends. In the middle of an answer to a question I asked about what he sees as the relationship between land and labor in Planting Justice's work, he made the following nuanced observation that speaks to how restorative food justice resists oppression:

> I think that relationship is important to make in terms of how
> interconnected, interlocking oppressions actually are. The land is a
> place, a space where we can see where that all plays out. It is a
> really interconnected, interlocking place to resist. . . . It means that
> taking care of the land and building a relationship with the land is
> a very beautiful humanizing experience [and] is a way of resist-
> ing. . . . We try to teach about labor that is humanizing and that is
> based on reciprocity. . . . Again that is the way that PJ [Planting
> Justice] is doing that [their work] . . . based on what Grace Lee
> Boggs calls not so much critical mass, but critical connections.

The strategy to foster "critical connections" begins with creating living-wage work and equitable relationships to land, which are some of the hallmarks of radical food justice practice.[57]

Planting Justice developed an economically sustainable base on which to put its commitments to work. Two mutually constitutive programs produce income streams that account for 80 percent of the budget, while 20 percent of the budget comes from grants.[58] First, Transform Your Yard is a fee-for-service permaculture-landscaping program. Upon reentry, some of those who completed the Insight Garden Program inside San Quentin end up working for Planting Justice on teams installing and designing landscapes. Clients, mainly homeowners, pay in full for about three-quarters of these edible landscapes, while the organization subsidizes or gives away free the other quarter to working-class people or community-based organizations. As of April 2016, Planting Justice had built 380 gardens, 25 percent of which were free. This program shuffles capital from middle- and upper-class homeowners to create jobs starting at $17.50 an hour. Although it took four years, all staff members eventually became full-time salaried workers with health insurance. Second, the canvassing program, which provides the same wages and benefits, also organizes and fundraises throughout the Bay Area to support such well-remunerated work, including finding and channeling clients who want edible landscapes. It raises over $150,000 a year for Planting Justice's operating budget through small local donors. Equally as important is the public education. As their website states, "Sparking conversations about the prison system, corporate food control, backyard gardening and green job creation—the canvass team spoke to over 51,750 people on the streets about food justice issues since its inception in 2012."[59]

While there is no single remedy for dealing with the violence and marginalization experienced at each stage of the prison pipeline, jobs, along with other restorative practices, help intervene at the point of reentry. Regarding the postincarceration experience, the civil rights lawyer, legal expert, and prison reform advocate Michelle Alexander is less than sanguine: "They enter a separate society, a world hidden from public view, governed by a set of oppressive and discriminatory rules and laws that do not apply to everyone else . . . and are permanently relegated to an inferior status."[60] But such a conclusion forecloses on a dialectical process. There are strategies to illuminate the challenge of reentry that generate solidarity to navigate a criminal justice system intent on reincarceration.

Antecedents of Restorative Food Justice

Restorative justice promotes healing. Although practices vary, it focuses on the needs of victims, reintegrates offenders, and works with the local community to rehabilitate victims and offenders.[61] It therefore rejects the carceral logic of exclusion and segregation inherent to mass incarceration. The roots of these practices lie in some forms of indigenous community-based restorative justice.[62] In sentencing circles, the community engages deliberatively, often with the victim, to address a crime and restore peace. In healing circles, prisoners or the formerly incarcerated create a space to undertake individually and collectively their victimization and crimes. In restorative conferences, communities of care intervene with youth before any court proceedings to try to solve the problem.[63] These restorative justice practices are powerful not because they can supplant a retributive criminal justice system, but because of the strong social bonds that emerge through voluntary association. These bonds are the basis for transforming selves, communities, and the criminal justice system.[64] Moreover, formerly incarcerated people are more self-confident and capable of giving to those around them and develop tools and new networks that reduce the chance of returning to prison.

Recent practices around the world indicate that the articulation of food justice by Planting Justice and its allies in Oakland is part of a wider movement to develop methods for increasing social equity at the point of reentry. Restorative justice is merging with "greening justice" initiatives.[65] Successful practices with formerly incarcerated adults in Australia, England, and Norway and Native American youth in the United States nurture a connection to nature through food and gardening, develop green jobs skills and certifications, and facilitate ties to local social movements. These initiatives create a foundation for psychosocial healing, empowerment, and community reintegration.[66] People experience greater levels of contentedness, space for reflection, deeper levels of communication with others, and an opportunity to practice caring through communion with nature.[67] Politically, the shared tactile experience helps reduce social distance between people and generates greater trust, which generates the visceral capacity to mobilize bodies into a social movement.[68]

The Practice of Restorative Food Justice

In response to the U.S. Supreme Court order for California to reduce its prison population, the California legislature passed Assembly Bill 109, the Public Safety Realignment initiative. While this reduced the state's prison population, it shuffled the prisoners to county jails, where the state has allowed discretion in how counties spend funds for "rehabilitation." More money for reentry programs became available, but because county jails are also overcrowded, the debate between advocates for jail expansion and recidivism reduction was intensified. In March 2016, a white organizer with Planting Justice named Nicole Deane wrote a blog post for the organization taking advantage of the political opportunity provided by Assembly Bill 109 to call for more state resources for reentry initiatives:

> We know that incarcerated people are perfectly capable of successfully returning to their families and communities and becoming valuable assets to those communities because we see it every single day at Planting Justice. All seventeen men who have come through our re-entry program have not only stayed out of prison and beat California's sky-high recidivism rate; they are becoming leaders in their communities, building community gardens, mentoring high school students, and supporting others who are making the transition out of California's brutal prison system. Our entire organizational budget is approximately 0.002% of the budget the BSCC [Board of State and Community Corrections] just approved for jail expansion—and we have a 100% success rate against recidivism. . . . Justifying half a billion dollars in jail construction spending in anticipation of maintaining these high rates of recidivism does a profound disservice to the communities most impacted by mass incarceration. We need to start investing in formerly incarcerated people—not more incarceration.[69]

Strategic interventions to support formerly incarcerated people vary, but the marginality that comes with imprisonment means that any resistance to California's notoriously high recidivism rates almost necessarily emerges from interstitial spaces not completely colonized by the state, capitalism, and institutional racism.[70] These interstitial spaces offer the

Figure 2. Presentation by a formerly incarcerated staff member in front of Compost the Empire mural at McClymonds High School. Photograph used with permission by Planting Justice.

freedom for resistance to grow to problems like mass incarceration.[71] This is the essence of what organizers at Planting Justice mean by "compost the empire." They create spaces, such as gardens; cooking demonstrations; healing circles; and communally run houses to support the reentry process with a focus on healing and reintegration. First, having a job helps instill a sense of self-worth that reduces the likelihood of reoffending.[72] Second, when formerly incarcerated people become "wounded healers" who mentor those who have been to prison, there is empowerment for both the giver and the receiver.[73] So while reducing recidivism is desirable, there are other benefits. The practice of restorative food justice in Oakland acknowledges the challenges identified by formerly incarcerated people and creates spaces to undo social and psychological forms of confinement.

As the Public Safety Realignment initiative started to roll out, many counties expanded their jails, but some came under public pressure to provide funds for reentry programs. One of these counties was Alameda County. The county gave money in 2013 to a two-year pilot program called Pathways to Resilience, which several nonprofits and companies cosponsored.[74] Planting Justice was one of the anchor sponsors. Together they asked, "Could an integrated program of culturally relevant, experiential permaculture design education; meaningful, values-aligned, and entrepreneurial work; and wrap around services reduce recidivism by healing and restoring participants' connections to the community and the environment?"[75] In addition to an eighteen-month program in San Quentin that served 250 participants, Pathways to Resilience offered a reentry program that focused on psychosocial healing and graduated twenty-one permaculture designers, many successfully attaining living-wage work or starting businesses.

Like many social movements responding to the carceral conjuncture of mass incarceration, Pathways to Resilience found intersectional ways to respond. The initiative received the wise leadership of Pandora Thomas, a black organizer and permaculture expert who cofounded the Black Permaculture Network. Along with Starhawk, an author, activist, and permaculture designer, Thomas coauthored a solidarity statement under the banner of the network, in which they wrote:

> We, the members of the undersigned permaculture groups and organizations, wish to publicly state our support for the Black-LivesMatter movement and the ongoing fight to end all police violence against communities of color. Permaculture is a system of regenerative ecological design rooted in indigenous knowledge and wisdom. Its three core ethics, care for the earth, care for the people, care for the future lead us to call for accountability for police who currently target, harass and murder people in communities of color, and especially the black community, with impunity. . . .
>
> At this time of grave environmental crisis, we recognize that the divisive impact of all forms of discrimination and prejudice hamper every effort to shift the path of our society off of the road to ruin and onto the path of regeneration. Our economic, political and social systems can only find ecological balance when they are founded upon justice. One of the core permaculture principles is that diversity creates resilience. We are committed to envision, design and create a world in which we affirm and celebrate human diversity, where we can learn from one another's perspectives and support one another's struggles.[76]

This attention to what environmental sociologist David Pellow refers to as *socioecological inequality* looks to challenge intersecting inequalities and hierarchies beyond social and ecological divides in order to build more inclusive and cross-cutting social movements.[77] Therefore, training primarily black formerly incarcerated people in permaculture through Pathways to Resilience has expanded the network of black permaculturalists, thereby deepening the integration between food justice and restorative justice.[78]

The restorative practices that stem from these ideological commitments include several rituals. Each helps counteract the stigma of incarceration because it is symbolic and emotive, is repeated as necessary, involves community, focuses on achievement, and involves "wiping the slate clean."[79] Of primary importance, healing circles anchored the Pathways to Resilience program. In a circle, everyone can see everyone else, which rejects the spatial logic of segregation and incarceration. This fosters the freedom to address the trauma of prison and create solidarity and trust with others going through the reentry transition. Both inside and outside of prison, the people I interviewed discussed the importance of having safe spaces to address their own victimization, the crimes they committed, and their vision of the future. Speaking to the power of healing circles, Gene offered, "I felt safe and secure. . . . It's like a platform that I could use to either dump some stuff in people's lap I was dealing with from the week or what I had been through. . . . It was a time to be able to get things out so I could grow and move on." Joan, a white woman who worked with Pathways to Resilience and is an expert on the restorative justice process, said, "There's a sort of collective wisdom that comes out of that circle process [that is] . . . giving people a sense of community." With this communal foundation in place, other rituals built on the practice of healing circles.

The programmatic culmination for each cohort of Pathways to Resilience participants was the rites of passage ceremony. As one graduate noted, "We opened the day in circle, with the sound of drums, as one community member led us in a ritual of calling in the four directions as well as the earth and sky to set the space as sacred. Another member encouraged us to speak aloud the names of our family, ancestors, and important figures that have shaped our lives and whose shoulders we stand on. Each of us also had a chance to put our own voices in the circle . . . each expressing the gifts and offerings we bring to the circle."[80] The graduates then individually approached a golden bowl full of fire and incense, dropped in a paper identifying something that they wanted to release from their past, and then announced this to the attendees. Afterward they walked through an archway of the entangled arms and bodies of family and friends and received a crystal from one of the Pathways to Resilience educators.

The rites-of-passage ceremony symbolically crystallized one stage of healing and set the foundation for entering food justice activism. The internal and interpersonal work required by Pathways to Resilience empowered formerly incarcerated people to participate in prefigurative urban agriculture projects that dialectically reimagine food justice. Restorative justice deepens food justice by calling attention to the trauma of mass incarceration and offering ways to meet the immediate needs of people inside prison and upon reentry. Although food justice activists are committed to social justice, their typical methods and skills are insufficient to work with formerly incarcerated people, which necessitates fusing restorative practices. Reciprocally, organizers at Planting Justice used their extensive understanding of agriculture and creating viable economic paths to deepen healing and provide the necessary resources for economic mobility.

Maintaining a good job and developing skills are vital upon reentry, as they help foster a sense of self-worth.[81] In other words, the value of restorative food justice, like beautifying a client's yard or using new skills to build one's own garden or urban farm, is empowerment. As Maurice exclaimed, "I think having a meaningful job makes a big difference, as far as staying out of prison. Because you'll do anything it takes to keep that job, if you care about it. You're not just trying to change your life, you're changing everybody's life."[82] Speaking about the empowerment that came with completing the Pathways to Resilience program, Jamal said, "They gave me the ability to believe in myself. . . . So that was real big for me, man . . . because I don't have to be the angry black man and just talk to you about it. I now have the skills and knowledge and understanding to go do it myself. So that's pretty invaluable."

Permaculture design and food production become innovative tools in the restorative process when they link working with plants to healing individuals and strengthening community bonds. As one of the cofounders of Planting Justice once told me,

> The work that you're doing is actually healing you from the inside out and it's enabling you to recognize your own power because

you're transforming physical space into something beautiful. So much of our cities have been . . . completely destroyed to the point where, you know, people are being born and dying on asphalt. . . . Being able to just take whatever kind of spaces back to life . . . is very healing on the inside. Because I feel like a lot of us, whether we know it or not, have been really harmed by the destruction of our ecology in so many ways that we can't even see, and so being able to very tangibly transform a space has the ability to hit us on some inner levels. And so to have a job that enables you to do that, and at the same time enables you to connect with your community and help provide basic needs for people in your community, is something that we really need.

Many of those who completed the Pathways to Resilience permaculture design course or work for Planting Justice feel transformed and regularly confirmed this healing experience. "It's just something magical, man; something spiritual happens when you are able to . . . grow your own food and sustain yourself," beamed Jamal. He continued, "Especially coming out of prison, we've been deprived of certain human rights. . . . There's

Figure 3. Building a trellis during a free garden build in East Oakland. Photograph by Wiley Rogers.

nothing better getting out of prison than to build a relationship with the earth to really go down and become grounded in that."

In terms of some of their public engagement, I witnessed palpable enjoyment when Planting Justice provided free gardens to community-based organizations and working-class families. Indeed, formerly incarcerated people build private edible landscapes that serve nonmarket functions and free gardens in public spaces or for nonprofits that increase cross-cultural collaboration and civic participation.[83] For example, Planting Justice collaborated with the thirty-five-year-old Canal Alliance, which works with undocumented Latinx communities. The Canal Alliance contacted Planting Justice in 2011 because it wanted to create new food production spaces to improve the well-being of its community. Therefore, Planting Justice taught a permaculture course in Spanish to eighteen youth in the summer of 2011 and started six different community gardens in the Canal District with these youth. To build these gardens, the organization convinced the owners of apartment complexes to use the land, essentially communalizing private space. Growing food expressed communal empowerment.

The process of beautifying yards, working as teams across social boundaries, and receiving positive feedback ruptured social and internalized stereotypes and created new opportunities to strengthen community. Mateo, a Latino high school graduate who completed a food justice culinary arts program run by Planting Justice and became a permaculture landscaper, shared, "Having people come up to me and be like, 'Thank you for coming out to my house and building this garden,' that fills that part in your heart that lets you know that you're actually doing something for your community. You are the change you want to see." Reflecting on how people would tell him during free garden builds that local government fails their communities, a formerly incarcerated black man named Lawrence shared the significance of supporting disinvested communities: "We prepped the land, we planted trees, and plants. We tried to upgrade that type of community. . . . And while we're doing it, the people that live in that area would stop by and thank us." Working collaboratively to overcome the institutionalized disposability of racialized people and places brings communities together.

Another way that Planting Justice built communal bonds was through educational outreach. The Food Justice Education Program engages in what it refers to as "education for liberation" by offering workshops for

Figure 4. Planting Justice mural at Fremont High School. Photograph used with permission by Planting Justice.

students, prisoners, affordable-housing residents, and the public. The program links practical skills such as companion planting, cover cropping, and integrated pest management to lessons about farmworker rights, the Black Panther Party's Ten Point Program, and a historical timeline of racial and economic justice struggles that inspire the food justice movement. To reinforce this liberatory education, Planting Justice worked with the Community Rejuvenation Project to paint two murals. At Fremont High School in Oakland, which is 98 percent students of color and majority Latinx, there is a large mural alongside a row of fruit trees, raised vegetable beds, and compost bins that proclaims, "Planting Justice," and celebrates campesinos and indigenous varieties of corn. At McClymonds High School, which is 99 percent students of color and majority black, there is a prominent mural across from a large enclosure containing over ten raised vegetable beds in the middle of what is otherwise a concrete desert, which states, "Compost the Empire"; and creatively displays a large face and a compost heap out of which grows marigolds, poppies, and milkweed that attract pollinators.

In each high school, formerly incarcerated men educated students about permaculture, set up smoothie stands with fruits and vegetables from the garden, and testified to their experiences motivating a commitment to restorative food justice. As people who grew up targeted by law enforcement because of their race, they empathized with high school students facing similar social contexts. Mac, a young black man who came through the Insight Garden Program and Planting Justice, always wanted to support his school and community for all he was given. "I was kind of a bad kid, so to speak, got suspended . . . so in summertime I went to summer programs. . . . I appreciated those programs and it was able to give me my first job." Mac reflected, "I always wanted to give back. . . . We work at schools now and so this is a way for me to do some mentoring." Given his criminal history, he reached youth in a way relevant to their neighborhood experiences. Mac divulged, "I got a wound on my head and it was from a bullet graze. I've been asked about it. . . . I have a story and good advice and mentor the kids that need it." He would tell youth to stay in school and then give students statistics about the high number of homicides in Oakland, which regularly tops out at over one hundred a year. Although he tailored his advice based on the situation of the student he was speaking with, he made sure to be clear about "the importance of the people who you are with, you know and you're guilty by association, so watch who you're with, don't just be with anybody," and always encouraged youth to be "respectful to yourself."

As a political arm of Planting Justice, the canvassing program furthered liberatory education and organizing. More than raising money, it was a food justice strategy that helped people "learn democracy," which is important given laws that politically disenfranchise ex-felons by preventing them from voting.[84] Confirming research that suggests civic reintegration helps develop a positive self-identity postincarceration, formerly incarcerated staff members felt empowered through public engagement.[85] Through the canvassing program, they would often teach the public about the human toll of the prison pipeline and challenge the criminalization of working-class communities of color by leveraging their supporters to back relevant campaigns and policy initiatives. For former prisoners such as Jerry, the civic skills are empowering. In an interview, he told me, "Canvassing really helps you to communicate more and better with people on the street. If you're not a public speaker, you will be." These skills are politically important, especially when tied to other public communication tools. Upon a year after his release from prison, Maurice became the first media apprentice at Planting Justice. In this position, he used the platform of Planting Justice's blog to educate the public on the slave-like conditions of prisons and call on people to act in solidarity. In one post he explained the importance of supporting the 2016 nationally coordinated prison strike against prison slavery, which took place on the forty-fifth anniversary of the Attica Prison uprising.[86] In reference to his experience with the family visitation strike in 1996, he wrote,

> Today we are still taking that stand and we are still saying in one voice, "NO MORE!" We are now only adding demands:
>
> NO MORE mass incarceration!
> NO MORE putting our kids away for life!
> NO MORE slave labor!
> NO MORE 3 strikes!
> NO MORE death penalty!
> NO MORE mental, physical or sexual abuse!
> NO MORE forced sterilization!
> NO MORE inhumane treatment of prisoners, men and
>   women alike!
> NO MORE unhealthy food!
> NO MORE deplorable living conditions!
> NO MORE inadequate medical treatment! . . .
>
> All I ask is for you to also stand up and support these brothers and sisters, men and women, whichever you prefer, in their time of need. It is never too late to be a part of something big.[87]

By organizing the public, Planting Justice devised a strategy to mobilize skills common in the food justice movement, such as building gardens, and tied them to reentry-related political campaigns. For example, the organization fought to make the most of the political opportunity afforded by the Public Safety Realignment initiative and pushed for money to be spent at a county level on reentry services instead of incarceration. In Alameda County, which is home to Planting Justice's work, 62 to 77 percent of realignment money was spent on running the Santa Rita Jail.[88] A formerly incarcerated man named Tyan Bowens, who graduated from Pathways to Resilience, fought for a different funding split alongside a

Figure 5. Rally in 2015 demanding half of Alameda County's public safety realignment budget for community-based reentry programs and services. Photograph used with permission by Ella Baker Center for Human Rights.

broad coalition of grassroots organizations called the Alameda County Coalition for Criminal Justice Reform (now the Justice Reinvestment Coalition). He avowed, "These programs work, they just need more funding. . . . A lot of people would probably turn back to what they used to do if they didn't have a program like this."[89] With the testimony of people like Tyan Bowens, activists pushed Alameda County to spend 50 percent of their realignment money on community-based reentry programs.

Food Justice, Creativity, and Reading the Social Context

Most food justice activism in the United States aims to eliminate inequities related to access to healthy, affordable, and culturally appropriate food.[90] The main strategies are urban farming, integrating more produce into local markets, creating community-run markets and grocery stores, and elevating the issues of race and racism in the food system and food movement. With the rise of the influential Occupy Wall Street and Black

Lives Matter movements, left-wing activists have focused more on addressing conjunctures stemming from capitalism and institutional racism. For food justice activism, this backdrop informs the simmering tension between strategies to meet immediate needs and strategies to take on the social forces producing problems to begin with.[91] Food production strategies are often based on the assumption that because food is lacking, people need to work with those groups experiencing food insecurity and fill the void.[92] This is a temporary, often patronizing, and ultimately insufficient approach. But instead of just forgoing strategies to meet people's immediate needs, they can be combined with mutual-aid strategies to dismantle the social relations and practices that perpetuate the underlying inequity.

Creative extensions of food justice emerge when activists dialectically reinterpret histories of structural inequality, pressing inequities, and previous and ongoing social movement resistance through food. The activism at the core of social movement networks that link food and carceral politics, exemplified in this chapter by Planting Justice and Pathways to Resilience, reveals that radical imagination work is a prerequisite to practice food justice differently. Instead of seeing food as an end, food becomes a means for social change. Nowhere is this clearer than in the practice of restorative food justice. By beginning with carceral conjunctures that disproportionately impact working-class communities and communities of color, the same communities struggling against inequities in the food system, the strategic response changes.

There is then the practical question social movement organizations always ask: How do we mobilize enough resources to maintain a presence capable of making economic, political, and social changes? Answers to this question will vary by context. As an organization that longs for radical changes but must deal with the choices available to nonprofits, Planting Justice developed programs to create enough economic independence to respond to problems as it sees fit. By witnessing firsthand the devastating effects of incarceration on the lives of black men in Oakland and listening to these men's plight, the organization developed restorative reentry programs. This prefigurative strategy generated income through edible landscaping while the canvass program *both* made money *and* built political support to reform discriminatory laws targeting formerly incarcerated people. There is interdependency between food justice programmatic work and cross-movement alliance building. Together these efforts weave structural critiques, ideas and tactics from other social movements, and strategies that create economic mobility and reform local policy into interventions into the institutional racism that maintains mass incarceration.

3

Taking Back the Economy

Fair Labor Relations and Food Worker Advocacy

California is home to a vast food system that undervalues work and exploits workers.[1] Since the late 1800s a revolving door of immigrant farmworkers have been subjected to institutionalized forms of discrimination. Their pay and benefits are abysmal. They suffer from pesticide exposure and the hazards of farm equipment and large animals.[2] Additionally, unhealthy housing conditions and barriers to health care are daily burdens.[3] Workers in meatpacking and food-processing facilities face similar difficulties. With a workforce of documented and undocumented immigrants, employers manipulate social differences to discipline workers and thwart resistance to the dangers of working with heavy machinery and possibly fatal tools.[4] For those working in warehouses and distribution facilities, a largely nonunion sector, workers are once again exposed to the dangers of working with heavy machinery, under extreme heat and cold, and with managers and owners resistant to improving wages and benefits.[5] The grocery retail sector is the one food sector where there are slightly better wages and benefits as well as working conditions due to the historical successes of unions. Nevertheless, there is an industry-wide race to the bottom in the United States due to the infiltration of anti-union corporations such as Walmart on the budget end and Whole Foods on the ritzy end. Even within alternative food networks, many small and midsized organic and sustainable growers and community-supported agriculture (CSA) operators engage in self-exploitation and rely on apprentice labor, while urban agriculture initiatives depend on a mass of volunteers with little prospect of reliable living-wage work.[6] For those working in everything from corporate chain restaurants and fast-food joints to farm-to-table restaurants, poor pay and benefits and workplace discrimination and harassment are rampant.[7]

Resistance to this state of affairs has long been present. Whether in the guise of the Wobblies and Communists organizing farmworkers and cannery workers, the United Farm Workers using boycotts to pressure growers for better wages and working conditions, or the persistence of labor unions like United Food and Commercial Workers (UFCW) fighting for meatpacking and grocery workers, organizers have struggled for economic justice in California's food system.[8] Mirroring efforts throughout the United States, fast-food workers in California led a movement for a $15 minimum wage and the right to form a union. Taking on companies such as McDonald's, workers and their supporters protested the rise of low-wage work after the Great Recession and demonized these companies for preying on working-class communities. The Fight for $15 movement leveraged these grievances to demand that cities and states raise the minimum wage. Consequently, cities such as Los Angeles, Oakland, and San Francisco passed laws to increase the minimum wage to $15 and pegged wage increases to inflation. As I cover later in this chapter, there have also been many fights against Walmart, the world's largest grocery retailer.[9] With few other places to expand except large metropolitan areas populated with liberal residents and labor unions, the company has faced stiff resistance, especially by UFCW and the worker-led OUR Walmart advocacy group.

There are also countless efforts to take back the economy with alternatives to the corporately concentrated food system that build on the communal organic farming and food cooperative movements of the 1960s and 1970s.[10] This represents a prefigurative food politics aimed at circumventing powerful food system actors with alternatives to transition into new economic relationships that replace exploitative labor relations. In the last two decades, there has been rapid growth in urban, biodynamic, permaculture, and organic farms and direct-to-consumer marketing. A large cross section of Californians are also starting worker-run food cooperatives, such as grocery stores, bakeries, and farms, as well as food-buying clubs.[11] When considered in addition to the labor struggles mentioned above, there is a widespread determination to improve the livelihoods of all those who work in agriculture and with food.

As an idea and a praxis, food justice includes a commitment to revaluing work and exchange with a variety of alternatives. Yet, for food justice to deepen, food justice activists need to join with food-chain workers in the conventional food system in fights for economic justice. In Robert

Gottlieb and Anupama Joshi's breakthrough book *Food Justice*, the authors argue that the food justice movement must include confronting the abuse of workers in the food system. This emphasis acknowledges labor is intimately related to physical health and social reproduction. It is thus necessary to have a food system controlled by workers that protects human rights and advances social justice. Equally important is that food-chain workers fuel a food system essential for human survival, which means social stability and development require improving labor conditions and revaluing food work in all its forms.

While support for food-chain workers can expand the scope of food politics, alone it obscures poor labor practices within many alternative food initiatives, which experience capitalist market and labor pressures. However unintentional or peripheral, Gottlieb and Joshi's seminal notion of food justice assumes labor problems exist only in conventional food supply chains, and alternatives are somehow better on labor because their production practices are more environmentally sustainable or local. But labor problems emerge from common conjunctures that permeate conventional *and* alternative food systems. On the one hand, the United States has institutionalized weak labor protections and the power of capital. There are legal exceptions for farmworkers and restaurant workers, a minimum wage system that has trailed cost-of-living increases, attacks on and membership declines in labor unions, and no comprehensive national food policy.[12] On the other hand, the rollback of social welfare produces gaps that civil society works to fill. Because so many food justice initiatives run on inadequate budgets, activists tend to accept the time it takes to develop fair labor practices or simply overlook poor labor practices. These conditions obstruct the food movement from tackling economic problems outside of developing alternative food initiatives. Overall, this suggests a weak class-consciousness and shallow commitment to workers' rights.[13]

One of the implications is that while in theory, food justice includes fair labor practices and the human rights of all workers, in practice, activists, especially those embedded in nonprofits, often prioritize their immediate needs and revaluing work in their own projects. Moreover, there are social boundaries between food justice activists with different degrees of power and privilege and greater access to resources and food-chain workers who are often first-generation immigrants facing xenophobia and institutionalized discrimination.[14] As a result of the underlying neoliberal ideologies and libertarian proclivities that run through these food politics, developing alliances is inconvenient.[15] This dilemma is understandable when survival, chasing grant money, and trying to keep up with the whims of consumers who love kale one day and kelp the next day feels like a Sisyphean endeavor of well-meaning work versus "the system." From another perspective, the variability in labor contexts means there are many organizing entry points to advance the interests of workers. Whether or not food justice activists develop class-consciousness, eliminate economic exploitation in their workplaces, and engage in confrontational food politics in solidarity with other workers is central to the labor conjunctures presented in this chapter.[16]

To emphasize these points, I first discuss the context within which, and how, San Diego Roots Sustainable Food Project revalues food work. This case offers typical experiences and pressures faced by local food activists working in nonprofits. The social position of these local food activists, who are largely white and well educated, alters how they think about food work, which for many of them means taking back the food economy from corporate agribusiness. In contrast, the experiences of grocery, meat-packing, and food-processing workers in Los Angeles reveals the almost mundane forms of exploitation reserved for working-class communities and communities of color. Instead of seeing this as an intractable problem, labor unions such as United Food and Commercial Workers (UFCW) Local 770 confront the political and economic drivers that harm workers. Also significant is the fact that food justice activists have worked alongside UFCW 770 and other labor advocacy groups to promote healthy food and quality jobs in the face of entrenched poverty. Revaluing food work is necessary, but it often benefits already-privileged groups and leaves many workers out. Conversely, confronting political and economic elites to support food-chain workers and the working-class communities of color where they often reside reduces inequities and expands food justice for subordinated groups. Resolving labor conjunctures depends on both strategies.

Postcapitalist Prefiguration? Local Organic Farming and Voluntary Labor

It is incontrovertible that place shapes social life and that social life shapes place.[17] The relationship morphs over time and depends on trajectories set in motion by the built environment and the people who interpret, interact with, and modify it. Most commonly, however, the local is the discernible conjunctural terrain. It is also the terrain of prefiguration. The history of social movements that use food to advance racial and economic justice resonate in the ideas, organizing, programming, and initiatives of the food movement. This dialectical motion refracts through local economic, political, and social relations. For example, the industrialization of agriculture coupled with reduced barriers to global trade, such as international trade agreements, has depressed the livelihoods of food-chain workers everywhere. However abstracted at a macro level, activists confront these pressures differently in Los Angeles, Oakland, and San Diego. Creativity is an important adaptive political strategy. Instead of accepting food workers' alienation from the food they produce and consumers' alienation from the labor that makes eating food possible, there is a food politics afoot throughout California that is fighting to revalue work.

Beginning in 2001, a group of organic farming and local food activists—who would go on to form San Diego Roots Sustainable Food Project (San Diego Roots)—joined to save 160 acres of organic farmland in a fertile riparian zone from the onslaught of suburban development, a common occurrence for San Diego's farmland. At the time, they were volunteering with Good Faith Farm, a small, three-acre plot leased from the farmer who owned the 160 acres. Land tenure was insecure. Most of the people joining the effort to save the farm were college-educated, white, middle-class members of Ocean Beach People's Food Co-op and looking for a place to volunteer on a farm. Because the co-op bought from Good Faith Farm, a working relationship set the foundation for sending out volunteers. This history of volunteerism and cooperation drives a shared culture around their importance. For example, Nancy, a white homeschooling mother, volunteered at Good Faith Farm. As she recollected,

> I called up the farmer and said, "Hey, can I come out and
> visit your farm with my kids." He said, "Sure, but I need your
> help." . . . He told me all the problems he was having like trying to
> farm because he wasn't a trained farmer. . . . He was trying to
> learn farming with no background in it. He was talking about all
> the different regulations for organic agriculture and workers, and
> all the red tape he had to go through just to get people to work on
> his farm and economically how hard it was to farm in Southern
> California. . . . I just started going out there on a regular basis

volunteering . . . and then I'd work a day at the farmers market
every week and sell the produce. I got to understand the challenges
of farming and also got paid in vegetables, which made me happy.

While the motivations to volunteer varied, from wanting to reconnect to
nature, to teaching one's children where food comes from, to learning
how to farm, eventually a core group formed A Local Organic Farmland
Trust (ALOFT) to buy the land themselves. Lacking resources to incorporate their group, they became a project of the Back Country Land Trust.
The hope at the time was to acquire the land to begin a family of farms
that grew food for the local community and provided an educational
space for organic farming.

Although ALOFT members were unable to raise the six to eight million dollars needed to save this farmland from development, they learned
many people were unaware of the number of organic farms in San Diego
County, the loss of farmland, and the value of supporting local farmers.
Most people they spoke with would ask why they should save farmland,
which led these burgeoning activists to start a conversation about organic
farms and local food systems in San Diego. In 2003, three members of
ALOFT then founded San Diego Roots. They consider themselves "a
growing network of citizens, farmers, chefs, gardeners, teachers, and students working to encourage the growth and consumption of regional
food. From farm to fork, we focus awareness and work toward a more ecologically sound, economically viable and socially just food system in San
Diego."[18] From the outset, the organization committed to educating
locals about the plight of family farms and the financial hardships of
small-scale organic farming. In the United States, small family farms
account for almost 90 percent of all farms, yet operate only 50 percent of
the land, accounting for 25 percent of the value of production.[19] These
farms also heavily rely on the labor of the operators and their spouses, and
most tend to have a negative operating profit margin.[20] San Diego Roots
also wanted to develop organic and permaculture demonstration sites to
model collectively growing ecologically sustainable food. Although California has the most certified organic farms in the United States, conventional capital-intensive and large-scale commodity production dominates the landscape.[21] Like many local alternative farming initiatives,
embedded in San Diego Roots' prefigurative commitments is a central
contradiction that illuminates the promises and pitfalls of its food poli-

tics.[22] Its approach to work questions the wage labor system *and* obscures the economic difficulties of organic farming.[23]

San Diego Roots' revaluing of farming reflects a broader shift in the food movement to expand home and community gardening so that people can connect their labor to the food they eat.[24] Viewing organic farming as the most immediate way to scale up this vital socioecological connection, San Diego Roots turned to finding farmland, and in 2010 started Wild Willow Farm and Education Center. Through fundraising, San Diego Roots raised $80,000 for their first year on the farm and with the help of many volunteers put in the work to transform the land into a productive space. When I was conducting fieldwork in 2012, Wild Willow Farm was transitioning from a permaculture experimentation site to more traditional row cropping, with a productivist orientation and a desire to make the farm profitable. The farm hired a food-marketing person and a lead and assistant farmer. Along with volunteers and an internship program, this expanded programming to teach people how to farm at a small scale with organic methods and to create a year-round CSA with a reliable set of crops and special seasonal varieties. These were two essential sources of revenue for an organization that otherwise did not receive much grant money.[25] With the freedom to create labor relations as San Diego Roots saw fit, the farm exemplifies resistance to the capitalist logic of California's industrialized agricultural economy.[26]

In its promotional materials, Wild Willow Farm brands itself as a place where people "Learn and Grow and Connect." This pithy tagline fuses a commitment to teaching people the cultural significance of small-scale organic farming with the value of working the land to build community. The farm school, which farms the six leased acres, is a litmus test of the values informing San Diego Roots' farming and labor practices. James, a white San Diego native and longtime organic gardener, farmer, mycologist, and native plant encyclopedia, was the teacher and mentor for these courses at the time of my fieldwork. In one of the first lectures, titled "The Spirit of Organic Farming," James told the story of the Luiseño. In one season, this indigenous tribe would walk from the coast to the peak of what the Spanish colonizers named Palomar Mountain,[27] which is on the northern edge of San Diego County. They followed the cyclical nature of the food supply, an ancient form of human organization strategizing survival in the form of food acquisition. These nomadic people created seasonal camps. Each season edible wild plants would be gathered and

Figure 6. Wild Willow Farm mural. Photograph by the author.

taken into camps. Eventually seeds would sprout out of old compost piles left after the Luiseño moved to another camp. The Luiseño eventually determined that they could be sedentary by cultivating these plants. This started the process of plant selection and breeding and animal domestication. Grains and tree seeds were the first plants grown because they were easier to use in different ways and their seeds were sturdy and durable. Due to flooding in the area, many nutrients flowed down from the mountains. People would farm when the flooding season ended. But with the onset of colonization and the gradual advancement of water management technologies, the agricultural landscape changed as the integrated agro-ecological land management strategy gave way to capital- and resource-intensive agriculture. As James viewed this history, people and nature became things to dominate. He ended his lecture by assessing that farming is now more about "bushels per acre . . . to improve our economy."

There is a voluntary simplicity at the heart of how San Diego Roots hopes to take back the economy through organic farming, with an ethic of stewardship that reflects some of the lessons of the Luiseño. The question, however, is whether San Diego Roots and their ilk in the food movement are reproducing neoliberal subjectivities or revaluing labor through more fair and sustainable livelihoods.[28] The first farmer to run Wild Willow Farm, Sam, framed the motivation behind the farm school and internships thusly: "I felt like if we were going to educate the next generation of farmers and gardeners in San Diego we needed to do more than offer one off Saturday volunteer days." Their educational model relied on unpaid labor, which accounted for most work hours to run the farm. Although the farm school eventually replaced the internship program, these educational spaces were pivotal for inspiring new organic farmers.[29] For example, Janelle, a Latina former lead farmer, fondly reminisced, "I found Seeds [a one-acre working farm at San Diego City College] and decided to do an apprenticeship there. Wild Willow had just been started and was taking interns. I did this as well. I had about a year where I was not going to work and just full on got into farming." Usually a short-term disinterest in money or materialism allowed people like Janelle to take on internships and apprenticeships. While volunteer labor may aid actualizing the collective vision, it may also create economic pain for the individual. "You can't expect someone to run a farm or school garden on very minimal pay or volunteering," Janelle, who no longer works at Wild Willow Farm, suggested. "Right now because there are so many people interested in this, they are willing to give a lot of their time and it makes it seem like it is all right." Behind this labor conjuncture in organic farming is the tension between the privilege to farm without pay and barriers to gaining the needed experience to start or work on a small organic farm.

Although imperfect, the projects of San Diego Roots are a prefigurative alternative to capitalist wage labor systems. As J. K. Gibson-Graham contends, we need a diverse economy, one predicated on "different kinds of *transaction* and ways of negotiating (in)commensurability; different types of *labor* and ways of compensating for it; and different forms of economic *enterprise* and ways of producing, appropriating, and distributing surplus."[30] In the spirit of reimagining a farm as a place for community, San Diego Roots hosts regular potlucks. "You know we have a lot of people that come out to the potlucks, but don't come out to volunteer previous to that," Laura, a white former board member, observed. "It's just one of the realities; people like to socialize but not necessarily get dirty and work hard." Yet, for every person who wanted to share food, there were those who gave their labor freely to promote the development of the farm school. Nonmonetary values and voluntary association fostered opportunities to learn about farming and created new markets for food produced locally, organically, and on a small scale.

While the postcapitalist spirit thrived, it could not escape state regulations. This was a common point of contention for San Diego organic farming activists who felt law enforcement inflexibility obstructs building a more diverse economy. Jenna, a white former staff member, recounted how labor laws regulating farm apprenticeships have led to the closure of farms fined for not providing legal compensation, which made the development of a fee-for-service educational model at Wild Willow Farm even more pressing: "It's one of those catch-22s: 'Well I want to learn about this, but I have no experience and you're not going to hire me to do that.' . . . So Roots is really responding to that in terms of providing a legal way that people can get this knowledge and have some experience so that they can come to some of our really successful organic farms and get a

Figure 7. Local and sustainable values drive the work at Wild Willow Farm. Photograph by the author.

job there." The history of La Milpa Organica Farm provided organic farming activists with a parable to solidify their skepticism of the state. La Milpa was a for-profit farm that for seven years relied on apprentices, which ultimately put the farm in conflict with labor authorities. One day in 2010 an inspector from the Department of Industrial Relations visited the farm and found people lacked any benefits, such as worker's compensation; were compensated with free room and board; and when paid with cash, it was not reported. According to supporters, these apprentices were happy. The farm owner, Barry Logan, served a night in jail, paid a $4,000 fine, and ultimately shut down the farm.[31] Eddie, a former board member at San Diego Roots, reasoned, "Maybe this is an example of the intent of the law is very well and good, and it needs to be there for the people who abuse that sort of law. . . . It's applying the right law to the right people and having exemptions when they make sense." In a final public speech at La Milpa, Barry Logan expressed similar sentiments:

> I want to apologize to you for abandoning these fields. I am not
> clever enough to simultaneously inhabit the natural world of a
> living organic system and its antithesis, the modern state with the
> bizarre and unnatural conditions it dictates. Unfortunately,
> growing food, and living as free people is not compatible with the
> ill-considered and unjust mandates, rules, laws and regulations
> that are imposed upon us. . . . Our society needs experiments. We
> need places where we can freely explore these questions and build
> new models for a rapidly changing world. Freedom is a word that
> has been accorded great reverence in the lexicon of this thing we
> call America. I believe that we need more of it.[32]

This speech discloses a radical longing to provide a space for freely associating people to decide how and where they want to spend their time. La Milpa was already on the social margins, so when the state enforced labor laws, it catalyzed further distrust by the local food movement, and yet paradoxically, the perpetuation of legally acceptable organizational forms, such as nonprofits.

Even though there are limitations to volunteer and apprentice farming models, San Diego Roots heeded the warning of La Milpa and created a 501(c)3 nonprofit.[33] This allowed them to address the extensive loss of farmers and farming skills associated with the industrialization of agriculture with intensive educational classes.[34] But their skepticism of the state endured, evidenced by the rejection of capitalist wage labor relations; their response to the incongruities in labor law was an appeal to the value of self-sufficiency. Contradictorily, this often reinforced neoliberal subjectivities. Ned, a white longtime board member, contemplated, "If the shit really hits the fan, it's [farming] a really good skill to have." Mirroring an organizational ethic, he then implied that to acquire organic farming skills, one must give freely of oneself, usually free time. Yet there was also the common belief that growing one's own food is a nonmonetary form of payment. "You can get paid in a sense for what you do," Titus, a black former farmer at Wild Willow Farm, celebrated. "You do this and you get this, you get some food, you get eggs, you get milk, you get cheese, you get beer, all that local stuff." Many of my interviewees likewise expressed that learning to grow food has social impacts. The shared value of organic farming can foster a communal purpose. As Sherry, an Asian former intern, told me, "We all have to share the environment, so if we learn tools in order to mitigate our destruction of it, I feel like we have a better thing to share amongst ourselves."

Despite the many benefits of the prefigurative food politics of San Diego Roots, like the weekly box of vegetables provided to interns, local food activists sometimes questioned whether these labor models advance food justice. Speaking of the lead farmer at the time, Laura divulged, "He's not getting paid what he should be getting paid because we can't afford it. That's not right either; that's not food justice." Food justice, then, includes not only noncapitalist kinds of exchange but also fair remuneration.[35] Wild Willow Farm has generated increasing levels of revenue from farm-school tuition and produce sales since 2012, but there was concern at the time that the labor model was unsustainable. A white former staff and board member named Cindy expressed, "What we see in a concrete way at the farm is that if we can't pay people like we want to pay people to do this work, then we understand why nobody can. How do we create that job, the money for it? I don't know." In response to some of these economic constraints, and struggles during the Great Recession, many San Diego Roots members questioned the hegemony of wage labor systems. Melissa, who is white and one of the founders, asked, "How do we sustain ourselves without having to depend on an illusive money economy?" She was interested in the prospect of developing models predicated on alternative modes of exchange. "I see [fewer and fewer] people that have the

Figure 8. Assistant farmer and instructor tending the corn at Wild Willow Farm. Photograph by the author.

nine-to-five job because the jobs aren't there," Melissa suggested. "That means that people are going to be sharing resources more. They're going to be bartering time. They are going to trade; I'll grow this and trade this for you."

Seeing the need to respond collectively to the realities of a precarious labor environment inspired reimagining work and exchange, but the labor power required to run the farm ultimately led to new strategies. Turn interns into students who pay tuition to work Wild Willow Farm, which helps to pay the other staff needed to run the organization.[36] This model has maintained a critical financial base for the organization to expand its reach throughout San Diego.

What is important in this case is there are both neoliberal and radical implications of working in the interstitial spaces of capitalism to learn about and engage in small-scale organic farming.[37] There are many alternative food organizations similar to those in this study that begin with social priorities such as self-determination, community, health, and environmental connectivity, which provide a platform to reimagine and rebuild local food systems.[38] When considering whether these organizations and their social movement networks possess the capacity to advance food justice, we need to consider the context within which "actually existing radical food projects" take place.[39] This does not mean ignoring how ethnoracial and class privilege intersect with neoliberal practices that elevate the market and ignore the need for political confrontation.[40] Rather, instead of setting up a Gibson-Graham-like deconstruction, scholars need to read dialectically for difference *and* domination.[41] Central to such a pursuit is evaluating the liberatory capacity of the practices considered food justice work.[42] There are many anti-capitalist and anti-statist sentiments that inform the food politics that guide the exchange and labor practices of alternative food initiatives. Yet it is apparent from research on the political economy of food and agriculture in California that prefigurative practices are insufficient to restructure the conditions under which San Diego local food activists and organic farmers might produce a radical food justice politics.[43] While a commitment to prefiguration across the food movement is a necessary condition for a postcapitalist food politics, the movement cannot fully transform labor relations in the food system without confrontational tactics. The following sections reveal why.

Organized Labor against Racial Capitalism: Standing with Food-Chain Workers

Almost a three-hour drive up the coast from Wild Willow Farm, in downtown Los Angeles, sit the offices for United Food and Commercial Workers Local 770. The rise of this local began in 1937 with a produce clerk named Joseph DeSilva and six other food market employees who affiliated with the Retail Clerks International Union (RCIU) and formed Local 770. Facing terrible working conditions, seventy-two-hour workweeks, $18-a-week pay ($0.25 per hour is $4 per hour in 2014 dollars), and no benefits, they managed to lead the charge that improved the lives of retail clerks. At first, the large chains were recalcitrant, only willing to accept a fifty-four-hour workweek. Once World War II began, RCIU 770 pushed the War Labor Board to increase wages in Southern California. After being rebuffed, RCIU 770 won a rehearing and the first guaranteed forty-hour workweek in 1945. While wages remained frozen throughout World War II, RCIU 770 continued fighting for better pay; equal pay across race, national origin, and gender; and overtime and benefits. In the spirit of racial inclusion, RCIU 770 also worked to find jobs for its Japanese American retail clerks returning from internment camps throughout 1945, much to the consternation of the public and mainstream media. Then in 1947, after a fourteen-day work stoppage, RCIU 770 won on all fronts, most important, winning nondiscrimination clauses, decades before the inscription of nondiscrimination into federal law.[44] In its second major work stoppage in 1959, the union asked for better health-care benefits and a cost-of-living clause in the pension, which they won after twenty-eight days.[45]

Negotiations in later years expanded to include the interests of other food-chain workers after RCIU 770 merged in 1986 with Meat Cutters Local 421 and Butchers Local 274 to become the current UFCW 770. As of 2014, UFCW 770 represented thirty thousand workers throughout Los Angeles County, primarily in grocery retail but also in meatpacking and food processing, and drug stores and pharmacies, including cannabis dispensaries. UFCW 770 is one of the largest locals in the country and is part of the largest private-sector labor union in the United States. Its assets, which in 2014 sat at over $41.1 million, give the union the resources to help shape the landscape for all workers in Los Angeles, particularly grocery workers.[46] This is despite the dire realities of organized labor. Los Angeles labor unions experienced a 1 percent overall membership decline between 1988 and 2004 because of major membership gains in 1990 and 2002. Although this is hard to see as anything more than a modest victory, comparatively, there were 2 and 5 percent membership declines in the same period for California and the United States overall.[47] In total in Los Angeles, unions represent 9 percent of private-sector workers and 58 percent of public-sector workers, bringing the total unionized workforce to 1.1 million people.[48] One of the motivating structural factors for the strong labor movement is entrenched economic insecurity, particularly in immigrant communities and communities of color.[49]

The two months I interned in UFCW 770's Organizing Department and my archival research provide a clear sense of the dialectic between racial capitalism and frontline labor struggles. As a historical and ideological force, capitalism perpetuates and builds on racial hierarchies endemic in society.[50] The imperative of capital accumulation is to advance white supremacy by racializing workers and underdeveloping black, Latinx, Asian, and other racialized communities.[51] Representing the dialectical response to these conditions, UFCW 770's strength comes from a commitment to build working-class power by fighting racism. One central strategy has been to develop leadership from working-class communities of color that are most exploited by a racialized food system. The politics of representation is important because it allows for what the political philosopher Iris Marion Young refers to as a "differentiated relationship" that allows for a different "social perspective" among those engaged in a political process.[52] She contends pointedly, "In a society of white privilege, for example, the social perspective of white people usually wrongly dominates the making of many public discussions, and it should be relativized and tempered by the social perspectives of those positioned differently in the racialized social structures."[53] Toward these ends, leaders such as Art Takei spent forty years with UFCW 770 diversifying the leadership and supporting the creation of labor advocacy groups for people of color. Now the staff primarily consists of people of color and women, many of whom are multilingual. While the union relied on white male leadership in the top positions for most of its history, the executive office is now run by one Latino, one black woman, one Asian man, two white men, and one white woman.[54] Field representatives, whom shop stewards and workers consult if there is a problem in the workplace, include seven white women, four Latinas, three black women, one Asian woman, eight Latinos, and four white men.[55] For those in the Organizing Department during my fieldwork, the staff consisted primarily of Latinx and Asian organizers.

Labor organizers, union representatives, shop stewards, and union management regularly related stories about their family or personal experiences working in the food system. The recurring themes were the abuse associated with the work and the need for labor unions. A Latina union organizer named Marta has parents who were farmworkers. At one point, her father was experiencing wage theft, so he started a campaign to recapture these wages. The farm owner fired one leader, effectively stopping the campaign. Her mom, however, was part of a campaign that increased the number of breaks strawberry pickers receive. Marta boasted, "That was my mom's mini labor campaign and I thought that was really cool that they won something." For many UFCW 770 organizers, they saw their work tied directly to the legacy of Cesar Chavez and the United Farm Workers. A field representative named Ray, who works with meatpacking and food-processing workers, recalled a transformative experience at one of his first labor organizing trainings in Delano, California: "[I saw] this mid-seventies older man on his knees ... bleeding picking grapes; it was a sight that brought tears to my eyes. ... All I remember him saying was, 'Thank you for the work you are doing. It is helping us.' At that moment I realized this is what I want to do." These encounters with the exploitation of racial capitalism compelled some organizers to work with unions to halt racialized labor abuses and improve workers' livelihoods. Speaking to an example closer to the realities of Los Angeles workers, Jill, a Latina labor advocate with Los Angeles Alliance for a New Economy (LAANE), has a grandfather who worked at a union grocery store. "He lives somewhat comfortably at his older age," she beamed. "It's made a huge difference because he never went to college."

The belief that UFCW 770 represents the diversity of Los Angeles's working-class community leads other labor organizers to conclude that labor politics should be vital to food politics. An Asian organizer with UFCW 770 named Ann contended, "We should be people who as leaders of a private-sector food-processing [and grocery retail] union ... be at the forefront talking about food justice [and] ... we should be talking about green jobs. ... We should be at the forefront talking about every single one of those issues. ... When they [workers] go to work, they see these problems and they are able to tell you. If you represent hundreds of thousands of workers, you have to speak that much louder because you have that many voices [whom] you are speaking for and representing." Relatedly, labor organizers recognize the labor struggles of food-chain workers pertain to their social position within their community or neighborhood. Mark, a white former packinghouse worker and now leader in UFCW 770's Executive Office, asserted, "We should have a say ... organizationally because that is the most effective way to talk. ... When you look at the production of food, you have to look at those who produce it. ... The human element involved in the production of food is critical. Whether it's slavery, some rank industrialism where people are exploited tremendously or whether people are paid a living wage and seen as pillars of the community, those are all reflective of the kinds of communities that they are a part of." The corollary is that the form food justice takes reflects community values. For many union representatives, organizing with a Los Angeles labor union means prioritizing economic and racial justice to earn the respect of workers. Felipe, a Latino packinghouse shop steward with UFCW 770, told me a story about a Latina he met who now works at Farmer John Food Services, a plant with a union contract. She worked for Hoffy, another food processing plant, for fifteen years, making only $9 an hour the entire time. Felipe said, "When she asked for a raise, the HR [Human Resources] people told her, 'Pick any door you'd like because we aren't going to give you a raise.' So she . . . went to Farmer John. Less than a year working here, she is already making $11 an hour. . . . I've been using her story: 'This is your pay without a union, this is your pay with a union. It's always going to be a dollar or more at a union plant.'" The larger lesson is that unions not only advance the interests of food-chain workers but also expand food justice.

Poverty, Demand-Side Solutions, and Reimagining Food Justice

The focus on food access by many food justice activists runs up against the desire of labor organizers to advance economic equity in the food system. As a result, there are few examples of where food politics bridge food access and labor issues. Moreover, advocates of alternative food initiatives typically ignore conventional food-chain workers because their labor supports an environmentally and socially undesirable food system. They also purport to want to know their local farmer, but often fail to understand the role of farmworkers in local food production.[56] These perspectives dovetail with an agrarian ideal that drives the creation of alternative economic models but obstructs allying with working-class people.[57] Complicating matters further, the whiteness and class biases of the food movement often exclude food-chain workers, who tend to reflect different socioeconomic groups.[58] On the labor union side, there are intense economic and political pressures to maintain, let alone grow, union density.[59] Unions have sustained heavy losses in many labor strongholds and are scrambling to develop campaigns to unionize corporate-dominated food sectors such as big-box grocery retail and fast food. These conditions can produce myopic labor campaigns focused on economic reforms at the cost of the environment or public health. The labor movement is also much more entrenched in the political system, which many food activists view with skepticism, preferring instead to purchase their way to a solution. Relatedly, the labor movement focuses more on winning political campaigns, which requires large amounts of money, time, and union member organizing.

Speaking to these tensions, in the mid-1990s, the Los Angeles Food Policy Council (LAFPC) started the arduous process of gathering information about each sector of the local food system to figure out how best to prioritize its efforts. One of the major issues was the abandonment of full-service supermarkets from working-class communities of color. Organizers in these communities wanted better access to healthy and affordable food. However, representatives of UFCW 770 at an information-gathering session at this time essentially said this was not their issue. They had yet to experience the full-frontal assault of Walmart on urban markets like Los Angeles or the attacks by unionized supermarket chains on hard-fought labor victories. Therefore, UFCW 770 instead preferred small unionized markets even if they charged more for food, lacked fresh produce, and prioritized selling nonhealthy items like liquor and cigarettes.

What was required to shift perspectives and find common ground between labor and food justice activists in Los Angeles? Because the predominant food justice narrative stipulates that places without food need a grocery store, UFCW 770 and their allies in organizations such as LAANE and the LAFPC focused on poverty. As the critical food scholar Julie Guthman has argued, not only are capitalism and institutional racism overlooked when food justice simply equates with filling grocery gaps, but so are the most effective strategies for intervention.[60] Michelle Obama's Let's Move campaign is a prime example of this oversight. As part of this campaign, major grocery retailers promised in 2011 they would open up fifteen hundred stores in places designated by the U.S. Department of Agriculture as "food deserts." According to Michelle Obama's 2014 progress report, only 602 stores opened, providing 1.4 million people with new grocery stores out of the eighteen million lacking easy access to one.[61] Missing completely from the First Lady's campaign, as well as many food justice initiatives, is the need to end poverty so people can afford to eat the most nutritious food. In other words, we need a food politics that creates demand-side solutions.

When labor organizers center the structural economic position of workers, there is a higher likelihood solutions prioritize improving a person's social mobility. Consider, for instance, the relationship between neoliberal capitalism in a post–Great Recession context and the discontent of the Occupy Wall Street movement, a robust Fight for $15 movement, and the Democratic presidential race of Bernie Sanders. But there are strategic challenges, given consumers' desire to keep food costs low; cheap food usually tops food-chain workers despite their being interrelated.[62] In response, labor organizers discursively overemphasize labor. A Latino union representative named Emiliano who works with meatpacking workers reminded me in an interview, "We can't forget that when you eat chicken, beef, pork, or even tofu, it took a worker, it took somebody to pick it off, like a soybean, it took a worker to slaughter a cow or pig or chicken. Whether you believe that's necessary, that's everybody's opinion, but as far as making a living for somebody, or giving somebody a job, that's what we're about." There are practical and ideological reasons driving this analysis. Marta reasoned, "If they aren't jobs you can raise a family on or make a decent living [on], that is obviously a problem for the economy as a whole. . . . The disparity in wealth can only be gained by workers . . . by organizing and taking back some of the money that these companies have been hoarding." Marta's redistributive perspective identifies the structural problem; most of the capital derived from food-chain workers is shuffled upward into the hands of owners and investors, which is inversely related to a thirty-year trend of stagnating wages and benefits.[63]

By giving workers primacy, labor organizers challenge a prevailing form of food politics that focuses on eating local, organic food. In response to a question asking about differences in how labor and food justice activists address food insecurity, a Latino labor organizer with LAANE named Adrian revealed that he grew up in a neighborhood with poor food access. "If we aren't going to directly subsidize organic grocers or organic industries and make them cheaper like we do for the corn industry, then we really need to be working on wages of people and making sure they can afford it," he suggested. Focusing on wages and benefits is also a matter of human dignity. Offering the worker perspective, Felipe reasoned,

> If your boss or the owner of the company you work for tells you, "The minimum wage is $8 and I'm paying you $10. What else do you want? I'm giving you a vacation . . ." If you feel, "That is true. Why should I fight for that when I am making more money [here] than other places?" That means you believe in them and you don't care about yourself and your own family. In order to live in LA, how much money do you need to live? . . . I would say $25 an hour to live decently. Not necessarily to buy a house but to be able to rent a decent house for your wife and family, to send your kids to college, you have your own car to come to work and to have money to enjoy your life. You work during the week and you have

weekends to spend time with your family. . . . That is why you work! To eat and to enjoy your life.

Felipe discloses that in addition to the importance of fair remuneration, there is also symbolic value. Pay reflects the degree to which people can enjoy more leisure time and perhaps enjoy local and organic food. Labor organizers also shared some of the critiques made by food justice scholars that neoliberal market-centric alternative food strategies reproduce white privilege by overlooking racialized labor pools. For example, Jill questions organizing explicitly around food when it elevates health above the realities of work under capitalism: "You can create the program or the market, but what is ultimately going to allow people to become healthier and have less health disparities?" The answer resonates with many of the other labor organizers I interviewed: improve labor standards and end poverty. Starting with an abstract thing like food, which is a product of human labor and embedded in systems of social stratification, overlooks inequities in the process of social reproduction. Speaking to some of these class and racial fissures, Adrian remarked, "While I appreciate . . . personal health and the environmental-type concerns, I immediately started recognizing the whiteness . . . of the food movement. . . . Our priorities might get left out as [those of] a person of color. . . . It's affecting us too. We should have a voice."

Despite concerns that the food movement and many food justice initiatives focus on supply-side solutions, labor organizers have pushed the issue of poverty and built strong alliances to avoid a trade-off between healthy food and quality jobs. New political opportunities emerged in 2010 when a representative of the United Farm Workers joined the LAFPC. Then in 2014, although UFCW 770 was at first reticent to address food insecurity and the need for access to healthy food, the LAFPC invited John Grant, the secretary-treasurer, to sit on the Leadership Board. While this formal relationship expanded the perspective of labor organizers to consider food access, their primary analysis of the conjuncture is through a class-conscious lens that confronts blind consumerism. As Mark reflected, "You can drive through town on your way to work, and sometimes you have to really concentrate to identify all those people who you are passing that are working. They become part of the landscape. They don't really step out of that role." This perspective highlights how workers are largely a means to an end in a consumer society. The common adage "The customer is always right" makes it hard to see workers. Such neoliberal ideologies influence social practices that reproduce poor labor conditions, even in the food movement. For example, bucolic promotions of the small family farm can overlook how consumers face intense marketing pressures that inscribe change at the individual level through the market. Neoliberalization is a socialization process that elides worker exploitation. The moral for allies in the food movement is not to forget the importance of economic justice. Amy, a Latina labor organizer supporting Walmart workers, claimed activists of many kinds "forget about the workers and their mistreatment. In terms of animal rights or environmental justice, a lot of people get centered on the types of justice that are important to them but when it comes to economic or worker justice, they neglect it."

Navigating Corporate Power, Food Insecurity, and Bad Jobs

Directly related to claims for a food justice that integrates economic justice is the fact that where supermarket chains once stood as bastions of community stability, they are increasingly sites of corporate power and malfeasance. Anti-union companies such as Walmart perfected the chain model of its predecessors, but without providing the same quality of food or employment. Armed with its neoliberal tagline "Save money. Live better," Walmart has fought to enter communities throughout Los Angeles to colonize the urban food landscape. The bland branding of a "Walmart medium blue" logo followed by the tacky "Walmart yellow" spark are a visual reminder that where there were grocery stores that provided a communal space for money to flow back into the local economy, there now stands an extractive big box. Framing such interpretations are documentaries such as Robert Greenwald's *Walmart: The High Cost of Low Price*, which portrays Walmart as a greedy corporation. Nowhere is this more apparent than in the gross disparities between the wealth of the Walton family and Walmart workers. The Walmart 1%, which was a project of the UFCW campaign Making Change at Walmart, calculated, "If Sam Walton's dependents actually worked for their Walmart dividend checks this year, they would be handed $1.5 million every hour. Meanwhile, Walmart workers get an average of $8.81 per hour and are routinely denied full-time work."[64] Conversely, corporate and development boosters tout big-box retailers as job creators and cheap commodity providers for working-class communities. After the Great Recession, low-wage jobs replaced middle- and high-wage jobs, so many people see big-box retailers as saviors providing at least some form of employment and food at a price that matches a growing low-wage economy.[65] This constitutes the chief contradiction driving the emergence of a local food politics that refuses to compromise one basic need for another.

Finding common cause across interest groups to overcome the uneven development of cities is no easy task. The labor movement is historically complicit in environmental degradation and poisoning the public on the basis that the workers powering industry receive their share of the profit.[66] Driven on by the capitalist growth imperative, workers, with the support of organized labor, have often overlooked the ways in which urban industrial facilities produce negative consequences. Left in the wake of these development patterns are working-class communities and communities of color who suffer the health consequences. Contradictorily, if these communities eliminate a toxic facility, they may also remove a source of employment to economically stabilize the neighborhood.

In similar ways, UFCW has not always been the best steward of the environment or of public health. They represent grocery workers who sell not only fresh produce but also highly processed foods derived from corporately controlled supply chains lambasted by the food movement. So while Walmart may be a particularly formidable company, major unionized supermarkets like Kroger and Safeway are still embedded in a capitalist industrialized food system. Indicative of this trend is the "Buy blue" ethos of labor organizers. Around Thanksgiving, UFCW was advertising union-made products available at union supermarkets. Under the banner "Have a Union Thanksgiving," replete with a plump turkey in the background, were brand logos for companies such as Kraft, Ocean Spray, Foster Farms, Betty Crocker, and Butterball. This suggests labor unions, at least to some degree, are parasitic on a corporately concentrated food system.[67]

Even when it comes to solving food insecurity, there have been tensions. Before Marta was organizing workers in Los Angeles, she was in Oakland. UFCW Local 5 was invited to a community town hall discussion about whether to open Walmart in a food-insecure neighborhood. She was concerned that it felt like "UFCW versus the poor black residents of Oakland." Many residents wanted the store, but UFCW Local 5 was ultimately successful in helping to prevent its opening, as it had been in obstructing the entrance of other nonunion supermarkets. Speaking similarly to the complicated relationship that UFCW 770 had with food-access activists in Los Angeles, a public health report titled *Food Desert to Food Oasis* recommended that the city not force grocery stores that serve "food deserts" to pay living wages or allow unionization.[68] The report reflects the perceived need to check the influential political power of UFCW 770 in grocery zoning decisions. While these instances make UFCW appear deaf to the dietary health needs of the public, Marta recognized the false dichotomy dividing the labor movement from the food movement: "The only 'real' solution is if all retail stores are union and provided good jobs and were a source of food."

Union density in grocery retail has declined over the past few decades, which has further pressured labor unions into economic concessions. The historical narrative offered by UFCW 770 goes something like this. Union decline came with the penetration of new large supermarkets and the merger of medium-sized supermarkets. Incidentally, larger supermarkets negotiated with unions to secure preferred contracts, which displaced smaller union grocery stores. Coupled with the ability of major supermarkets to drive down food prices by controlling their supply chain, smaller grocery stores disappeared. As supermarkets grew into (multi)national corporations, they developed the capacity to operate across time and space in ways local labor unions' organizational structure hinders. Moreover, corporate consolidation drives unevenness in labor standards, grocery retail development, and therefore consumer shopping patterns. The resulting race to the bottom harms grocery workers.[69]

Add in inevitable capitalist crises like the Great Recession, and there is the problem of how economic precariousness translates into food insecurity. In 2011, there were 50.1 million food-insecure people and 44.7 million people receiving food stamps.[70] California has 4.1 million food-insecure adults, with Los Angeles County accounting for 1.2 million of these people.[71] When you drill down to look at food-chain workers, they disproportionately experience these realities. Thirteen percent of all food-chain workers, almost 2.8 million workers, relied on food stamps in 2016.[72] This is 2.2 times the rate of food-stamp usage of all other industries.[73] In 2011, 23 percent of food-chain workers in California were using CalFresh food assistance versus 11 percent of the general population, while 54 percent of California nonsupervisory food-chain workers lacked health insurance.[74] These experiences are also prevalent in Los Angeles County, where 18 percent of food-chain workers are food insecure.[75]

Many of my interviewees recognized the cruel irony of food-insecure food-chain workers. In Huntington Park, which is the neighborhood where most of UFCW 770's unionized meatpacking and food-processing members live, a number of union grocery stores closed. Nonunion Latinx grocers such as El Super and Northgate González Markets were the replacement. Having lived and worked in the area for decades, a former Latina meatpacking organizer named Isabel reflected, "People go to them and do their shopping because their money goes further. You can't blame them." UFCW 770 would like to improve this situation but faces logistical obstacles. Dave, a white researcher and organizer with the union, told me that many of these Latinx chains are small, which makes them tough targets. They offer working-class Latinx communities nutritious food options, but remuneration for workers is poor. "In no situations could we go after a company that has standalone store after standalone store," he acknowledged. "It has to be some sort of agreement with a corporation for neutrality with their chain to be able to do it [unionize] for it to make sense." A neutrality agreement "contain[s] a pledge by the employer that it will remain 'neutral' in the union's organizing campaigns conducted in the employer's nonunion facilities."[76] Unless coordinated labor unrest disrupts an entire chain's stores, it is unusual for a company to allow a unionization drive that might diminish the gap between economic and food insecurity.

Partially in response to food-chain workers' dual marginalization, UFCW 770 is working with the food movement to reduce the dietary deficits of working-class Angelenos. Alliances have emerged for three main reasons. First, the high visibility and success of labor campaigns led by Los Angeles labor unions and advocacy groups over the last fifteen years lend legitimacy to the labor movement. Second, the integration of activists with direct knowledge or experience of food work *and* food insecurity into the food movement bridges previously distinct movement domains. This enriches and diversifies the field of food politics. The food movement has grown in Los Angeles to include the interests of food-chain workers because many activists from communities that lack living-wage jobs and healthy food recognize the entanglement of these problems. Last, labor organizers accept the need to increase access to healthy food and have found they can work alongside the food movement through the lens of poverty. UFCW 770 hears about its members' food insecurity and sees how building or joining coalitions can address demand-side root causes.[77]

The social conditions for food and labor movement alliances are auspicious. Angelenos have supported the confrontational labor campaigns of grocery workers since the large Southern California grocery retail strikes of 2003–4. Then after slowing Walmart and other big-box retailers' entrance into Los Angeles through the 2004 big-box ordinance, labor organizers attempted to block Walmart's new tactic. As Luciana, an organizer with LAANE, explained, "In order for them to grow into other urban areas, Walmart has changed their strategy in how they expand." The company has seized on "use by right" clauses in city zoning laws, particularly in places banning big-box retail stores. They allow Walmart to avoid serious local government review before opening their "Neighborhood Market" in a smaller retail space already zoned for such uses. This allows the company to avoid building new superstores and the costly battles that come with public oversight and permitting requirements. One of the perceived problems is that Walmart undermines their claim that they benefit communities by abusing laws that permit them to avoid any verification. As Jae, an Asian political operative with UFCW 770, asked, "What do you have to hide?" In the most contentious of these conflicts, Walmart endeavored for years to open a Neighborhood Market in Chinatown deploying "food desert" rhetoric to succor an "underserved" community, even though the community had ample local access to food. Although Walmart eventually outmaneuvered the opposition for a short time, the defeat precipitated further challenges to Walmart.

Since 2012, UFCW 770 has supported OUR Walmart. This worker-led advocacy group has staged unfair labor practice strikes to call attention to terrible wages and benefits, insufficient hours, and a lack of workplace respect. Although there were never more than a couple hundred workers who went on strike on Black Friday in 2012, 2013, or 2014, they embodied public grievances that helped inspire the resurgence of labor unrest throughout the United States.[78] These direct-action tactics did not lead to unionization, but they did shame Walmart into improving workplace conditions.[79] Although the number of workers actually participating in these actions was low, they galvanized social media, the blogosphere, and the mainstream media to create the impression of widespread discontent.[80] In Los Angeles, these forces sustained criticism of Walmart. Public oppo-

Figure 9. The largest protest against Walmart in history took place in 2012 in Los Angeles, California. Photography by Mike Chickey.

sition, like the largest-ever-recorded anti-Walmart march in 2012, did not prevent Walmart from entering the heart of Los Angeles in Chinatown, but it did help contribute ultimately to the company's retreat.[81] These confrontations positively reinforce the benefits of opposing corporate power and reveal the complicated political terrain that activists navigate.

In the middle of ongoing labor struggles in the grocery retail sector, UFCW 770 was also involved in policy initiatives and civic engagements to address food insecurity, which have produced wins for both the labor movement and the food movement. In 2008, a Blue Ribbon Commission convened environmental, faith, food, health, and labor representatives. The commission found "food deserts" were expanding throughout Los Angeles due to "supermarket redlining," grocery stores pay worse in working-class communities, and these same stores mandate fewer programs to reduce environmental impacts.[82] To incentivize grocery stores to locate in underserved communities, the city of Los Angeles made community redevelopment money available. This money often follows where city planners, developers, and politicians see inflows of capital.

Downtown Los Angeles did not have a grocery store for many years, even as hipsters and techies flooded into the area. However, as downtown gentrified, the calculus switched. UFCW 770 capitalized on this new demand by working with city leaders and community groups to shuffle redevelopment money to Ralphs for a unionized grocery store.

In contrast, communities such as South Los Angeles face pressure to accept nonunion retailers. Unionized grocery chains divested from this community, labor organizers refuse to accept a Walmart, and yet the demand for healthy food remains. Therefore, food justice activists have had to devise other strategies. Tapping into the California FreshWorks Fund, a public-private partnership focused on helping fill grocery gaps, Northgate González Markets opened in South Los Angeles in 2014. Food justice activists were happy with this outcome, and so was UFCW 770 because the company signed a community benefits agreement (CBA).[83] In short, CBAs are contracts usually signed between a broad-based community coalition and a developer or operator. Such agreements outline a set of standards, amenities, or mitigations that are the developer's responsibility and require the coalition to publicly support the project. The Northgate González Markets CBA mandated living wages, benefits, and local hiring practices. Unlike a strictly neoliberal response that sidesteps local government, CBAs build in legally enforceable elements that create greater inclusivity and accountability in land use decisions.

The victories of labor unions such as UFCW 770 and their willingness to build new alliances have made it easier for food activists to embrace labor issues and commit to breaking down barriers in the name of improving the local food system.[84] Despite the historical wariness of allying with the food movement, the labor movement's entrance into spaces like the LAFPC has provided a set of political tools that integrates an explicit concern with economic justice. Ultimately, these social interactions strengthen campaigns to take care of food-chain workers. The objectives laid out in the LAFPC's Good Food for All Agenda illustrate this shift. They aspire to three things: "a thriving and good food economy for all; strengthened agricultural and environmental stewardship throughout the region[; and] better health and well-being of residents."[85] Although there is no comprehensive food policy in the city that mandates meeting these objectives, they compel the leadership board and working groups to work across food movement boundaries. The social learning emerging from this process has symbolic value because it represents a more participatory and deliberative democratic model.

One of the major LAFPC victories has been the creation of the institutional procurement pledge called the Good Food Purchasing Policy (GFPP). Not only is this important locally, but it has become a model program that the Center for Good Food Purchasing is spreading throughout the United States.[86] The Center for Good Food Purchasing estimates that demand from major institutions in active GFPP cities is 2.2 million meals, the economic impact of which is worth $500 million. The pledge encourages buying from small and midsized food and farming operations and ensures the food meets high environmental sustainability standards and is nutritious and cruelty free, all of which works to scale up alternative food networks. It also recommends that food-chain workers receive fair compensation and work in safe conditions. This incentivizes purchasing from companies with unionized workforces or that rely on third-party certification systems like fair trade. The GFPP is not a policy mandating a monolithic set of practices, but rather a voluntary set of standards institutions adopt to meet a range of goals. If an institution meets commitments, the GFPP awards star ratings like how LEED (Leadership in Energy and Environmental Design) certification works. After conducting a baseline assessment, the GFPP will provide technical assistance to help an institution meet its goals and regularly verify it meets these goals. If successful, the certifiers recognize the institution based on their level of commitment in each of five categories: a strong local food economy, environmental sustainability, a valued food industry workforce, the humane treatment of animals, and high nutritional quality. To maintain its rating, the institution must improve continually the "goodness" of their purchases. To date, the City of Los Angeles, the Los Angeles Unified School District, and Guckenheimer (a company that provides meals for Google LA and Roll Global) have signed onto the GFPP. Combined, they serve over seven hundred fifty thousand meals daily.[87] Collaboration between the labor movement and the food movement has helped improve local food supply chains in terms of food access, nutritional quality, and labor standards.

. . .

The activism of UFCW 770 and its food justice allies enriches food politics in Los Angeles. Taking back the economy in this context means workers capturing more of the value produced by their labor. One key strategy is leveraging the power of the state to enforce and create better labor laws. Where corporations are concerned, it means organizing workers, shaming poor labor practices, and using the legal system to extract concessions. Unlike at San Diego Roots, where taking back the economy manifests in mutual association and is less reliant on wage labor, the case of UFCW 770 reveals that challenging corporations that mistreat workers is a prerequisite for increasing the availability of healthy food.

These two orientations to taking back the economy reflect the dialectical openness of food justice. On one end of the spectrum sit activists whose food justice economics, if you will, reimagine and re-create exchange to reflect the values of trust and cooperation. They eschew some of the typical monetary exchanges that predominate in conventional and alternative food systems. Strategically, this economic secession represents an affinity with anarchist and anticapitalist Food Not Bombs activists and "freegans" committed to living on the food waste of capitalism while simultaneously working toward its dismantlement.[88] On the other end of the spectrum sit activists pushing employers and the government to improve the livelihood of workers. This reformism relies on confrontational tactics to compel businesses to increase wages, benefits, and workplace conditions and democracy. Relatedly, the labor movement, which includes labor unions, worker centers, and advocacy groups of all kinds, can ally with immigrant rights activists to reform labor and immigration laws.

Food justice economics vary depending on strategic targets and intents. Yet different perspectives are not mutually exclusive. Taking back the economy will require confronting exploitation in the food system to ease the suffering that food workers experience. It will also require developing economic models that revalue food work, eradicate hierarchy, and create participatory models that prioritize environmental sustainability and equity to match workers' needs to their abilities.

4
_____

Immigration Food Fights

Challenging Borders and Bridging Social Boundaries

Given the prevalence of immigrants in California, their prominent role as workers in the food system, and their visible resistance to social marginalization, immigration conjunctures directly shape all three of my cases.[1] This suggests the need for strategies that can dismantle social boundaries to deepen multiracial and multiethnic food justice coalitions.[2] California has more immigrants than any other state in the United States. More than ten million immigrants live in the state and represent almost 30 percent of the population. A little more than 50 percent of the foreign-born population comes from Latin America, mostly from Mexico. Although most immigrants are documented residents, a sizable minority, 25 percent, are undocumented.[3] The experiences of immigrants and native residents in California have broad implications. Seven million people live in border counties, thirteen million reside within sixty-two miles, and a whopping seventy million are residents of border states.[4] The food system thrives on these conditions; foreign-born workers account for 20 percent of all food-chain workers, and in sectors like farming, scholars estimate undocumented farmworkers account for between 25 and 50 percent of the workforce.[5] Undocumented workers are also highly exploited. They are more likely to be harassed, abused, and exposed to dangerous workplace conditions; receive low-wages; and experience wage theft.[6]

The racialized social boundaries in the food system in the United States go back to settlers' expropriation of indigenous land and agriculture's colonization of people and nature as it proceeded west.[7] During roughly the same period, an estimated 388,000 Africans were sold into the plantation economy of slavery.[8] Lest whites have to perform the most arduous labor, the food system became reliant on an ethnic succession of immigrant workers until the very present. We disregard this history and its consequences for achieving food justice at our own peril. Ignorance is acquiescence to white supremacy and the exploitation of foreign-born workers through practices of "imported colonialism."[9] Whites have driven a de facto system of segregation that uses guest farmworker programs to import racialized foreign workers and then legally and socially exclude them from the polity. The historical antecedents producing these boundaries echo on in many of the daily food politics of the food movement, such as preferences for ecological values or white farm imaginaries that ignore racialized immigrant farmworkers.[10] One of the major food justice political projects must be to confront institutional racism and xenophobia that excludes and demonizes immigrants.

The task of dismantling social boundaries in the food system mirrors other social movements that navigate the complex process of building solidarity. Throughout the left in the United States, there is greater awareness of how identity influences the experience of oppression and movement participation. While there was an era when movements fought for "civil rights" for entire categories of people, like blacks, women, gays, and lesbians, we now live in a time of increased sensitivity to the failure of grand narratives to capture nuance. There is also more focus on individual and collective complicity, however unintentional, with systems of oppression. Take the Black Lives Matter movement, which was started by queer black women. Although mainstream attention focuses most on the dehumanization of black men at the hands of white police officers, the creators of Black Lives Matter have pushed the movement to adopt intersectional lenses. It is not just that generalized black lives matter. How particular blacks experience racism matters, whether they are women, queer, trans, disabled, or undocumented. Conversely, radical politics must honor specific needs and inequities and take measures to leverage privileges to intervene in these inequities. Challenging oppressive social boundaries to achieve equitable social relations requires reflexivity and a commitment to adjusting strategies.

Any attempt to transform the food system is entangled in a system of violence that produces and maintains differences based on citizenship.[11] Social boundaries initially produced through settler state colonialism, ecocide, genocide, militarism, and institutional racism can continue to have detrimental effects through both active and passive forms of maintenance.[12] As this pertains to immigration, attention to the conjunctures in San Diego, Los Angeles, and Oakland shows how difficult it is to develop a food politics that can overcome the divisiveness of citizenship. In each city, organic farming and local food activists navigate immigration within the contradiction between the status of undocumented Latinx immigrants and the food system's reliance on exploitable and deportable labor.[13] Moreover, the view of immigration taken by San Diego Roots, UFCW 770, and Planting Justice is refracted through their demographic makeup, mission, geography, and food system entry point. I focus on social boundaries to highlight the discursive and practical opportunities to disrupt these historical trends. By comparing food politics in different contexts, I conclude that resisting the supposed essential social difference assumed by white supremacist and xenophobic notions of exclusivity and superiority is central to reimagining food justice. Challenging social boundaries opens the possibility for a food politics opposed to borders and the detrimental impact they impose on people, many of whom end up working in the food system.[14]

Organic Farming, Immigrants, and the U.S.–Mexico Border

At Wild Willow Farm, San Diego Roots, like hundreds of organizations and farms around the United States, engages in the important work of educating a new generation of organic farmers and revaluing labor practices with nonwage forms of exchange.[15] Because the farm sits along the U.S.–Mexico border, it offers the opportunity to reflect on the contradictions of farming amid divisions between farmers and farmworkers, organic and conventional, and eaters and workers. This location exemplifies the connection between conceptual distinctions people make to categorize groups and their social consequences for all farms, whether or not they directly rely on immigrant labor. It also offers a visceral reminder for many organic farming and local food activists of the need to transcend the associated social boundaries. Yet the racialized and militarized nature of the space creates obstacles. First, activists navigate typical stereotypes about immigrant farmworkers. Second, activists witness the militarization of the border and the monitoring of migrant bodies. This contrasts the ethnoracial, class, and citizenship privileges they are afforded farming on the U.S. side of the border. Together these factors inhibit a food politics capable of breaking down social boundaries and reforming labor laws to protect migrant farmworkers and immigrants from detention and deportation.

Not only is California agriculture reliant on a racialized workforce that devalues labor in order to shuffle more capital into the hands of growers, but also it benefits from a dehumanizing immigration and surveillance regime. Based on manufacturing fear over things like crime, terrorism, and the economy, the law enforcement arm of the state frames foreign nationals, especially those from Latin America, as a threat.[16] In a post-9/11 context, the state relies heavily on military and security methods to monitor and control these populations. The combination of militarized surveillance practices and threat narratives produces social boundaries.[17] Therefore, in San Diego, which boosters refer to as "America's Finest City," immigrants remain invisible to many whites and those whose families have been in the United States for many generations. This hiddenness is not just optical or experiential. Invisibility is ideological and produced through racialized discursive strategies that turn immigrants into an unknowable other subject to society's desire for cheap labor.

Figure 10. Border fence at Friendship Park on the U.S. side of the San Diego–Tijuana border. Photograph by Chantae Reden.

Stereotypes and Misperceptions of Immigrant Farmworkers

Attention to how San Diego Roots activists internalized and maintained social boundaries reveals the significance of stereotypes to divide native organic farmers from foreign immigrant farmworkers. One of the consistent views was economic marginalization is not ideal, but new immigrants are working through the typical occupational hierarchy to achieve economic prosperity like immigrants before them. This operated through a few key racialized perspectives. First, the problems farmworkers experience are intractable. Second, higher labor costs equate with higher food costs, which entails the economic precariousness of farmworkers. Third, farmworkers undertake backbreaking work most American citizens are unwilling to perform.

Although many farm-school participants, staff and board members, and volunteers recognized migration has economic and political drivers, they considered this a typical condition in California agriculture. In conjunction with what scholars have found, I was told free trade agreements, guest farmworker programs, and the industrialization of farming in Mexico and Central America have pushed and pulled migrants northward.[18] Then I always heard the caveat that the history of California agriculture is a story of one ethnic group replacing another one in search of better opportunities. These two narrative threads support each other. Underlying them both is the assumption the United States is a desirable place to migrate to, which dovetails with the assimilationist ideology of the United States as a "melting pot" and the belief in an "American dream" where people are economically free to choose their destiny. The problems associated with immigration are therefore intractable. Historical path dependencies, political and economic expedience, and the abstract liberal belief of "freedom of choice" erect barriers to solidarity. Together these beliefs located social change outside of the control of San Diego Roots, which instead must stay afloat in a competitive food movement nonprofit sector.

Sustaining these perspectives was the narrative that cheap labor is required for affordable food. A white organic farmer named Wayne asserted, "I know that if we didn't have those workers here, our local agriculture industry would come to a screeching halt and food prices would skyrocket. We would have to import stuff from farther away and increase food costs like crazy." Such statements exaggerate the impact of increasing the wages of farmworkers and overlook the economic incentive citizens might have were the remuneration adequate to the arduous task of farming. Farmers receive a small share of every retail dollar for the fruits and vegetables they produce, about 30 percent, and a third of this pays for farmworkers. Philip Martin, a labor economist who focuses on farmworkers and immigration, found in 2016 that a 47 percent increase in farmworkers' wages to $15 an hour would pull farmworkers out of poverty and translate to consumers spending on average about $20 a year more on fresh fruits and vegetables.[19] And as Julie Guthman discovered in her study of organic agriculture in California, weak labor laws contribute to keeping farms afloat by allowing them to deflate labor costs and turn a greater profit through the valorization of their organic products.[20]

Although perceptions of social boundaries varied, there was the common racialized sentiment that immigrant farmworkers need less. A white unpaid staff member named Amber replicated this typical stereotype: "Their quality of life, where they come from, people from Mexico, they have a lower quality, so they don't need as much." Racialized self-perceptions supported the projection of immigrants' presumed needs. Specifically, there were racially coded beliefs that differentiated native-born white San Diegans as unwilling to perform farm work. Sean, a white volunteer at Wild Willow Farm and a chef at a hip local food restaurant, projected a reversal of the ethnic succession in agriculture if food cost more: "If food gets more expensive, then I definitely think we can afford to pay local [i.e., white] people to do it." Under this scenario, the only way to improve conditions for farmworkers is to pay more for food. This would certainly help. But the sovereignty of consumer choice mandates cheap food and eclipses the legal urgency to protect farmworkers or pass laws to prevent the exploitation of immigrants.[21]

In a similar line of reasoning, some people at San Diego Roots normalized the plight of immigrant farmworkers, while market pressures and neoliberal subjectivities of individuality and personal responsibility justified inaction. Reflecting the slow transition the organization was going through in 2012 to become economically stable, a white board member named Sharon compared this to the experience of being an immigrant farmworker: "We're still struggling to make ends meet every month. It's the same thing that the migrant workers are facing. . . . They can't be really thinking about too much more." Sharon made this comparison to demonstrate economics comes before social solidarity. When I asked later whether the organization should support immigrant farmworkers, she replied she would like to see more social interactions that increase cultural exchange: "It'd be good to be a part of that community, educating everyone around us, having cross-cultural events where we can go to some of the farms that are across the border and have relationships with them, learn from the farmers that come across." Explicit political commitments did not accompany this well-meaning desire for greater social interaction. While the economic pressures San Diego Roots faced are common to food movement nonprofits, there is not a mutually exclusive tradeoff between maintaining financial solvency and finding ways to advocate on behalf of farmworkers.[22] Even as the organization stabilized financially, the focus remained on sustainable living, organic farming, and fostering beginner farmers despite the glaring contradictions of working along the U.S.–Mexico border.

Border Militarization and Monitoring Migrants

On one of the first days I interned at Wild Willow Farm, a Border Patrol agent in an SUV drove up and interrupted a conversation I was having with a few people from San Diego Roots: "Have you seen anyone run through here?" We all responded, "No." After he drove away, Alan, a white founding member of San Diego Roots, quipped, "This is the nature of working right on the border." He followed up with, "You have to defend 'national security,' " as he made air quotes. He then pointed to the close imposing wall running east-west along the border for as far as the eye could see. Later in the morning, I mentioned to Titus what happened. He saw the person in question crossing the border and running through the farm. Upset with the Border Patrol, he replied, "Those guys are assholes." Janelle, who was also at the farm all the time, agreed: "Fuck Border Patrol." Titus then noted that a few days prior he had found a fresh pair of clothes left behind some bushes to aid migrants; he often tried to leave out food. As we harvested tomatoes, reflecting on the morning events, helicopters flew overhead looking for border crossers.

The militarized and surveilled feel of Wild Willow Farm juxtaposed how San Diego Roots used the farm to demonstrate the merits of organic farming and build community. Although many participants recognized the inequity of the ease with which they could farm and the travails of immigrant farmworkers, I rarely heard of any policy prescriptions or action plans. Perhaps one of the reasons for this is the prevalent military culture within San Diego, which some of my interviewees proposed produces feelings of *insecurity* that stymie resistance to border militarization. As Jayla, a black San Diego activist and scholar working in food politics, explained, "You don't recognize the fact that people feel a daily insecurity about the border. . . . For a lot of the people here that's because they may not be documented . . . [and] really feel the impact of the border policing. We have a strong military presence here. . . . There are people . . . very concerned with using that lens of homeland security and military defense to how we build our economy." Despite the influence of the military, border enforcement, and defense industry, the perception of people at San Diego Roots was that border crossers face the greatest threat.[23] Raquel, a Latina former staff member who lived on the U.S. side of the border for years, noted empathically, "I see the Border Patrol with their semi-automatic weapons and the new fence going up. We hear the rustling in the bushes . . . and people are crossing this heavily militarized area. . . . You feel kind of caught in the middle of . . . a crime almost. . . . But at the same time, I'm empathetic." The implication here is that the social boundaries produced by the border reinforce the symbolic differences of citizenship and the legal risks of resisting its militarization.

A prominent military and immigration enforcement regime contributed to a politics of quiescence.[24] Speaking to this reality, Melissa, reflected, "Politics in San Diego is interesting because it's not something [border issues] that people engage in. . . . Especially people in the progressive community working on food issues, you know, tend to not dwell on that stuff." Her comments illuminate how organic farming and local food activists bracketed social problems related to immigration and the border to deemphasize their significance and foreclose on taking action. Merging with this hesitance was the perceived tendency in San Diego for people to avoid confrontation over controversial topics. Referring to her experience trying to have conversations about capitalism and institutional racism, Jayla told me, "If you're really vociferous about your opinions either you're a quack, you know, or you have to either go running or surfing or something." The policing of acceptable ideas and topics emulates the regulation of bodies and the default security framework looming over the city's social movements. These conditions even manifest in the built environment at Wild Willow Farm in the form of fake closed-circuit surveillance cameras that pepper the tool shed, Quonset hut, mobile office, and outdoor kitchen and barn. Ostensibly, the cameras dissuade potential burglars, but they also notify farm visitors and border crossers alike that they are under scrutiny.

Mobility Privilege amid Racialized Restrictions

Wild Willow Farm is embedded in ethnoracial and economic relations stratified along lines of human mobility and segregation in San Diego. In a collection of oral histories by Kelly Mayhew in a book highlighting the voices of nonvacationland San Diego, an undocumented college student from Mexico named Geraldo discloses, "My people don't tend to mingle with the first-class citizens. I don't see a lot of my people going to the theater, or going to nice restaurants. Why? There are not a lot of us who have the careers that would allow us to do these things."[25] While white and middle- to upper-middle-class San Diegans usually experience greater mobility privilege than Geraldo, they hold negative views of Tijuana, and seldom cross the border. A poll conducted in 2003 found those with unfavorable perceptions of Tijuana rarely, if ever visit, and a majority would like more restrictive border policies or are content with current enforcement standards.[26] Latinx residents, on the other hand, more frequently visit and overwhelmingly hold positive perceptions of Tijuana. The differences in mobility reflect some of the history of xenophobia in San Diego that trickled into the larger California polity in the 1990s. Racist language and policy have long informed white San Diegans' relationship to their Mexican neighbors.[27] This intensified after Pete Wilson, the former San Diego mayor and California governor, relied on the "Latino threat narrative" to argue that "illegals" were receiving far too many state resources during a Southern California recession.[28] Pete Wilson also supported the passage of Proposition 187, which restricted undocumented immigrants from receiving public education, health care, and other social services. Although the courts ultimately deemed the proposition unconstitutional, the underlying sentiments inform how white San Diegans imagine the border, which affects the movement of both documented and undocumented immigrants.

Exacerbating some of these tensions in October of 2007 were some of the largest wildfires in San Diego history. While the mandatory evacuations and disaster relief efforts were largely compassionate, a racist undercurrent affected many Latinx residents and undocumented farmworkers. First, Latinx evacuees at relief centers were accused of stealing donated items and as a result faced deportation by Border Patrol. Second, police officers monitored evacuation zones by arbitrarily detaining and requesting identification. Without identification, people faced deportation.[29] Third, many farmworkers working in mandatory evacuation zones also lived in precarious housing in nearby canyons. Wayne criticized these living conditions as inhumane: "The so-called housing they provide, they say, 'You can stay in that canyon right there, and here are some blue tarps. Just don't burn the place down when you cook all your food there in the canyon. Use the bottom end of the canyon as your latrine.'"[30] While farmworkers were not blamed for these fires, Wayne's comment recognizes their marginalized social status; they did not receive relief services.[31] Even one of the oldest and well-regarded organic farms, Be Wise Ranch, forced workers to toil in hazardous air quality in order to save the strawberry crop. Most farmworkers stayed for fear of job loss or deportation by Border Patrol.[32]

The racialized restrictions placed on immigrants and farmworkers contrast starkly with the mobility privilege of those who travel to the border to connect with nature at Wild Willow Farm. Many people who otherwise had little experience farming idealized small-scale farming, which downplayed the privilege of being able to experience the natural beauty of the Tijuana River Estuary. For example, participants at monthly potlucks when I attended the farm school consisted primarily of people driving from Central San Diego to see an organic farm and share in the joys of eating local food. Similarly, most interns and students at the farm school drove from other parts of San Diego County. Although whites made up only 28 percent of the population in Central San Diego and 22 percent in the South Bay, these potluck-goers and interns were largely white.[33] Some people minimized these politics of racial representation. A white staff member named Pam offered the following color-blind analysis: "I saw this picture of a religious family praying, saying, 'Thank you God for the food,' and underneath it this Mexican farmer says, 'De nada' like 'You're welcome.' . . . I'm kind of touchy when it comes to racial classification because there's just so much built around it. . . . I accept people and just kind of tend to get away from the politics. It's just a natural response to a lot of negative connotations and racial issues that obviously we all face." Shutting down discussions on immigration also obscured the privilege associated with whiteness. This manifested in perceptions of farming at Wild Willow Farm, which contradicted the reality faced by

Figure 11. Community potlucks at Wild Willow Farm consisted of many people from Central San Diego and few border locals. Photograph by Gregory Berg-Enso Photography.

most farmworkers in the region. "I like to work happy jobs," exclaimed a white intern named Amanda. "From what I see working on this farm, sustainability comes into it. It is not work that drains on you . . . [or] damage[s] your body." Albeit unintentional, the privileging of white bodies that can move through and work in a border zone without fear of reprisal misses an opportunity to compare this to the racialization that undervalues the bodies of immigrant farmworkers.

Not only are Wild Willow Farm and many other surrounding farms located in an ecologically diverse and agriculturally fertile riparian zone; they sit in a demarcated zone that is highly significant for national security. After 9/11, an "enforcement first" strategy led to border enforcement agencies receiving a massive increase in funding to police borders and criminalize immigrant communities. With the creation of the Department of Homeland Security, funding for these agencies doubled from $6.2 billion to $12.5 billion between 2002 and 2006, and by 2012, the funding grew by another 43 percent.[34] Specifically, border enforcement received the largest budget increases for that decade, resulting in roughly 3.5 million deportations. Thus, there is a major disparity between how organic farmers and law enforcement view the border zone. For farmers I spoke with, this contrast revealed something about the stratification of the freedom of movement for different groups. A neighboring farmer, commenting on the constant buzz of helicopters from the nearby U.S. Navy helicopter training ground, and the overwhelming Border Patrol presence, insisted, "That protection feels excessive." Instead, "We just want to grow food to feed people.... We want to learn the river; see where it rushes and where it is calm. I want to know the names of the plants and trees and shrubs. Which six animals left their paw prints in the mud?" Surveillance produced a desire for transcendence. Cory, a farmer who used to work on that farm and at Wild Willow Farm, reasoned, "Borders in the environment don't exist.... We have birds that migrate from Mexico to our side. We have squirrels that climb through ... they also go back the other way. Working with nature you start to realize that borders are this man-made thing ... in many ways an illusion." Yet he later contradicted the idea that borders are an illusion: "Some of them [Mexican farmworkers] would drive across the border every day to come work at the farm [but when] ... their visas expire, were not allowed to come back." Herein lays the crux of the problem. These desires to dissolve borders and increase freedom of movement fail to translate into practices that resist ethnoracial and citizenship divisions.

· · ·

Local food activists and organic farmers working along the U.S.–Mexico border face many obstacles. Capital, people, power, privilege, and non–human nature flow unevenly across this territorial boundary, which throws into stark relief the competing uses and views of the space. Given that San Diego Roots is confronted with the world's largest military and security apparatus, and its concomitant effects on the lives of immigrants and agriculture, it is easy to see why the organization might not add solving these problems to its mission. However, I occasionally heard and witnessed acts of solidarity with crossers, such as Titus, who used to leave food and clothes in some of the neighboring willow groves. I also never heard anyone express sympathy with the position of Border Patrol agents or other law enforcement agencies. As Wayne once retorted, after helicopters briefly drowned out his organic farming workshop, "They come out here to see what homeland security actually looks like: food security. You are all dangerous people." Underneath this antipathy is a frustration with the political mandates driving the militarization of the border. But organic farmers are not enough of a threat to the state to turn the border region into a verdant space with no social boundaries between themselves and immigrants.

What the experience of San Diego Roots illustrates is that practicing food justice in the context of immigration conjunctures cannot simply entail creating alternatives to a food system viewed as undesirable given that powerful actors in the food system exploit ethnoracial and citizenship differences for profit. The food movement faces a choice of whether or not to branch out beyond the confines of the typical ecologically driven food politics, such as organic farming. These decisions offer insight into the difference between what food justice requires, such as the dissolution of divisive social boundaries that perpetuate inequities, and the role that local context plays in influencing the perspectives behind activists' food politics. For comparison, I now turn to how organizers in Los Angeles and Oakland conceive of their role in supporting immigrant rights and their strategies for confronting social boundaries.

Demographics, Immigrant Rights, and Food-Chain Workers in Los Angeles

A few hours up the coast in Los Angeles, UFCW 770 is engaged in labor politics at the intersection of immigration-driven demographic shifts and the grocery retail and food-processing sectors. According to recent statistics, immigrants account for 35 percent of Los Angeles County's population, 53 percent hailing from Mexico, El Salvador, or Guatemala (41, 7, and 5 percent, respectively). Undocumented Latinx adults account for 27 percent of these people.[35] In response, there is a proliferation of grocery chains catering to the city's large Latinx population. Most of these are not unionized. Many exploit undocumented workers. These abuses are widespread; Latinx people make up 46 percent of grocery workers in California, 22 percent of whom are foreign born.[36] Food processing, which includes meatpacking, also relies on a high concentration of Latinx immigrants.[37] According to low estimates, at least a third of the workforce is foreign born and Latinx.[38] Historically, many of these workers are undocumented. As the prominent rural sociologist William Heffernan sharply put it, "Employers can take advantage of these people because they can threaten to send them back. . . . It's the race to the bottom. . . . Companies started breaking the unions, moving the plants to rural areas and hiring immigrants a long time ago."[39] Los Angeles, then, is a hotbed for organizing Latinx immigrants because the business community would like to diminish the influence of labor unions.[40] Were the business community to succeed, the result for immigrants would be dire. Immigrants are integrated culturally into the fabric of the city, but their economic standing is weak. They have low access to affordable housing and low homeownership rates, low wages and high levels of poverty, and inadequate workforce preparation.[41] This economic precariousness stems from structural disadvantages that come with immigrating to a new place and lacking access to politically powerful or savvy social networks that can protect against prejudice and discrimination by receiving communities.[42] Therefore, supporting immigrant workers is important strategically for UFCW 770.[43] To ignore immigration would undermine the growth potential of the union and alienate other progressive allies dedicated to the human rights of immigrants.

Despite the historic immigrant composition of the working class and immigrants' significance to building labor power, the labor movement in the United States has repeatedly failed to bridge ethnoracial and citizenship divisions to expand unionization. In fact, labor union leaders since the late 1800s have appealed to racist and nativist sentiments to claim immigrants are "unorganizable."[44] While this has consistently proven to be false, the labor movement has at times strategically demonized new immigrant groups as a threat to preserve the victories of previous generations.[45] Ironically, after European immigrants were integrated into labor unions and assimilated into American society, they became white, which placed them atop the racial hierarchy. They also became labor leaders who oversaw the rapid decline in union membership. This presented the labor movement with the dilemma of how to proceed with mobilizing the working class. Once Latinx workers started entering the labor market in larger numbers in the 1980s, the economy was undergoing major neoliberal restructuring, the working class was comparably weaker, and Latinx immigrants were treated like pariahs for taking away low-wage jobs and stagnating wages. As the labor movement started to accept the arrival of neoliberalism and mass immigration, it turned away from restrictionist policies and toward policies that provided legal work opportunities and pathways to citizenship.[46] It turns out that Latinx documented and undocumented immigrants *want* to join labor unions and may in fact be *more likely* than native-born whites to organize and develop the collective power necessary to advance their interests.[47]

Several major political opportunities have helped the labor movement to ally with the immigrant rights movement. In 1994, the California labor movement worked with a broad coalition against Proposition 187, a proposed ballot initiative targeting immigrants backed by Republican governor Pete Wilson. "We could not look away," asserted Mark. He added, "Electorally, we knew we had to have numbers of people vote against it who were not a part of the labor movement. . . . We went deep into the community of those who've immigrated or relatives who immigrated." In addition to this work, there was one of the largest mass protests in California to date, where roughly one hundred thousand people marched in opposition to this ballot initiative. One of the unintended consequences of Proposition 187 was that it catalyzed an immigrant rights movement and the rise of Latinx voices within the labor movement. In 1996, the growing power of Latinx communities was seen in the election of its first-ever representative, Miguel Contreras, to head the Los Angeles County Federation of Labor.[48] Shifts in ideology and leadership at local levels foreshadowed nationwide changes. In 2000, the AFL-CIO reversed its policy positions to support a legal process that provides amnesty to undocumented immigrants and dispute laws that sanction employers who hire undocumented people. This pragmatic shift, based in the belief that current laws put immigrant workers in precarious positions and that immigrants could help prevent the decline in union membership, began at the grass roots in places like Los Angeles but became a movement-wide position.[49] It was no surprise, then, when the labor movement supported the 2006 nationwide protests against the Border Protection, Anti-Terrorism and Illegal Immigration Control Act. The bill sought to increase border militarization and the criminalization of undocumented immigrants and those offering them assistance. These mass mobilizations, their concomitant activists and organizations, and the increased participation in electoral politics helped launch the current undocumented youth–led DREAMers movement. Correctly reading the conjuncture back in 1994, President Ricardo Icaza of UFCW 770 wrote in an opinion piece published soon after the march against Proposition 187, "For Latinos, that march . . . was a glimpse into the future. Most marchers were young people who more accurately reflect what Los Angeles is and will increasingly become, youthful and ethnically diverse. . . . Ironically, as more and more of them participate in the political process it will become more difficult for cynical politicians . . . to ride the wave of cultural and racial backlash at the polls."[50] In this way, UFCW 770 is part of a larger progressive political shift in the region shaped by immigrants' visions of economic and social justice.[51] Conflicts over immigration and the economy continue, but organized labor now recognizes the importance of addressing the plight of immigrants for building broader and more powerful social movements.

There are similar implications for the conceptualization and practice of food justice. Labor organizers and workers show how working-class people and progressive social movements have greater power when they enlarge their base by fighting alongside those marginalized due to their foreign-born status. Expanding the vision of food justice to work across social boundaries can shore up the strength of the food movement with a broader base from which to demand the elimination of social inequities. An explicit commitment to these struggles increases the likelihood of successfully navigating the impediments that come with confronting the racialization of immigrants. How UFCW 770 and its allies grapple with these circumstances suggests that there is a strategic significance and moral imperative to deviate from typical urban food politics.

Building Solidarity with Immigrants through Multiracial Organizing

Two of the major decisions a social movement faces are whom to recruit and whether to branch into new contentious arenas.[52] The labor movement historically views its role as the vanguard for the working class. This has led unions to ignore fractious identity politics. But given that ethnoracial, gender, and sexual identity, to only name a few, intersect with class position and occupation, the experience of labor is uneven. As waves of civil rights movements in the United States have wrestled with the politics of recognition within the polity, they at the same time have fought for equitable participation and remuneration in the economy. Although multiracial organizing is now central to the success of UFCW 770, historically, the union is part of a labor movement that, as Diego, a Latino organizer, recounted, "negotiated our way out of jobs [and] . . . existed in a vacuum, and because of that we have existed our way into extinction." Given that unions have lost millions of members over the last five decades, Diego continued that in order to transcend the micro-concerns of unions such as work breaks and minimum wages, "we had to go back and say, 'We stand for immigrants and immigrant's rights, whether the workers are documented or undocumented . . . for racial equality [and] . . . that we believe a healthy workplace with healthy workers that have living-wage jobs produces a product that is better for consumers.' "[53] This new angle is not just about responding to demographic changes; it is tied to addressing the political demands made by immigrant rights' activists and connecting this to eaters, who otherwise overlook the experiences of these workers.

The strategic emphasis on ethnoracial identity and class depend on the campaign, but racial and economic justice are mutually constitutive. From my conversations with UFCW 770's community partners and political allies, I gathered that there is a shared analysis of the problem based in a historical understanding of ethnoracial relations in the United States and the food system. As Lillian, an organizer with Food Chain Workers Alliance and an ally of UFCW 770, observed, these groups work in "the lower-paid jobs in the food system and have lower access to healthy and affordable food. . . . It's interconnected. It is structural racism. That is how the food system was built, on the backs of slaves and exploiting Native Americans, and it's still exploiting people of color and immigrants." Of equal importance was that many communities of color experience this legacy in the form of economic hardships, which compels fighting on the front lines for better working conditions. "Many of them are not going to go to school and need a quality job," asserted Jill. "They are going to start families early and need . . . upward mobility. . . . It's not just about anonymous workers. . . . A lot of the workers who come to our rallies and do this work are from those communities."

With a large and growing Los Angeles Latinx community, the Latinx supermarket sector has expanded. While UFCW 770 and some of its partners, such as LAANE, prioritized the interests of working-class communities of color, they did not blindly accept poor labor practices just because an immigrant ethnic group sold culturally appropriate food. Some of the worst labor practices occur in Latinx grocery chains.[54] From Jill's research, she found that "a lot of ethnic markets have flourished in low-income areas . . . but many of them are not unionized. You are seeing a huge expansion of them since LA is becoming more and more diverse. Most of those stores don't have standards for their workers." From what I was told, many employers pay undocumented workers under the table, usually below minimum wage. The acceleration of these trends and Latinx grocery chains' resistance to unions have spurred labor organizers to wage major campaigns that deploy a range of tactics.

The most visible campaign to date targets the grocery chain El Super. El Super acquired seven unionized stores (all other El Super stores are nonunion) when they bought out Gigante in 2008. The trouble began when the four Southern California UFCW locals, representing about six hundred workers, attempted to renegotiate their contract when it expired in 2013. These negotiations floundered, and so these UFCW locals began a consumer boycott on December 20, 2014, after working without a union contract for over a year. Workers demanded better remuneration and working conditions only to have El Super try to convince union members to vote out the union. Ultimately, workers took a vote on whether to stay in the union, where more than 90 percent of eligible workers voted three to one to stay with UFCW. Increasing protests, civil disobedience, public opposition, support from major labor organizations and leaders such as the Los Angeles Federation of Labor and the United Farm Workers veteran Dolores Huerta, and financial losses have pressured El Super to take controversial measures. It fired Fermin Rodriguez, a cashier and union leader who had worked for El Super for nine years. UFCW filed a complaint with the National Labor Relations Board (NLRB), which ruled that El Super violated federal law and had to rehire Mr. Rodriguez. With his resolve deepened after going back to work, he made the following statement: "For more than two years, my coworkers and I have been fighting to win a 40-hour guarantee for full-time workers, adequate paid sick leave, seniority protections, fair wages, affordable health benefits, the right to organize without retaliation, and respect. We wanted to achieve a fair contract at the bargaining table without a strike, but this company persists in unlawful conduct denying us of our rights under federal law. El Super only responds to direct pressure. El Super workers will not tolerate any more of the company's illegal behavior."[55] Although El Super returned to bargaining in August of 2015, the union did not receive company information that it believed was necessary to bargain for a fair contract. Therefore, the union continued to pressure the company by bringing more unfair labor practice claims before the NLRB. As a result, in April of 2016, El Super was ordered to pay back wages to almost 550 current and former employees.[56]

This campaign against El Super shows how a labor union can mobilize workers and the public against a company with ties both to the United States (it is managed by the Paramount, California, Bodega Latina Corp.) and Mexico (Grupo Comercial Chedraui owns an 81 percent share

Figure 12. March to El Super in 2016 to demand respect and a fair contract. Photograph used with permission by UFCW Local 770.

of California Bodega Latina Corp.). The implication is that at a local level, labor unions and their community supporters can intervene to prevent companies from exploiting immigrant communities. Nowhere is this more obvious than in charges brought by UFCW 770; LAANE; Project on Organizing, Development, Education, and Research; and the Frente Auténtico del Trabajo labor federation in Mexico under the North American Free Trade Agreement (NAFTA) and Organization for Economic Cooperation and Development (OECD). The NAFTA charges were brought against Chedraui for its "sham unions" in Mexico that opponents claim serve the interests of management over unions. The OECD complaint against El Super called for an end to the company's campaign against workers and UFCW, and in this way mirrored the union's efforts in the United States to leverage the NLRB.[57] Labor organizers used these transnational governance systems to illuminate anti-union practices and force the company to end its anti-union retaliation and to negotiate in good faith.[58]

These immigrant-focused campaigns raise some questions about the complicated overlap between conjunctures. How do labor organizers understand citizenship and immigration status in relation to occupational

status? Is a group's shared class ultimately more important? While strategizing can begin with the desire to improve labor practices in an industry, winning over immigrants requires investment in their workplaces
and neighborhoods. On the one hand, Jae proposed, "If one community
has good working conditions, why shouldn't other communities have it?
That is what binds us all together." When UFCW 770 confronted exploitative Latinx supermarket chains, it established trust in the working-class
Latinx community. On the other hand, there was a reflexive understanding of the importance of people from similar backgrounds involving
themselves in and leading the organizing. As Dave contended, "We can't
just have a white male leadership at the top and expect rank-and-file workers who are people of color and women to throw their blood, sweat, and
tears behind the union's program. . . . They have to believe by doing the
work [that] . . . there is a path to leadership." There need to be mechanisms
to integrate the interests of those marginalized due to their foreign-born
status. Dave proceeded, "They have to see it being directly connected to
their lives." Representing the concerns of Latinx immigrant communities
makes UFCW 770 a part of the immigrant rights movement.

Immigrant Organizing in the Face of Deportability

Despite the dangerous and economically marginal conditions faced by
food-chain workers, activating these workers is difficult because many are
non-English-speaking immigrants; they are easier to exploit and harder
for native English-speaking white society to identify with. Moreover,
many legal tools, like employer sanctions and systems like E-Verify and
I-9, dissuade employers from hiring undocumented workers. Unless
unions recognize these distinctions and commit to challenging discriminatory laws targeting undocumented immigrants, workers are less likely
to join union ranks.[59] In succeeding waves of food-chain workers, from
Chinese farmworkers and Irish meatpackers to Mexicans and Central
Americans now predominating in each of these occupations, companies
have increased profits by abusing the precariousness of each group. Without the guest worker programs or amnesty options available to previous
generations of farm and food-processing workers, the specter of deportation is real. Yet there is a disjuncture between the constant fear of deportation by undocumented workers and the cautiousness of labor unions to
support the immigrant rights of workers.[60] Unions like UFCW 770 want

laws to protect immigrants from deportation, but those unions can still fail in how they support immigrant communities and workplaces.

These challenges are apparent in Vernon, an industrial city south of downtown Los Angeles. This city, population 115, is known for its concentration of warehouses; apparel, electronics, furniture, and paper manufacturing; and meatpacking and food-processing plants. With over eighteen hundred businesses, employment exceeds fifty thousand people.[61] UFCW 770 used to enjoy influence in the food-processing sector, which prior to the 1980s represented a large segment of Vernon's economy. In the late 1970s, there were two packinghouse locals representing roughly thirty thousand workers, but by 1982 when the two locals merged, there were just over ten thousand workers. Following trends in the United States, unionized packinghouses began to decertify or close only to reopen in anti-union cities or countries. There also began an influx of Mexican and Central American immigrants looking for work, while union roles were diminishing rapidly. Attempting to stanch membership loss, workers carried out a series of unsuccessful strikes UFCW 770 never fully recovered from twenty years later. In September of 1985, union members at Farmer John, the largest pig packinghouse on the west coast of the United States, voted to go on strike over medical and pension benefits and promote a boycott of their products such as the Dodger Dog. After already suffering a major defeat in 1982 by agreeing to a two-tier wage system where people performing the same work but who started the job at different times made different wages, the union hoped for a successful strike. Ultimately, the strike failed. Mark, who was a meatpacker at the time, lamented, "Nineteen eighty-five was the worst year for strikes, at least on the West Coast. We had a dozen strikes, three-quarters of a million lost in worked days, five deaths, a number of the plants decertified; some went out of business; contracts were horrible." By 1986, UFCW 770's packinghouse division only represented around six thousand workers. Fifteen years later, the division fell into disrepair with fewer than one thousand union members.

Despite the heavy loss of union members, UFCW 770 still recognized the importance of representing food-processing workers. The industry is rife with workplace safety violations, no worker compensation, employer retaliation against workers attempting to unionize, poor labor law enforcement, and abuse of new Latinx immigrants.[62] Commenting on the experience of food-processing workers at the unionized Overhill Farms, a

Latino worker and shop steward named Santiago told me many undocumented workers are afraid of standing up for fair labor practices: "The companies don't want smart people. They want people who do what they are told. No complaining. 'I'm going to give you one dollar for tomorrow and you are going to start at four and finish at three the next day.' They say, 'Yes, boss, okay.' That's the kind of people they want." Even when assertive, many experienced line workers who wanted to work as a lead in some department faced discrimination. According to Santiago, the Human Resources person knew Spanish, but she only wanted English speakers in these positions even if they lacked experience.[63] Yet, with ten to fifteen years of experience, Santiago insisted, "They know the work; they don't need to speak English; they can read and they have been doing that work for so many years. . . . That's not right."

The union is aware many of its members are undocumented or perceived as such and harassed by bosses and law enforcement. Dave stated, "We just can't depend on our own union membership power to win. We have to be able to tap into the other sources of community power. The places where we organize, a lot of those are led by people of color. It's an essential precondition for our success." The union appropriately modified its organizing tactics. Unlike previous campaigns that targeted only Vernon plant workers, UFCW 770 tried to work with groups such as Coalition for Humane Immigrant Rights in Los Angeles to open and run worker centers.[64] These worker centers represent trends in the "alt-labor" movement to have entities not beholden to labor unions that can independently agitate for worker rights. In addition, because they take the form of community coalitions or nonprofits, they have the flexibility to carry out certain kinds of organizing that unions cannot undertake. As a practical matter, UFCW 770 has limited capacity to support more meatpacking and food-processing workers. Their grocery retail organizing is paramount. It is a growing and stable industry, it makes up a majority of the union membership, and it faces intense race-to-the-bottom pressures from low-wage and anti-union companies. The union leadership distributes resources accordingly. In the food-processing sector, it can organize only one plant at a time. Supporting worker centers is a strategic way to simultaneously incubate labor activism regardless of its influence on union membership. This builds the labor movement's capacity and broadens the network of labor advocates supporting workers.

Developing new ways to support undocumented immigrants reflects the legal complexities of hiring practices like employee verification. After

UFCW 770 achieved a significant membership drive at Farmer John in 2010, there were around 350 workers without legal work documents. The company slowly let these workers go, knowing they wanted union representation. To accomplish this, a new internal policy required all workers to sign a letter stating that their Social Security Number matched their identity. One reason for requiring these letters is that the Social Security Administration occasionally sends out "no match" lists showing discrepancies between names and numbers. Needing work, many undocumented people sign the letters. Employers still hire them, knowing many forge their identities. If undocumented workers ever became a problem for management, there is a pretext for firing them. It is also a way to discourage them from joining unions. Illustrating this reality, Felipe related a story about a woman who worked at Farmer John for eleven years. Management fired her in 2010 during the membership drive. He said that in the process of trying to get her to join the union, "she had one foot in front and one foot backing up, saying, 'Am I going to get fired today?' . . . For the last eleven years she was thinking that way. She said, 'What can I do?' Exactly, what can *we* do? . . . As a union, we can't do anything because she already signed that letter." The union does not require members to provide their legal status, instead leaving it up to the workers and their employers to navigate those legal channels. As a result, these workers would face their undocumented status alone were it not for other support networks like immigrant rights organizations or legal centers.

One of the most visibly contested examples of labor union weakness in the face of the mass firing of undocumented workers occurred at Overhill Farms in 2009. At the time, Overhill Farms was a $200-million-a-year company providing packaged and processed food for American Airlines, Jenny Craig, Panda Express, and Safeway. After a "desktop raid" by the Internal Revenue Service found mismatches between Social Security numbers and employee names, the company fired 254 workers, over a quarter of the workforce. While the government took no action against the workers, and did not mandate the cooperation of Overhill Farms, the company still fired workers. As thirty-eight-year-old Bohemia Agustiano, a mother of four, seethed, "We killed ourselves on the assembly lines for years; many of us have injuries from repetitive motion. Now we're worth nothing. We're out on the streets. This is unjust; no one should be treated this way."[65] The ire of workers was also directed at UFCW 770. As another fired worker named Erlinda Silerio insisted, "The union should try to stop people from losing their jobs. . . . It should try to get the company to hire us back, and pay compensation for the time we've been out. It should communicate with us and keep us informed."[66] UFCW 770 claimed it supported the workers, but this did not bring back their jobs.

Although UFCW 770 advocates for immigrant rights, workers were upset with the response to this mass firing. UFCW 770 took an institutionally sanctioned route. Despite paying union dues for many years, workers experienced the brunt of a hamstrung union that could only try to dissuade Overhill Farms, file grievances after the fact, and direct workers to social service resources. UFCW 770 opposed the sanctions that led to the firing, but lacked recourse to reinstate the jobs.[67] Because the union could not prevent the exploitation of the deportability of immigrants, workers sought the assistance of the immigrant rights organization Hermandad Mexicana Latinoamericana to organize numerous protests in front of Overhill Farms. The group was founded in 1951 to defend Latinx immigrants. Hermandad saw an opportunity to support workers by engaging in active resistance. Representing a more radical and grassroots approach to the problem, Hermandad claims, "One of the main objectives of the organization is to organize immigrants into unions, and assist those unions committed to organizing immigrant workers into their union. The organization is also dedicated to assisting immigrants who are already members of a union and are involved in fighting for union democracy and assuring that their union adequately represents them, particularly as this relates to immigration issues that have the potential to undermine the member's social and economic situation."[68] Even with this final grassroots push, the fired undocumented workers did not recover their jobs. Instead, many found work in other nonunionized food-processing facilities, while Overhill Farms walked away from the conflict unscathed.

Given similar experiences throughout the United States, unions have fought for major immigration overhaul, especially as the Great Recession harmed Latinx immigrants more than whites.[69] Union proposals vary, but many labor organizers I interviewed agree with Emiliano, a Latino organizer of meatpacking and food-processing workers: "If we don't get some kind of amnesty or some kind of pathway, then it is always going to be a challenge for unions to organize." Because companies rely on hidden scare tactics, it is rare for a union to file charges claiming discrimination against undocumented immigrants. Even when unions unearth illegal intimidation tactics, workers may not want to proceed with filing a grievance for fear of retaliation. In the experience of a Latina labor organizer whose father was a union packinghouse worker, Susana declared, "There goes your witness. . . . You think you can try to back them up but they get scared. They do not want to get deported." The deportability of undocumented workers explains why much of the labor movement now supports a pathway to citizenship. Employers can diminish labor solidarity when workers have different levels of legal protection. Providing citizenship to eight million workers would also be a boon to unions all over the country.[70]

Labor unions also have the capacity to stand up for immigrants who are unwilling or unable to be vocal. There are indications that the Overhill Farms experience inspired reflection within the union. Some UFCW organizers have started to take more direct action. For example, in October 2013 in Washington, D.C., at a major immigration reform march, police arrested four UFCW organizers including Rigo Valdez, who at the time was the director of organizing at UFCW 770. He affirmed, "I was arrested today to stand up for the workers who cannot stand up for themselves. In twenty years of organizing, I have witnessed exploitation of workers because of their immigration status. We can no longer allow the abuse of any workers in our country, and must fight and demand that all of us are treated with dignity and according to our rights. Comprehensive immigration reform is not only morally right, but necessary to guarantee the long term economic and social health of our nation. If our lawmakers will not act, then we will."[71] These actions mirror the direct actions and protests organized by the DREAMers, an indication that the labor movement is not so ossified that it is incapable of adjusting to the needs of undocumented workers throughout the food system.

Although imperfect, UFCW 770's approach to immigration is encouraging. It is possible to engage in food politics that expand beyond typical social movement domains by advocating on behalf of those marginalized by their ethnoracial identity and citizenship. This in turn pushes the dialectical development of food justice. Besides UFCW 770's commitment to economic justice, a commitment to racial justice for immigrants precedes strategies that broaden the pool of potential comrades. Instead of viewing immigrant food-chain workers as competition for low-wage jobs, labor unions like UFCW 770 and many of their allies in Los Angeles see these workers as accomplices in the fight against abusive corporations. For instance, breaking down social boundaries by hiring second-generation immigrant rights activists who speak Spanish fosters trust. Or taking public positions against deportation and restrictions on the use of social services and education provides evidence that a labor union takes social inequities as seriously as it takes economic inequities. There is more than the ethical imperative to bridge gaps between citizens and noncitizens, and Latinx immigrants and other social groups. There is a strategic significance. Building collective power across many constituencies creates a broader base to reform the food system and develop equitable alternatives.

So far I have focused on the specific structural impediments faced by immigrants. While the Mexican or Salvadoran migrant faces a militarized U.S. border upon entry, she would experience different circumstances while working in a meatpacking plant in Los Angeles or on a farm in San Diego. The barriers between activists and immigrant food-chain workers also vary. Labor unions whose rank and file come from Latinx immigrant communities have greater sensitivity to immigration than does a nonprofit like San Diego Roots, whose members consist primarily of white native English speakers. From working in the organizing department at UFCW 770, I witnessed that because most of the organizers were fluent in Spanish, they were well equipped to communicate, an obvious prerequisite to dissolving social boundaries. All the materials for the El

Figure 13. Protest against El Super in 2016 after UFCW 770 found out its vice president contributed to Donald Trump's presidential election campaign. Photograph used with permission by UFCW Local 770.

Super boycott are available in Spanish, countless YouTube videos have interviews in Spanish with workers, and UFCW 770 has targeted the Spanish-language press and television media. A key lesson is when organizers work across social differences, the chance for greater economic and racial justice increases. This becomes apparent if we ask a counterfactual question: what would have happened were UFCW 770 not to have supported immigrant rights over the past twenty years? The likely answer is there would be greater divisions between immigrant food-chain workers, the food movement, and the labor movement.

The Urgency to Dismantle Social Boundaries

In late 2015, as the holiday season was under way, the Obama administration ordered Immigration and Customs Enforcement (ICE) to round up and deport families from Central America who came to the United States in large numbers in 2014 to escape drug wars and violence. These raids were part of a larger 2016 plan to return some fifteen thousand people, mainly mothers and their children from Guatemala, Honduras, and El Salvador, who came to the United States seeking asylum but lost their cases and were ordered to leave.[72] These raids produced immediate backlash from immigrant rights activists and left-wing social movements. Anger over the use of raids to round up people already traumatized from the experiences that initially drove them to the United States, coupled with concern that raids would exacerbate distrust of law enforcement in immigrant communities, led to protest and public condemnation.[73] As Marisa Franco, who is director of the national #Not1More Campaign, an organization fighting deportations, protested, "These raids are part of a pattern of abuse and intimidation woven into the fabric of the immigration enforcement agency."[74] With roughly four million deportations since 9/11, these raids pushed immigration reform into the public spotlight and mobilized immigrant communities into coalition with many left-wing social movements. After the xenophobic presidential campaign of Donald Trump was launched with a speech to an overwhelmingly white audience in which he told the crowd that Mexico is sending drugs, crime, and rapists into the United States, which therefore required building a wall along the entire southern U.S. border, life for undocumented immigrants became arguably worse.[75] Whereas President Obama engaged in the mass deportation of immigrants but publicly invoked Cesar Chavez's "Sí

Se Puede!" throughout his presidency to gain the trust of the Latinx community, President Trump has aligned his racist "bad hombre" rhetoric with white nationalist–infused policy.

The food justice movement faces the choice of whether to remain passive or to engage in food politics that resist the conjunctures of the post-9/11 immigration regime. To engage requires leveraging the influence of one's organization to speak out against policies or practices that divide people. Recall the most famous lines in Martin Luther King Jr.'s "Letter from a Birmingham Jail." He wrote, "Injustice anywhere is a threat to justice everywhere. We are caught in an inescapable network of mutuality, tied in a single garment of destiny. Whatever affects one directly, affects all indirectly." In Oakland, Planting Justice sees itself similarly as a force for social change. One of its underlying commitments is to anti-racist racial projects that tie people together across many different social boundaries. So Planting Justice practices mutual aid to advance food justice by advocating for the dignity and human rights of marginalized groups. While known more for working alongside formerly incarcerated people, Planting Justice also supports immigrant rights. The organization's engagement reflects less-quoted lines from King's famous letter that speak out against xenophobic fears: "Never again can we afford to live with the narrow, provincial 'outside agitator' idea. Anyone who lives inside the United States can never be considered an outsider anywhere within its bounds." This obviously includes the more than eleven million undocumented immigrants who currently live in the United States or come to its shores seeking asylum. Solidarity requires mutual recognition of the inherent dignity of all people.

In 2009, seventeen-year-old Salvador Mateo-Escobar, who became a permaculture designer and leader at Planting Justice, experienced the deportation of his mother.[76] According to Salvador, she had applied for a work permit with immigration authorities in San Francisco. They proceeded to lie to her in a phone call saying her work permit was ready to be picked up. When she arrived, they handcuffed her and told her she was being deported. Salvador's father had been deported when he was four years old, and so he was the only one left to take care of his little sister. The trauma of this experience extended beyond the emotional loss of being separated from one's mother and the pressure of taking care of a younger sibling as a high school student. Salvador and his sister were also evicted from their house because they could not afford to pay the rent.

Their mother toiled to raise them, always working two jobs to pay the bills. She was rarely home and lacked the time to cook for her children. As Salvador told me, when she had a break, she would leave them money and "a note saying, 'Go buy something at the taco truck or something.' And we had a fridge full of food, but none of us knew how to cook it. So that was more convenient for her because she needed her break and the last thing on her mind when she was coming home was cooking or cleaning or any of that."

Knowing her children were still dependent on her, she tried to cross the border again. She hired a *coyotaje*, one who helps smuggle people across the U.S.–Mexico border. People pay anywhere from $1,000 to $3,000 to receive help crossing the border.[77] However, once she arrived at the border, she was "sold out" to immigration authorities and incarcerated in an Arizona detention center. Salvador received the devastating news on a collect call from his mother, who proceeded to tell him that she would miss his graduation and would be unable to come back to the United States. At around the same time, Salvador met the cofounders of Planting Justice when they came to his high school to start a program that linked urban agriculture with a food justice curriculum. Planting Justice then sponsored Salvador and one of his classmates in a mentorship program that helped them start a youth venture to build backyard gardens. Although the venture did not last, he was hired by Planting Justice. With both his parents restricted in Mexico, Salvador repeatedly used the platform of a well-known food justice organization to raise awareness about immigration and to advocate for immigrant rights.

Salvador's story was publicized in a video on Facebook and used as a platform to encourage Planting Justice's movement network to act. In one part of this video, he argues that deportation is not a solution, and he offers a way for people to help:

> Families and individuals come to this country not to do what
> Donald Trump says, to like rape our women or take our resources
> or money, but to seek an opportunity just like the rest of us. To
> seek a well-paying job, to seek a job that pays you more than
> Mexico does, which is $5 a day. I mean, who is able to support and
> feed their families on $5 a day? You know what, it's disgusting
> what people have to go through just to come to this country and
> then to be harassed on a daily basis because they don't speak the

language, because they look different. It's always scary to wake up every morning and know that any day someone can come and just say that you are being deported. . . . On behalf of Planting Justice we would like to ask all our supporters to stand against deportations and the ICE raids that are going on right now. . . . Call the White House right now and let them know how this is affecting the communities, to stand up with our immigrant communities and families and let them know that we are supporting them and that we want them to stay in this country.

The story humanizes people impacted by deportation. Although it is hard to know how many people in Planting Justice's network acted, the video was viewed over 6,400 times. Even if ending deportations or raids is not included in the organization's official mission, food justice shares a common lineage with social justice movements that tackle racial and economic inequities. This lateral thinking responds to the immigration conjuncture and can develop a food politics that may otherwise be considered outside the purview of the food movement.

5

Radicalizing Food Politics

Collective Power, Diversity, and Solidarity

The food movement often advocates for "good food," a principle that combines environmental, economic, and social sustainability, and consequently the creation of a "good food table," a space for fostering community and new food systems.[1] In practice, this includes everything from mobilizing food policy councils to hosting community potlucks. Yet as an idea that encompasses the mainstream ethos of the food movement, this principle depends on many assumptions.[2] Most common is the notion that food is a mechanism to convene people across differences and to foster civic participation.[3] "Everyone eats," so the saying goes. This visceral fact means problems in the food system should inspire people to care about what they eat. Food is the optic of change. But this framing obstructs the underlying structural inequalities in the food system.[4] Moreover, a kumbaya politics dovetails with the postpolitical when it masks oppression and depoliticizes inequities. If good food simply means people make different consumption choices or convince government bureaucrats to encourage more farmers markets, then it is an insufficient frame for eliminating the problems driven by neoliberal capitalism and institutional racism. This is not to malign the ritual of gathering around food. Nor does it presuppose that food cannot be a vector around which to mobilize crosscultural exchange. Instead, there are political ramifications of ignoring the centrality of antagonism and social difference to democratic struggle. To unmask social hierarchies within the food system, which are contingent but present themselves as natural, is to acknowledge the viscosity of contestation. In the context of contemporary democracy, contestation revolves around inequities, a generative process necessary to advance the interests of subordinated groups.[5] Managing problems and mediating interests consensually present the real possibility that the inequities faced by groups become secondary to achieving some middle ground.

An alternative is to refocus the political imagination around the messy agonistic process of the struggle for food justice.

Food justice, as a historical set of ideological commitments and strategies aimed at eradicating oppression in the food system and society, is a promising way to *practice politics*. This is not without difficulty. Social justice–oriented food politics, from their expression in the agrarian populist movement on through to their countless forms in the current food movement, have not fully liberated people from the ravages of capitalism, state power, and institutional racism. Nevertheless, as part of a dialectical process of navigating different terrains of social struggle, they have succeeded in articulating, and in some instances achieving, greater collective power, freedom, and equity.[6] The dissent and some of the radical visions represent a nonlinear vision of conflictual democratic politics. The dialectical process of this antagonism, always open and reflecting different conjunctures, offers many moments for intervention. To recognize these moments is to assert the need for more divergent modes of political action. Within a democratic context, food justice practices develop through the process of tacking between relations of subordination, transformative yearnings, and reformative practices.

As the political philosopher Jacques Rancière has maintained, democracy is an anarchic principle that "implies a practice of dissensus, one that it keeps re-opening and that the practice of ruling relentlessly plugs."[7] Democracy is not a state where people with certain qualifications, such as education or wealth, rule and others are preordained to be subject to that rule. The "power of the people" can emerge only when there is politics, an arena within which the agency of the ruled can contest the power of the rulers and vice versa. Politics is not about *possessing* power, nor is it about the relationship between society and the state, commonly understood in terms of an assumed state superiority to act on an inferior citizenry. Politics is the capacity to act based on the assumption everyone is equal to everyone else. People consummate equality when they act to demonstrate their equality.[8] Think of the formerly incarcerated black activists in Oakland who, despite losing freedoms at different times in their lives, assert their equality through restorative food justice practices. Equality does not require the rulers to distribute equitably things to the ruled. This is what Grace Lee Boggs means when she asserts, "We want and need to create the alternative world that is now both possible and necessary. We want and need to *exercise power*, not take it" (emphasis added).[9] "Compost the empire," the ruptural notion guiding Planting Justice, reflects one mode of practicing food politics that strives for new configurations of power by broadening the scope of freedom in the face of oppression. As Rancière reasons, "The 'freedom' of a people that constitutes the axiom of democracy has as its real content the rupture of the axioms of domination."[10] He is referring to the human capacity to alter hegemonic relations as *the* political essence of democracy: "The citizen who partakes 'in ruling and being ruled' is only thinkable on the basis of the *demos* ["the people"] as a figure that ruptures the correspondence between a series of correlated capacities."[11]

Articulating food politics as a practice of dissensus sharpens what it means to engage on the terrain of the conjunctural. While structural inequalities are ubiquitous, dialectical humanism shows that a multitude of confrontational and prefigurative strategies can lead to new hegemonic relations that advance a radical and plural democracy. If one of the problems of the food movement has been the market as movement, then one of the ways through this impasse is to rearticulate the political and democratic practices that reject the neoliberal impulse for consumer solutions.[12] The reasons for this shift abound. Neoliberalism as hegemony presupposes the individual is the locus of action. From this follows a familiar line of reasoning. If an individual has a problem, say, a Latina grocery bagger is underpaid by the supermarket that employs her, then she should work harder to receive a raise. Dismissed by the neoliberal view is the political economy of the grocery retail sector and the food system within which it operates. The race to the bottom to squeeze capital out of racialized and gendered labor disappears as an explanatory variable. Similarly, inequities along the lines of race and gender melt into the language of individual rights and emerge only when there is an act of "discrimination." Even patterns of discrimination morph into aberrations in a post–civil rights era.[13] All of this is to say that the individual is superior to the collective; the social is dead, and along with it social problems and social movements.

Pushing against the neoliberal harbinger of the postpolitical requires more than democratic control over the economy in a typical Marxist sense. Drawing on Antonio Gramsci, Ernesto Laclau and Chantal Mouffe argue for a "radical democracy" predicated on a distinct view of social antagonism and hegemony. One of their central tenets is that "democratic struggle emerges within an ensemble of positions, within a *relatively* sutured political space formed by a multiplicity of practices."[14] Antagonism is part of everyday life. Views of others, social positions, organizations, and institutions are therefore open to change; social conditions can never ossify or eliminate difference. In other words, antagonism emerges around more than food (or the economy, the state, etc.). Food politics is one field within which social struggle is ongoing. Social groups are relative to one another with respect to their situation within a matrix of oppression. Consider the analytical and practical significance of the class, ethnoracial, and gender (and other) positions of the grocery bagger. As was the case at United Food and Commercial Workers (UFCW) Local 770, organizers understood that the large Latinx and black makeup of their union membership required supporting immigrant rights and food security campaigns. Perhaps unusual, but this labor union's food politics recognized other antagonisms to not foreclose on alternative political visions.

Food justice is one heterogeneous project among many striving for radical democracy, namely, for new hegemonic formations within the postpolitical and neoliberal moment.[15] This open dialectical project reflects Laclau and Mouffe's theorization of hegemony as a *"type of political relation:"* "The openness of the social is, thus, the precondition of every hegemonic practice [and] . . . the hegemonic formation . . . cannot be referred to the specific logic of a single social force."[16] Similarly, food justice, with its diverse historical roots and conjunctural engagements, offers an expansive terrain to practice food politics in a way that acknowledges social difference and strives for equity across a range of antagonisms. This is qualitatively different from gathering around food as some lowest common denominator that ignores difference by prioritizing consensus. Food justice is potent politically precisely because of the plurality of its social justice demands, which demarcate sites of social struggle to transform some relation of subordination.

Food justice is also a powerful movement-organizing principle. This raises the question, how does food justice–inspired politics unfold? The conjunctural analysis of Gramsci, the dialectical humanism of the Boggses, and the post-Marxist insights of Rancière, Laclau, and Mouffe on politics and radical democracy help account for this dialectical process. My focus on resistance to the problems of mass incarceration, labor exploitation, and immigration and social boundaries translates some of the universal commitments to equity into distinct social justice–oriented food politics. Together this means food justice can unify previously disparate political practices. But first, activists and scholars need to shed some of the shibboleths of food justice that reduce it to a narrow band of neoliberal or postpolitical practices (e.g., market as movement, white people bringing good food to black people). Instead, by accepting the centrality of antagonism to politics, focus can turn to tracing how intergroup conflict is generative of common emergent conditions that help advance food justice across unique contexts.

Strategic Considerations for the Emergent Practice of Food Justice

UFCW 770, in collaboration with other economic and racial justice groups, supported warehouse workers as part of a larger campaign against Walmart. This case points to how fighting for labor rights is central to food justice because it contests relations of subordination and reinforces the fact that agonistic political practices are necessary to eliminate practices like the corporate race to the bottom. Specifying this dialectical process illuminates *collective power, diversity,* and *solidarity* as common emergent conditions. For UFCW 770, these conditions are never given. They are goals that evolve based on historical victories and missteps to meet the needs of current campaigns.

Assembling coalitions across typical labor movement divides is difficult, but when unions can develop positive-sum coalitions that achieve victories, build their own power, and advance community interests, there is the increased chance of shifting political climates and activist cultures.[17] Central to the Walmart and warehouse workers example is the complex relationship between worker centers and labor unions.[18] Broadly speaking, with the industrial restructuring, decline of labor union membership, and increase in nonunion service jobs over the past four decades, worker centers have stepped in to support economically marginalized communities and nonunionized workers. These centers often focus on ethnoracial and linguistic commonalities and take a more holistic view of how to improve the lives of poor people. When collaborative opportunities emerge, say, in the famous coalition in Nebraska between UFCW and Omaha Together, One Community (OTOC), which successfully unionized hundreds of meatpacking workers, the role of local organizations like OTOC is critical to success.[19] With deeper connections to the community that workers come from, worker centers often prioritize social problems that intersect with economic conditions, like the documentation status of immigrant workers. Therefore, when labor unions are unable to step out of their typical top-down organizing models, communities might view them as paternalistic and overly focused on increasing their membership. Whereas in Nebraska UFCW initially viewed its role as a strategic supporter, as OTOC had years of buy-in from the community due to its organizing efforts, in Los Angeles UFCW 770 sought to co-opt and undermine Korean Immigrant Worker Advocates (KIWA), a community-based worker center organizing Korean grocery workers.[20] KIWA had succeeded previously in increasing wages for restaurant workers in Koreatown and sought similar advancements for grocery workers, but instead of coming up with a strategy to build collective power with a resource-rich labor union, they wanted to maintain their autonomy. While positive-sum coalitions can increase the overall power of workers, social movement history suggests that wins are not inevitable.

The week I arrived in the Organizing Department at UFCW 770, a host of labor unions and advocacy groups were in the middle of supporting a labor struggle of warehouse workers in Ontario, about an hour and a half due east in the elite-coined region aspiringly called the Inland Empire. A few years prior, in 2009, the Change to Win Federation (CTW), a new coalition of labor unions focused on increasing labor organizing, helped launch the worker center Warehouse Workers United (WWU).[21] The reason for forming WWU was to increase the presence of organized labor within the distribution and logistics industry. The Inland Empire was a logical place to center the initiative, as it is home to one of the largest distribution centers and warehouse districts in the United States. In the fall of 2012, warehouse workers, many of them immigrants from Mexico and Central America, were entrenched in a months-long campaign against NFI Industries. WWU and its labor allies targeted a company facility used exclusively by Walmart, which was part of a comprehensive campaign to associate Walmart with poor labor practices throughout its supply chain. Due to low wages and unsafe working conditions, workers participated in strikes, protests, and marches. With the help of WWU, they also filed complaints with government agencies and launched lawsuits. Because many of the one hundred ten thousand workers in Inland Empire's warehouse zone are temporary workers for subcontractors with giant corporations like Walmart, unionizing the industry was unlikely. Instead, organizers worked to build collective power with other allies.

The Organizing Division at UFCW 770 was two years old at the time and strengthening its labor ties throughout Los Angeles and the surrounding metropolitan area. For years, the union was losing members and bargaining power due to the entrance of low-wage grocery retailers like Walmart. An organizer named Ann remarked, "We have been beaten down. . . . We're constantly fighting back companies that are trying to cut wages or cut a retiree who deserves the pension they got. You find people who lost that battle after being lifelong union members now shopping at Walmart." Instead of accepting the irony of these circumstances, UFCW 770 recommitted to organizing. The union waged a multipronged campaign against Walmart consisting of efforts to keep the company out of Los Angeles, improve working conditions for Walmart associates, and support workers in Walmart's supply chain. They joined forces with those sharing this common enemy, an affinity that compelled support for WWU. With fewer resources than Walmart, building relationships with groups committed to economic and racial justice throughout the region was necessary.

There is a long history of labor solidarity at UFCW 770 informing their approach to battling Walmart. In 1985, for example, meat cutters at seven grocery stores throughout Southern California, who at the time had separate contracts from clerks in the same stores, were involved in a bitter labor dispute. During contract negotiations that year, the stores' bargaining representative, the Food Employers Council, first formulated what became a typical corporate position: we need labor concessions because of the entrance of big-box retailers like Walmart. Rejecting proposals to slash wages, benefits, and hours, nearly ten thousand meat cutters went on strike in early November. In solidarity with this action, twelve thousand warehouse workers and drivers represented by the International Brotherhood of Teamsters also went on strike to push for a better contract.[22] The intent of such labor solidarity was to apply pressure to corporate grocery stores like Vons by garnering public support for picket lines to harm store profits. The most contentious issue was a proposed two-tier wage system where new employees receive lower wages than those already employed for the same work, a concession that UFCW ultimately caved to after an eight-week strike.[23] Despite this loss for grocery

Figure 14. Unfair labor practice strike against NFI Industries by Warehouse Workers United in 2012 in Ontario, California. Photograph by the author.

meat cutters, which signaled the beginning of an era of corporate consolidation that compelled labor unions to come up with new strategies, building labor solidarity remains a key strategy.

It is unsurprising UFCW 770 supported WWU. Not only have warehouse workers backed grocery workers in the past, but also, given the flattening of wages and benefits since the 1980s and fewer union members, UFCW 770 politicized economic inequality alongside many left-wing interests in the wake of the Great Recession.[24] The important takeaway from this labor solidarity is that organizers paid constant attention to the shifting economic landscape and took advantage of political opportunities to knock Walmart off balance. As I explored in chapter 3, this strategy focused on the problem of poverty, which it used to mobilize many different interests in favor of better food access and quality jobs. In line with the cultural sensitivity of worker centers, WWU also highlighted how immigrant warehouse workers making poverty-level wages are more exploitable while at work. As a worker at an NFI Industries facility, Marta Medina, reported, "The work here is hard. When I was pregnant and asked for lighter work, they told me, 'We didn't hire you to have children. Work faster or leave.'" She was not the only one exploited at work: "We didn't know what our rights were, but we knew we weren't safe and needed to make a change."[25] Just like many other workers, instead of accepting these conditions, Marta fought back.

Mirroring a damning report into Inland Empire warehouse working conditions titled *Shattered Dreams and Broken Bodies*, a Latina WWU organizer spoke at a rally I attended on November 15, 2012, to end retaliation against workers.[26] Addressing a largely black and Latinx crowd of about 150 people, including people from labor unions like UFCW 770, workers from OUR Walmart, and Good Jobs L.A. coalition representatives, she drew attention to how this rally came at a time of national scrutiny of Walmart and its supply chain.[27] As we gathered in a large circle, she exclaimed, "At every juncture in Walmart's supply chain, workers are rising up. . . . We are at the warehouse because workers didn't have access to clean drinking water; their working equipment was broken; there is little ventilation and extreme temperatures in the summer. . . . Injury rates in the warehouse are extremely high." She went on to praise workers facing retaliation for railing against poor labor conditions throughout Walmart's supply chain: "In Walmart stores workers are silenced when they speak up about their jobs also. The two groups of workers as well as guest workers, who also work in the Walmart production facilities, are working together . . . to improve the working conditions and get the respect for thousands of workers in Walmart's supply chain." The importance of solidarity across the supply chain frames these confrontational tactics as part of a larger strategy, one increasingly common with food labor organizations like the Food Chain Workers Alliance.[28] This builds the collective power necessary to maintain pressure that translates into improvements for workers. One of the most significant of achievements was the settling of a $21 million lawsuit in May 2014 claiming rampant wage theft by Schneider Logistics Inc. of more than eighteen hundred workers at three of their warehouses dedicated solely to working with Walmart.[29] Vindicating the claims of workers at NFI Industries a few miles down the road, the judge ruled in this case that Walmart could be named as a co-defendant because it exercised incredible control over how Schneider Logistics Inc. ran its warehouses, essentially pressuring them to increase productivity.

Collective Power

Building collective power strengthens food justice as a social movement. If, as the famed social movement scholar Sidney Tarrow suggests, social movements are "collective challenges, based on common purposes and social solidarities, in sustained interaction with elites, opponents, and authorities," then the food politics of food justice activists are part of this process.[30] But to evaluate whether food justice "builds crossover appeal" with other social justice movements requires viewing food politics through the lens of whether activists build collective power around solving *underlying* problems.[31] This is what it means to engage radically. As the Latin etymology implies, a radical action is one that gets to the roots of the matter. Similarly, the modus operandi of the food justice movement, as a movement of movements that crosscuts social change agendas, is building collective power around shared interests to respond to structural problems.

Philosophers and social scientists have long studied power, a survey of which might fill a small library. For the purposes of understanding food justice as a force for social change, the sociologist William Domhoff offers a definition that builds on Bertrand Russell's insight that "power is the ability to produce intended effects." Collective power, then, "concerns the capacity of a group to realize its common goals. . . . It is what makes possible the existence of distributive power: if the group didn't have the collective power to grow and produce, there wouldn't be anything worth fighting over."[32] Such a broad definition of collective power converges with a dialectical explanation of how hegemony is a continually contested political project around economic, political, and social conjunctures. But why is building collective power necessary? Because collective power is a prerequisite for achieving outcomes, scholars and activists can identify the nature of the conjunctures driving food politics and evaluate whether they work toward food justice. Given that the fight for food justice is likely never ending, working collectively is a surefire way to build a base of political support to continually confront "elites, opponents, and authorities."[33]

When activists think like a movement, they strive to collectivize their struggles in ways that strengthen the food justice movement. Putting aside consumer politics, food justice may remain relevant as a mobilizing principle if proponents can expand their institutional and grassroots power. Carceral, labor, and immigration conjunctures uniquely illustrate what it means to partake in such movement-building practices. This includes expanding institutional power with the purpose of improving the lives of subordinated people. Strategically, this means working in alliance with grassroots organizations and advocacy groups, participating in political actions, gathering petition signatures, fundraising, lobbying elected officials, framing media messaging, and critiquing injustices. There are also prefigurative forms of power that require increasing grassroots leadership and control. This is where practices such as farming, gardening, cooking, eating, social boundary bridging, and environmental sustainability and social justice consciousness raising can be means for greater self-determination. The key is for such practices to sustain over time. As Planting Justice and UFCW 770 have shown, tackling complex social problems requires an ongoing commitment to mobilization strategies that draw on and build new social networks, organizational structures to coordinate collective action, and shared cultural frameworks and identities.

After years of food justice evolving from a sparsely used term to a diverse social movement committed to advancing social justice in the food system, it appears the conviviality of food is uniquely positioned to help build collective power. Planting Justice, for example, ties a commitment to permaculture as an integrative principle to its food politics. In one of many media interviews, Gavin articulated, "Mass incarceration rips people out of their land and from their communities and doesn't do anything to repair those relationships once they come home. . . . That is such a flagrant example of what happens when people and place and story and land have been disconnected. *It's where we are starting as a political act,* but also because those folks [formerly incarcerated people] are the leaders that we need in order to transform our society [emphasis added]."[34] When members of Planting Justice first started working with formerly incarcerated people inside San Quentin State Prison, they brought their urban agriculture and permaculture skill sets with them. Their commitment to social justice merged with an "'inner' and 'outer' gardening approach" that built connections and a shared sense that it was possible to end "ongoing cycles of incarceration."[35] As Julius, a middle-aged black man who after the Insight Garden Program went on to work at Planting Justice, related, "The program made me a better person. Now that I'm out, I'm more active in the community and in work. When the garden is planted, and the work is done, and the vegetables grow, it brings a lot of people together. That's the way community grows."[36] After spending two years and ten months in prison, he went on to build permaculture edible landscapes and support the development of a five-acre permaculture orchard. Reflecting on these experiences, Julius shared, "Looking at all these jobs we did in the past, you know what I'm saying, and the smiles on people's faces, you know what I'm saying, I put that there, I built that there for them."[37] In other words, his individual actions reflect prefigurative strategies that contribute to building collective power. Planting Justice often calls on its evolving social networks to take political action to support prisoners and engage in policy and legal efforts to reform the reentry process. This ideological and material affront shows the tenuousness of the carceral conjuncture.

Behind fostering new black food justice leaders whom society otherwise writes off as ready-made criminals with little chance for redemption is an appreciation of what the abolitionist Frederick Douglass famously wrote: "Power concedes nothing without a demand."[38] Given recent exposés of mass incarceration in the United States that liken this system to a "new Jim Crow" and a "racial caste system," Douglass's clarion call still rings true today.[39] Advancing human liberty requires continual struggle: "Those who profess to favor freedom and yet depreciate agitation, are men who want crops without plowing up the ground. . . . Find out just what any people will quietly submit to and you have found out the exact measure of injustice and wrong which will be imposed upon them, and these will continue till they are resisted with either words or blows, or with both."[40] Resistance for formerly incarcerated people and their allies in Planting Justice relies on a collective mutual aid strategy comprising a network of thousands of people. Together this supports formerly incarcerated people with living-wage work and a pool of allies to agitate for policy reform that helps them defy California's recidivism odds.[41]

Restorative food justice practices are the result of many different people acting in concert against the criminalization of low-income communities of color. Although Planting Justice and its allies reject the use of "blows," they rely on "words" like those of canvassers stopping passersby on busy Oakland street corners. These counterhegemonic actions rearticulate the process by which people become "formerly incarcerated people" by tying this to racist policies and practices. Such a strategy fosters an "us" mobilizing collectively to build power in opposition to the "them" responsible for perpetuating inequitable outcomes in terms of incarceration and reentry. For example, on November 12, 2015, Planting Justice joined a caravan to Sacramento led by Californians United for a Responsible Budget "to urge the Board of State and Community Corrections not to approve Sheriff Ahern's request for $54 million to expand Santa Rita [Alameda County's jail]."[42] The sheriff proposed to use the money for a mental health treatment unit, but opponents noted the recent history of inhumane conditions, violence, and human rights abuses in the jail. Planting Justice, along with many families of formerly incarcerated people, spoke out against what they believed was an attempt by the sheriff to co-opt the efforts of reentry service providers and grassroots criminal justice reform organizations with a "social service" jail proposal. Despite opposition, the board unanimously voted to use more realignment money for jails instead of reentry. As one board member was reported to have said, "Preventing recidivism is difficult or impossible."[43] However, the prefigurative strategies of Planting Justice and its allies show that collective power is necessary to prevent recidivism. While this battle did not result in the kind of distributional power activists hoped for, it reveals the line of opposition drawn against the state's disposal of formerly incarcerated people. While these kinds of sub–food justice politics will not always produce victories, without such mobilization, victories will always remain out of reach.[44]

Diversity

One hallmark of food justice is a commitment to racial equity, which manifests in an array of food politics. This includes building cross-race and cross-class alliances to challenge corporate power (UFCW 770), explicitly condemning institutional racism (Planting Justice), or reimagining divisive spaces that perpetuate the racialization of immigrants (San Diego Roots). Underlying these particularities, the issue of diversity crosscuts how activists practice food justice. But like any dialectical process, the unique inequities and constellation of actors and approaches shape the social relations.

Blindness to the ethnoracial context can contribute to white activists interpreting food justice to mean that they need "diversity," seen here as inherently beneficial, while overlooking how this flirts with tokenism. Unfortunately, this is a common occurrence. When one adds a black or Latina staff member, or when someone convinces a person of color to give a presentation about race in the food system, the issue of diversity equates with meeting quotas. It simultaneously may ignore the culture that produced the ethnoracial organizational makeup to begin with. Marcelo Felipe Garzo Montalvo, a food justice activist and former board and staff member with Planting Justice, wrote a letter to the food justice movement in which he addressed this and related topics. After expressing gratitude for many of the positive attributes of the movement, he critiqued what he sees as "our collective mis/understandings of 'power, privilege, and oppression,' and therefore how we strategize their undoing and/or transformation through food systems work."[45] Having spoken with him many times, I was aware that this grievance stemmed from a concern with activists not contextualizing a chosen solution within the reality of intersecting sets of social problems. Referring to a cultural tendency of food justice politics, Marcelo elaborated,

> I have been asked, or called in as a "consultant," to discuss "anti-oppression," "anti-racism," or other ways to engage the perennial (and very frustrating) question of "why are there no people of color here?" Or more often than not, "why is there a *lack of diversity* in our organization?" or "how can we be more *inclusive*?" It must be noted that "lack of diversity" and "inclusive" are often neoliberal code words for a space being already white-dominated. When I see a call for papers asking for a list of "how tos" for working with people and communities of color in food systems, I am reminded of the dozens of times I have been asked these sorts of questions, and the dozens of times I have been unable to offer the prescriptive answers these folks may be seeking. Many times when I hear these code words, I fear it is already too late. A space and culture has already been created and established that is so thoroughly white (corporate [we don't need to be a corporation to be corporate] and heteropatriarchal [dominated by the norms of heterosexual males]), that it contains within it one of the hallmarks of whiteness itself: white guilt and its accompanying savior complex.[46]

Indeed, whiteness, privilege, and thoughtlessness often permeate white-dominated food movement spaces.[47] While white activists need to reflect on their motivations for diversity, without an overarching anti-racist praxis, they may miss opportunities to advance a food politics capable of intervening in institutional racism.

It is common to think of diversity as something to achieve in an organization, institution, or movement that lacks people of color, but this creates the perception that people of color (or other underrepresented groups) are outsiders or at-risk victims.[48] This may reinforce exclusion and inequity. At the same time, diversity is not a sufficient condition to ensure that all groups have the same access and opportunities, say, to urban agriculture resources in a diverse city.[49] Given the prevalence of color-blind politics that correlate the assorted ethnoracial mix of a city with the notion that racism is dead and ignore the structural inequalities that predominate in communities of color, it is important to break down how food justice practices engage with this context.[50] Perceptions and actions in the name of diversity can reveal a lot about whether a mixture of socially distinct groups can work across social boundaries to create equitable forms of food politics that produce equally equitable results.

My cases highlight some of the ways that orientations toward diversity influence food politics. While a deficit model focuses strictly on disadvantages, an asset model prioritizes the cultural and social forms of capital that communities of color bring to their practice of food justice.[51] In the former, groups will use diversity to act on behalf of a statistical minority, usually with charity. The reasoning goes that we live in a post–civil rights multicultural society, so we should make sure that each group has its basic needs met. In the latter, diversity celebrates the distinct skills and forms of knowledge each group possesses. By bringing this to bear on social inequities, there is the recognition that social justice requires inclusivity, representative leadership, and working *alongside* marginalized groups to solve the root problems collectively.[52] For example, in Los Angeles, many antihunger groups operate from a deficit position. Reports such as *Rising Food Insecurity in Los Angeles County* by the Los Angeles County Department of Public Health conclude with major recommendations to increase government and nonprofit food assistance programs.[53] The irony is that the report spotlights the stratification of food insecurity among adults living in households with incomes less than 300 percent of the federal poverty level but only mentions fleetingly in a single bullet point the need for better wages. More than any other indicators, Latinx (63.5 percent) and foreign born (60.8 percent) correlate with food insecurity, so it is all the more a missed opportunity to tie other economic policies (e.g., fair housing statutes) to immigration reform (e.g., a pathway to citizenship that immediately extends greater labor protections and civil rights). In contradistinction, UFCW 770 is attentive to the plight of Mexican and Central American immigrant communities. Their food politics approach diversity by fostering leadership and working with these groups to improve their economic and social standing, which includes fighting off racist immigration proposals and supporting Latinx El Super workers.

Related to the relationship between race and diversity are strategy and diversity. Relations of subordination play out on countless terrains. Mutually constitutive of this reality is social antagonism, which means the subordinated and their allies adopt a plethora of strategies.[54] Speaking to this position, anarchist and author Peter Gelderloos explains, "A diversity of methods is necessary in our struggle because none of us have the answer regarding the one true strategy for revolution; because there is no one size that fits all and each of us must develop a unique form of struggle for our respective situations."[55] Conjunctures emerge in different times and places, which requires reading the internal contradictions of the moment to identify the best way forward. Practically speaking, because inequities manifest in the food system in so many ways, there is the need for the food movement's food politics to be nimble. This is one of the food movement's strengths. As Gelderloos argues, "Our movements are harder to repress when we replace a party-line unity with a broad solidarity, when we attack as a swarm and not as an opposing army."[56] Putting aside the appeal to revolution in the typical anarchist sense of smashing the state, the larger point about respecting the diversity of differently situated social groups and their political visions, both individually, and then collectively through solidarity efforts, emphasizes the benefits of strategic fluidity.

There are also questions at the interface of race, strategy, and diversity. The adoption of some collective identity (e.g., immigrant union member, black food justice activist, white locavore) draws lines of insider and outsider, a process that reflects activist goals and political opportunities and constraints.[57] The construction of collective identities when food justice–oriented food politics are considered runs the spectrum between exclusive and inclusive campaigns. On the one hand, there are historical precedents such as Fannie Lou Hamer's Freedom Farms Cooperative, which used agriculture as a form of resistance to support black sharecroppers and tenant farmers facing white backlash in Mississippi for exercising their right to vote. With the real threat of starvation promulgated by whites, black farmers pulled together into an agricultural cooperative as an act of self-determination.[58] On the other hand, there are countless examples of multiracial coalitions that set the terrain for contemporary articulations within the food movement. Prominent among these is the support of the black freedom struggle for the Mexican American–led United Farm Workers (UFW). As backers of UFW's boycotts, black activists found common cause as part of a broader movement for racial and economic justice.[59] This latter example is interesting in light of how organizations are more likely to be exclusive without an underlying commitment to social justice, a broad anchor that can hold groups together.[60] But ideological commitments go only so far if an organization does not reflect the community within which it works, either demographically or geographically.[61] The practical question concerns how to navigate the very diversity that makes a democratic struggle generative of greater social equity. These are ultimately strategic decisions regarding how people chart a path between sameness and difference.

For example, San Diego Roots created an inclusive identity around local food and a desire to democratize local food access. This reproduces a common food movement assumption that society's plurality is significant insofar as people can reach consensus across difference. After sharing that most food grown in San Diego County is exported while most food eaten in the county is imported, Mel Lions, the director of San Diego Roots, counseled, "My biggest piece of advice is that if you are interested in being part of the local food movement . . . you already are part of the local food movement."[62] If people have purchased local food or considered where their food comes from, or if they are eaters, then they are de facto contributing to the food movement. Wild Willow Farm as an education center is open to anyone in the community. But this construction of sameness, while encouraging people to share in the joys of local food, at the same time strategically forecloses on ethnoracial and class differences within "the community." Such discourses sidestep inequalities that require confrontation within local food spaces. While not discounting the bridging power of food, their model of diversity ignores working with the interests, assets, and needs of local Latinx or newly arrived Latinx immigrants living in the borderlands in favor of a party-line unity around local food. While representatives of these communities sometimes attend events like farm potlucks and share their culinary traditions, San Diego Roots undervalues the social and political motivations behind such cultural foodways.[63] In brief, San Diego Roots both encourages and excludes diversity in its framing. One of the mechanisms for engaging in food politics that both respect and inspire ethnoracial diversity is solidarity. This is a necessary condition for food justice in the pluralist context of democracy.

Solidarity

In a dialectical reflection on how globalization is reshaping the meaning and practice of solidarity, Grace Lee Boggs wrote about an experience she had learning about the displacement of Afro-Columbian farmers by paramilitary-backed palm oil agribusinesses. She explained how these farmers fought to reclaim their territory, which she identified with in her hometown of Detroit. "We are resisting by growing our own food," Boggs wrote, "struggling to bring the neighbor back into the hood, creating Peace Zones out of War Zones, and redefining Work to mean making a Life and not just a Living."[64] Sharing stories and struggles across social boundaries is one of the key practices of solidarity. Instead of withdrawing into the ethnoracial or class-atomized outcome of globalization—say, as a shopper who buys a burrito at a local Mexican *taqueria* ignorant of the deportation of the cashiers' undocumented cousin who emigrated to the United States after being displaced as a small farmer due to the post-NAFTA importation of cheap agricultural commodities—solidarity calls for finding ways to work with the unevenness.[65] Identifying the inequities embedded in relations of subordination offers new paths to becoming an accomplice on the path to dismantle structural conditions. Boggs concluded, "Solidarity is beginning to mean connecting grassroots communities who are resisting corporate devastation and displacement by creating ways of living that give us control over our lives."[66] Solidarity requires respecting what is distinct about a struggle *and* acknowledging that similarities can encourage new networks.

Activists in Oakland, Los Angeles, and San Diego had unique opportunities to reach beyond their immediate milieu. For Planting Justice, this meant acting in solidarity with formerly incarcerated people and groups committed to economic, racial, and restorative justice. UFCW 770 engaged in labor solidarity with workers in occupations outside the union's purview and with immigrant rights networks. Paulo Freire famously wrote, "True solidarity with the oppressed means fighting at their side to transform the objective reality which has made them these 'beings for another.' The oppressor is solidary with the oppressed only when he . . . stops making pious, sentimental, and individualistic gestures and risks an act of love."[67] For Freire, to love is to affirm the inherent dignity of dehumanized people with concrete communal actions that overcome that dehumanization. Saying that you care about someone is different from taking steps to support them. For example, San Diego Roots failed to act in solidarity with immigrants. While there were those like the former lead farmer, Titus, who tried to compel his compatriots to foster ties with Latinx borderland communities with actions like collaborating with a local community garden, this was largely isolated. There were more platitudes than actions. Warning against only partially supporting the oppressed, Freire suggested, "To affirm that men and women are persons and as persons should be free, and yet to do nothing tangible to make this affirmation a reality, is a farce."[68]

It is illuminating to explore solidarity through negative examples. Compared with Planting Justice and UFCW 770, San Diego Roots did not as actively engage in building solidarity with subordinated groups. Territorial border imperatives complicate the forms of political allyship pursued by San Diego Roots. The politics of the border are endemic to San Diego, especially for those working in agriculture. For much of the city's history, the border was a fluid space where people moved easily through. However, the militarization and securitization of the border in the past two decades reflects an entrenched local military culture and nationwide xenophobia propagated by the belief that immigrants are a threat.[69] In turn, local food activists overwhelmingly ignored issues faced by Latinx immigrants, most problematically regarding labor issues in the local food system. This internalization of ethnoracial separation coupled with a glossy "local food" emphasis limited San Diego Roots' engagement with the issue of immigration. Despite Wild Willow Farm's proximity to the border, the perspective by some local food and organic farming activists that their work was a form of "homeland security" foreclosed on a solidaristic food politics with the (trans) local Latinx community. Ironically, this discourse can also justify sealing off the border from those same people who cross the border to work in California agriculture by framing them as the problem behind cheap food. In the end, these notions obstruct solidarity by reproducing stereotypes that absolve growers and politicians for their exploitative practices by blaming immigrants and ascribing characteristics that mark them as different and therefore less deserving.

As an open political project, food justice necessitates thinking about and acting on a range of conjunctures. While activists at San Diego Roots regularly denounced "the corporate industrial food system" and prefigured taking back the economy with noncommodified forms of labor, they overlooked some entrenched ethnoracial inequities along the border. Although troubled by the racial profiling and deportations of Latinx people in 2007 after wildfires forced San Diegans to seek shelter at evacuation centers, many activists in San Diego Roots perpetuated a variety of popular racialized discourses. Chief among these was the notion that immigrant farmworker exploitation is unavoidable. The defeatism of such language naturalizes ethnoracial inequalities through the belief that food would cost too much if farmworkers received living wages. Some activists expressed discomfort with these arrangements, but in a context where white San Diegans rarely chose to cross the border and generally view Mexico with suspicion, San Diego Roots' choice not to expend resources addressing these problems becomes more understandable.[70] At the same time, the organization is primarily white and generally lacks Spanish-speaking skills. A popular discourse that foreign-born farmworkers labor in an industry undesirable by most (white) Americans perpetuated this demographic difference. In conclusion, while the militarized and racialized territorial mandates of the border offered a unique opportunity for San Diego Roots to think through how to achieve food justice along the U.S.–Mexico border, their imagination remained limited.

Planting Justice, on the other hand, provides more ideas for building solidarity as an act of ideological intervention to reimagine food politics. This is noteworthy because the typical framing of problems in the food system as *food* problems is often the major barrier standing in the way of identifying and then combatting oppression. While observers of mass incarceration might see this as just one of many social ills plaguing Oakland's black and Latinx communities, Planting Justice believed it was significant and that food justice could be an effective response. Their activism ties into a long history of prisoner solidarity movements in the United States, as well as those movements committed to supporting political prisoners.[71] As Paulo Freire reasoned, solidarity requires acting as an accomplice with the oppressed. Standing with people like former prisoners reaffirms their humanity in response to the curtailment of their freedoms and marginalization. Although the actions of Planting Justice did not generally include efforts to abolish prisons, they offered critiques and spaces for reflecting on the racism at the heart of mass incarceration.[72] Moreover, they supported prisoners inside San Quentin State Prison as they began the process of healing from the historical trauma of mass incarceration and then met the needs that formerly incarcerated people articulated once they left. Nicole Deane, an organizer at Planting Justice, asserted, "The dominant model of prisoner re-entry—which emphasizes policing formerly incarcerated people's behavior—is an undeniable failure and must be radically rethought. We can't keep building more prisons. We can't jail our way out of our own failure to 'rehabilitate' people." In response, creating dignified work for formerly incarcerated people is "a political statement that the labor of former prisoners is valuable and that their success and well-being is a worthy investment."[73] Solidarity is ultimately a political practice that builds connections across social boundaries by taking a risk with one's privilege and supporting from behind.

To conclude, solidarity is both an outcome of the configuration of institutional, organizational, and activist demographics and the condition for reconfiguring these relations in more socially just ways. While food can be a site of division, it can also forge solidarity across social boundaries. There is nothing inherent to food that makes bridge-building possible, but when activism engages reflexively with its context, it can inspire new political practices.[74] Acting intentionally is part of what facilitates learning about the most pressing social inequities. Then it is possible to speak out for food justice and form the alliances that can create change.[75] To forge solidarity across differences requires staying open to conflict and messy deliberation and working to identify commonalities.[76] The very diversity of problems in the food system compels solidaristic food politics.

Food Justice and the Hope for a Radical and Plural Democracy

Why is food justice a compelling perspective? Food justice can universalize social struggles around a commitment to equity to broaden the horizon of food politics. Regardless of whether the food movement embraces reaching out, there are always opportunities to build collective power by mobilizing beyond movement boundaries. The common ground that animates this possibility is the anchoring power of food justice. Adopting equity as an equivalence between social struggles generates greater

Figure 15. A Seeds of Resistance poster reveals the urge of social justice movements to build collective power, diversity, and solidarity. Art by Ricardo Levins Morales.

diversity and solidarity. Food justice is not a zero-sum demand. As Laclau and Mouffe assert, "It is only on this condition that struggles against power become truly democratic, and that the demanding of rights is not carried out on the basis of an individualistic problematic, but in the context of respect for the rights to equality of other subordinated groups."[77] With the liberation of one bound to the liberation of all, this entails recognizing the diversity of human needs and redistributing equitably the resources to live dignified and fulfilling lives.

Conversely, because food justice foregrounds equity, it offers a strategic path to respect the breadth compelled by the heterogeneity of social justice struggles. The "unevenness of the social" requires that the demand for radical democracy include a commitment to plurality.[78] Food politics that intersect with carceral, labor, and immigration conjunctures suggest as much. After all, these are disparate with respect to their unique economic, political, and social terrains. The widespread imprisonment of low-income people of color is dissimilar enough from the ways in which immigrants in the United States experience marginalization that there are scholars and social movements that enumerate the particularities. How these terrains overlap with the food system is equally distinct. Nowhere is this more obvious than in how food politics differ across my cases and therefore how context shapes interventions. Consider, for instance, the differences between how Planting Justice fights racial and economic inequities with food alongside formerly incarcerated people, while San Diego Roots sidesteps supporting immigrants. The opportunity for recognition is present. Yet the response varies. Even if San Diego Roots took steps to ameliorate inequities, its strategies, notions of solidarity, and collective action would reflect the conditions in local agriculture along the U.S.–Mexico border. From a theoretical and a mobilization perspective, it is necessary to recognize the plurality of social relations.

There are major lessons here for food justice activism and the food movement. Once we reject that the food system is the only space within which food politics can take place, a whole range of strategic opportunities opens to build different kinds of collective power to challenge the forces that drive inequities. This is not to ignore how the food system arranges social relations. What is important is how the food system is inside the realm of the political. It reflects and reproduces cohesion and separation that exists throughout society.[79] Yet, because the food system is not a self-contained totality that independently operates by immutable laws, it is gravid with opportunities for resistance. In the context of the longing for radical democracy, how the food movement goes from identifying needs to achieving ends is an urgent consideration. If resistance remains devising alternative food models that reproduce racial neoliberalism without considering the diverse needs of subordinated groups, then the food system will continue to wreak havoc on people and the planet. Alternatively, food justice requires a resolute commitment to identifying the structural inequalities undergirding capitalism and institutional racism, a willingness to let go of failed food movement strategies, and an imagination up to the task of achieving socially just outcomes for eaters and workers alike.

Notes on the Future of Food Justice

During my research into the historical roots of food justice, as well as its contemporary political expression in California, I was struck by the overriding significance of structural inequalities typically outside the purview of the food movement. By comparing dialectically across my cases, I found that food justice is an important optic to view food politics as well as an organizing principle to solve pressing social problems. It offers a utopian horizon and applies to actually existing conjunctures. Although mass incarceration, labor exploitation, and the interrelated issues of a racialized immigration regime and social boundaries exist in Oakland, Los Angeles, and San Diego, activists tend to strategically focus their food politics. What makes a dialectical comparison compelling is that despite the fact that activists interact with structural conditions in unique ways, similar ethnoracial and class inequities remain prominent. These inequities serve as universal equivalents around which the food movement can deepen its political engagement.

One interview in particular inspired an awareness of the dialectical openness of food justice. Gabriel, an organizer at Planting Justice, suggested that oppression and resistance are interconnected in a variety of ways, and therefore different social movement lineages can lead people to converge on food justice. However, this can also stimulate reflections on the challenges associated with food justice as a plural political project:

> What is the food part of this thing? There is a lot of work you could do that involves food. People eat food every day. It is a basic human need. To base a movement on food justice, and whatever that means, has been such a blessing and a curse in the sense that you have such an open movement and space that can be considered a social movement. There is this whole discourse in food

justice: everybody eats; therefore everybody can participate in this movement. Totally right on. The underside of that is a really convoluted, what are we really doing kind of movement. If food justice is a practice or a praxis, what is our theoretical background? If we talk about theory practice, I still don't know if there is any sort of agreement on any level as to where food justice came from. What is it an articulation of? For me, I think that is really valuable to think through and for a movement to articulate. For me personally, again, it has shifted so many times within the movement. . . . I feel like I have spent a lot of energy and time in the food justice movement defending our turf. . . . I got sick of that and stopped doing that because it was burning my own energy to negate other people. It comes from a rational place. There is a necessity for that to be able to assert what we are doing. . . . How are we going to formulate a platform that is a cohesive thing?

Five years and many conversations later, I arrived at some answers. The "food part of this thing" is subservient to the equity part of this thing. The feverish appeal of food justice is the value of a food politics that challenges structural inequalities and engages in political struggle across different social nodal points. I disagree that food justice is convoluted. Instead, due to many social movement influences, food justice has broad appeal. This helps explain its rapid discursive spread and ideological expansion. As an idea and a practice, food justice is positioned to keep building collective power, fostering diversity, and cultivating solidarity.[1] Debating the perimeters of the food justice movement matters less than strategizing how to direct this energy to spread the practice of a food politics that intervenes in structural inequalities.

From the vantage point of 2018, achieving food justice in the United States appears inopportune given the revanchist tenor of Donald Trump and congressional Republicans. After eight years of perceived losses on health care, same-sex marriage, the environment, immigration, and criminal justice and the anti-capitalist mobilizations of Occupy Wall Street and the anti-racist insurrections of Black Lives Matter, there was an opportunity for revenge. With Republican control of Congress and the appointment of cabinet members whose views appear to contradict the stated public interest missions of their agencies, many subordinated groups and left-wing interests have been relegated to an inferior position outside of an imagined time in the past when the United States was great. A time with no civil rights, environmental, health, or labor protections. Essentially, white, wealthy, and male interests trump.

Gramsci famously wrote, "The crisis consists precisely in the fact that the old is dying and the new cannot be born; in this interregnum a great variety of morbid symptoms appear."[2] With the presidential election of Trump, the contradictions of racial neoliberalism reached their apotheosis. The postracial presidency of Barack Obama never resolved the racism behind mass incarceration, the criminalization and deportation of millions of immigrants, and the exploitation of workers of color in low-wage occupations, of which agriculture and food make up a substantial share. Instead of responding to the Great Recession with more stringent laws and regulations to check the power of wealthy interests, the American public bailed out Wall Street while Main Street suffered through a weak low-wage recovery. Moreover, the "one percent" tightened its grip on the levers of government as money became more prominent in elections after the *Citizens United v. Federal Election Commission* Supreme Court decision. In the food system, corporate power only increased despite the planting of the White House Vegetable Garden and First Lady Michelle Obama's anti-obesity-focused Let's Move campaign. Trump stepped into the interregnum between all these neoliberal policies and no avowedly left-wing alternative with a savvy right-wing populist brand that tapped into white resentment and anger with celebrity bombast and an unapologetic corporate messaging. Therefore, the small gains made by the food movement over the last decade, such as the rapid growth in farmers markets and local food consumption, the Food Safety Modernization Act, food labeling laws, soda tax initiatives, and Fight for $15–inspired living-wage ordinances, are in peril.

Food justice is not up to the task of engaging each conjunctural terrain as a lone oppositional force. What makes it significant is how left-wing movements have integrated its principles and started looking at their interests through the lens of food politics. "You have to have a conflict before you can have politics," James and Grace Lee Boggs wrote. "*Politics involves taking sides.* It means proposing or supporting particular plans, programs, perspectives which you believe are right."[3] The Black Lives Matter, climate justice, environmental justice, and right-to-the-city movements, as well as parts of the labor movement, have all recognized and opposed inequities in the food system. They have also proposed or demanded solutions that align with their social justice commitments. For example, the Movement for Black Lives collective developed a policy platform that includes demands for the financial support of black alternative institutions such as food cooperatives, an end to food apartheid, the elimination of debt for black farmers, and land for black farmers.[4] In contrast, the Climate Justice Alliance in its Just Transition Principles advocates for regenerative ecological economies that include the democratization of local food systems and the right to clean and healthy food.[5] While the emphases respond to particular conjunctures, they share the recognition that food justice is a fundamental aspect of a larger political project.

This leads to another notable historical development: the use of food to break down social boundaries and foster solidarity across difference. Given the frontal assault Trump has waged on frontline immigrant, Muslim, black, Latinx, and poor and working-class communities, left-wing movements have engaged in a politics not only of resistance but also of alliance building to imagine alternative futures. The Dream Defenders is an anti-capitalist, anti-racist, anti-imperialist, and feminist "uprising of communities in struggle, shifting culture through transformational organizing" through projects like Day of Dinners.[6] Day of Dinners included partner organizations like the Women's March, Planned Parenthood, the Movement for Black Lives, United We Dream, Take on Hate, the American Civil Liberties Union, and the HEAL (Health, Environment, Agriculture, and Labor) Food Alliance. On June 25, 2017, over ten thousand people came together around a meal. The goal of this project was to use the conviviality of food to "break down the walls in our local communities" through potlucks with people from different class, ethnoracial, gender, and religious backgrounds. Some of the conversation starters included, "Describe your first experience of injustice. How did it change your worldview?"; "Whose liberation are you longing for?"; and "What is the vision of hope that sustains you?"[7] Day of Dinners was an event meant to nourish people for the social justice struggles ahead.

The current conjuncture also suggests that food justice faces co-optation and dilution in unique ways that require perseverance to assert a food politics capable of dethroning corporate rule, ending institutionalized forms of discrimination, and advancing social justice. One of the reasons is that food can be fetishized to mask underlying social relations. Under racial neoliberalism, the food movement can reproduce these racialized market conditions and economic logics.[8] Social change becomes about local food, family farms, and organic, where each represents inherent immutable qualities in their commodified form.[9] You may support the local family who grew your organic strawberries. But do you know the labor conditions of the farmworkers who picked them or the workers who made the packaging to hold those strawberries? Do you understand the racialized immigration regime and labor laws that influence that local farmer's decisions? Have you considered the ethnoracial and class inequities in the rural community where that local farm is located? The often-exclusive nature of these market-based strategies can exacerbate social boundaries, disadvantage groups further, and obstruct collective demands.[10] For example, in concert with urban gentrification processes, demand for organic food options by race- and class-privileged groups may bring in a Whole Foods that supersedes the cultural foodways and food landscape of less privileged groups.[11] The Whole Foods becomes a monument to health and sustainability, obfuscating place-based struggles against institutional racism and white supremacy. So (whole) food itself is more than its biological makeup and nutritional content. Food contains within it social struggle and power relations.

So how might we think about intervening in the present condition? Grace Lee Boggs suggests remaining practically and intellectually reflexive with a sense of both patience and urgency to synthesize hopeful approaches and strategies:

> We are all works in progress, always in the process of being and becoming. Periodically there come times like the present when the crisis is so profound and the contradictions so interconnected that if we are willing to see with our hearts and not only with our eyes, we can accelerate the continuing evolution of the human race towards becoming more socially responsible, more self-conscious, more self-critical human beings. . . . This is our time to reject the old American Dream of a higher standard of living based upon empire, and embrace a new American Dream of a higher standard of humanity that preserves the best in our revolutionary legacy. We can become the leaders we are looking for.[12]

Entangled Crises and the Development of a New Food Politics

Food Justice Now! has chronicled the conjunctural development of food politics and theorized through dialectics the historical congruities *and* continuities linking food, structural inequalities, and social justice. Yet it has proceeded by highlighting social struggles to argue for an evolution of political practice. Because a transformation of our food and social systems will not take place immediately, there are pragmatic reasons to formulate robust policies and regulations.

The major policy vehicle pursued historically by the antihunger, environmental, small-farm, and sustainable agriculture factions of the food movement is the Farm Bill. Over time, each faction has used the Farm Bill to advance its own agendas. However, in the lead-up to the 1996 Farm Bill, a large grassroots coalition that came to be known as the Community Food Security Coalition began to develop an inclusive policy platform. It used the language of "community empowerment, neighborhood and local action, [and] strengthening farmer-to-consumer links" to open political space for a more progressive agenda.[13] In the face of the Republican Revolution of 1994, when Republicans took control of the House of Representatives and the Senate, it was increasingly clear the food movement needed an antidote to powerful neoliberal forces. Although there was fierce debate and skepticism by some food movement stakeholders, the coalition succeeded in receiving authorization and funding for a Community Food Projects program, which created the political opportunity for more radical food justice voices to enter the fray.[14] Nevertheless, the 1996 Farm Bill, informally known as the "Freedom to Farm Act," fundamentally shifted farm policy by ending price supports and production controls, the two pillars of supply management. This reflected the growing strength of agribusiness and the livestock-grain industrial complex.[15] The rise of the Community Food Security Coalition did not fundamentally transform how the Department of Agriculture interprets its mandates as the enforcer of the Farm Bill through a limited number of lenses and historical relationships with agricultural scientists, corporate interests, growers, and ranchers.[16]

Some of the initial divisions in the food movement have healed, but challenges remain in developing an inclusive and systems-level approach to food policy. The growing presence of food justice as a political force indicates the arrival of a moment where the state, as an arbiter of democratic impulses, faces pressure to respond to social movement demands for economic and racial justice. But food movement coordination has been uneven. Consider the differences between resistance to genetically modified organisms, contestation over organic and nutrition standards, and fights over prisoner-produced food and the low wages of farmworkers. Given the patchwork nature of regulatory bureaucracy in the United States, there are few opportunities to coordinate across interests for a food *system* predicated on environmental sustainability, health, and social justice.[17] The food movement has learned some of the lessons from its decades-long engagement with the Farm Bill and state and municipal food policy initiatives and is converging around a broad regulatory solution. The revanchist right-wing tide demands as much. While the reaction is to resist, the need is to imagine a clear alternative to the corporatization of politics, white nationalist pride, xenophobic scapegoating of immigrants, and the criminalization of poor communities and communities of color.[18] The utopian horizons of food justice suggest an indispensable way forward.

Given the concern that President Obama would not live up to all the hopes of the food movement and a recognition that the Farm Bill alone cannot address all the problems in the food system, public conversation broke out in late 2014 around how to mobilize for a comprehensive food policy. Food movement leaders Mark Bittman, Michael Pollan, and Ricardo Salvador and the United Nations Special Rapporteur on the Right to Food, Olivier De Schutter, wrote an opinion piece in the *Washington Post* called "How a National Food Policy Could Save Millions of American Lives." The authors review the failures of current food and agricultural policies. They then urge President Obama to address food in his State of the Union speech:

> We find ourselves in this situation because government policy in these areas is made piecemeal. Diet-related chronic disease, food safety, marketing to children, labor conditions, wages for farm and food-chain workers, immigration, water and air quality, greenhouse gas emissions, and support for farmers: These issues are all connected to the food system. Yet they are overseen by eight federal agencies. Amid this incoherence, special interests thrive and the public good suffers. . . . A well-articulated national food policy in the United States would make it much more difficult for Congress to pass bills that fly in its face. The very act of elevating food among the issues the White House addresses would build public support for reforms. And once the government embraces a goal such as "We guarantee the right of every American to eat food that is healthy, green, fair and affordable"—it becomes

far more difficult to pass or sign a farm bill that erodes those guarantees.[19]

President Obama did not mention a national food policy in his State of the Union speech. More important, the opinion piece was a clarion call to the food movement to engage in a new kind of food politics.

A month later, the Union of Concerned Scientists hosted a National Food Policy Twitter chat. The food movement was finally strategizing beyond the myopic focus on alternative food initiatives. It included the authors of the *Washington Post* opinion piece minus Olivier De Schutter. Eleven questions organized the live chat, which each host answered. The questions set off simultaneous live conversations and interventions by many participants. Although the hosts hardly represented the diversity of the food movement, many segments of the food movement historically ignored were present.[20] These included groups like Food Chain Workers Alliance and the Coalition of Immokalee Workers, both of which brought the concerns of low-income workers of color and immigrants to the conversation. There were also vocal food justice activists who interjected concern with structural inequalities in the food system: Civil Eats, the go-to food movement blog; Anna Lappé, a highly visible author and sustainable food activist; and the food justice agitator and movement-building visionary Navina Khanna, the Director of the HEAL Food Alliance.

The conversation focused on the content of a national food policy; where in the federal government to house such a policy, especially in relation to the Farm Bill; how to build collective power to create and implement the policy; the role of equity and food-chain workers; and how to resist corporate power. This is a noteworthy list given the historical divisions in the food movement and the challenges of strategizing how to regulate the food system, engage in prefigurative *and* confrontational mobilization, and elevate the needs of subordinated groups. The W. K. Kellogg Foundation, perhaps a bit hyperbolically, was even compelled to tweet, "for 1st time food mvm't is working as 1: health, environment, agriculture & labor for a real food revolution."[21] But as in other social movements, there are "dividends of dissent" that come from infighting.[22] Disagreement allows activists to work through questions of strategy and identity on the road to solving their chief grievances. Although there were several celebratory tweets, it was clear the goal was not to reach some kind of false consensus to smother differences in the name of gathering around food.[23] In this moment, the food movement displayed a capacity to resist the postpolitical pull by deepening its agonistic political practices.

After participants had an ongoing discussion of movement building and excitement about finding ways to build collective power, the sixth question asked, "Do you see a national food policy as our best mechanism for addressing issues of equity? How?"[24] Although Michael Pollan's response was disappointing ("A food policy that make healthy calories more competitive with junk calories contributes mightily to equity"), his tweet received twice as many retweets and likes than Mark Bittman's tweet, which read, "I see it as part of the same struggle. You can't make big changes in food w/o making big changes in many other things."[25] Maybe this difference reflects the sentiment of the chat participants. If so, it confirms that many of the ideas informing mainstream food politics (e.g., "subsidies create problems for dietary health") grossly neglect underlying structural inequalities. Critical grassroots voices intervened at these moments to address concerns usually subservient to health and environmental goals. They lent legitimacy to the claims of organizations like the W. K. Kellogg Foundation that this chat was more than an exercise in reproducing the same hierarchy of concerns. A food justice activist from New Mexico named Rodrigo Rodriguez offered some especially incisive tweets. Two of them, "If we don't address the structural racism in the 'food movement' then a national food policy is nothing more than rhetoric" and "People of color farmers and communities are consistently marginalized in food and farming spaces where their voice is important," aired long-standing grievances.[26] He also tweeted, related to inequities enmeshed in other institutions, "I've yet to hear anything about migrant farm workers or land and resource removal in Black, Brown and Indigenous communities."[27] While it is hard to measure the full effect of such comments, they echo the concerns of many food justice activists who are organizing across social justice movements.

This conversation took place at the height of the Black Lives Matter insurrections, the Fight for $15 strikes, and ongoing climate justice direct actions against the XL Keystone Pipeline. Confrontational politics were in the air. This oppositional social change ethos melded with organizing throughout 2015 by the most progressive segments of the food movement to build on the initial national food policy conversation. The Plate of the

Union campaign was launched by Food Policy Action Education Fund, the Union of Concerned Scientists, and the HEAL Food Alliance. Their goal was to mobilize the public to push federal policy makers to enact progressive food policies. With the help of the HEAL Food Alliance, the campaign tapped into a grassroots food politics that is building the power of the food movement. In 2015, the theme of The Gathering, an annual food justice conference sponsored by the Growing Food and Justice for All Initiative, was "H.E.A.L Our Food System." Workshops included "Grassroots Organizing for Good Food Policy," "Just Labor within the Food Justice Movement? Analyses and Steps Forward," "Food Justice at the Federal Level: What Will a National Food, Health and Well-Being Policy Look Like?," and "Justicia Alimentaria Sin Fronteras—Food Justice without Borders." These ideological shifts show that contemporary food politics are radicalizing and merging with the concerns of a range of social justice movements.

Although most of the food movement could not imagine the rise of Trump at the time, the disappointments of the Obama presidency were enough to increase mobilization around economic and racial justice. With the existential threat of congressional Republicans and Trump to frontline communities, it is noteworthy that the development of a deeper political consciousness through conversations about a national food policy show the ideological advantages of food justice. The calls for structural solutions by food justice activists and the narrowness of the Farm Bill necessitate new policies that crosscut the federal government and that set a foundation for state and local municipalities. While many local solutions exist because experimentation and innovation face fewer hurdles, having a patchwork regulatory environment on matters such as public health, environmental sustainability, labor, and civil rights is insufficient.[28] In practice, this means political organizing must integrate numerous targets. The work of food policy councils and similar convergence spaces are important to build cross-sectoral and cross-interest networks, offer insights into successes and failures, and articulate democratic values upon which to rebuild food systems.[29] Similar efforts to create food movement convergence spaces (e.g., national food policy Twitter chat, national conferences, national coalitions, protests, demonstrations) will only deepen its politics by mobilizing across differences and pooling resources into efforts that restructure federal food policy.

Food Justice Policy Visioning

The expanding influence of food justice aligns with the urgency for a food politics that can limit revanchist movements and advance the interests of subordinated groups. Passing a national food policy under the Trump administration is unlikely given the overriding attention by left-wing social movements to resist right-wing attacks on immigrants, people of color, prisoners, public education, the poor and working class, the social safety net, and the environment. But this is not the first time, nor will it be the last time, that progressive and radical forces face daunting odds. In fact, there is a strong public desire for a clear left alternative with a vision that can mobilize people around a social justice agenda.[30] Not only did tens of millions of people embrace the avowed democratic socialist Bernie Sanders during Democratic Party primaries, but also organized left forces regrouped after the election to work together to stoke grassroots energy. In early 2017, The Majority, a coalition with more than fifty organizations, launched its first campaign, "Beyond the Moment." The Movement for Black Lives played a key role in convening people across climate justice, economic justice, racial justice, immigrant rights, labor, queer, and feminist movements. The Majority used the fiftieth anniversary of Dr. Martin Luther King Jr.'s "Beyond Vietnam" speech to call for intersectional analysis and organizing.[31] From the April 4 anniversary of the speech to May Day, the goal was to begin prefiguring the political actions necessary "to move masses of people nationally toward meaningful, trans-local actions designed to expand multi-racial, multi-sector and local long-term organizing capacity to strengthen the fight for justice, freedom and the right to live fully, with dignity and respect for all people."[32] The message of the moment was clear: radicalizing requires building mass collective power across differences.

In the realm of food, the response was similar. Voter research by Plate of the Union found public support for building a broad movement to reform the food system to ensure equal access to healthy and affordable food that takes care of workers, the environment, and farmers.[33] Knowing this, the HEAL Food Alliance quickly mobilized to oppose Trump's cabinet nominations. His picks for the Department of Health and Human Services, the Environmental Protection Agency, the Department of Agriculture, and the Department of Labor were especially devastating for the food movement. The right-wing résumés of these four wealthy white men included opposition to food stamps, improved nutritional standards, fair wages, environmental health protections, and climate science. Resistance by the HEAL Food Alliance was a stopgap measure with limited chance of success. Therefore, it was surprising when along with the Fight for $15 movement and groups like Food Chain Workers Alliance, Food Policy Action, and Restaurant Opportunities Centers United, they pressured labor secretary nominee Andrew Puzder to withdraw.[34] As the CEO of CKE Restaurants, the parent company of Carl's Jr. and Hardees, he actively opposed raising the minimum wage and oversaw a fast-food empire that routinely engaged in wage and hour violations, sexual harassment, and other unfair labor practices.[35] While this was a laudable victory, the Senate confirmed many other cabinet members not committed to running their agencies and departments in line with the broad goals of the food movement. The need to resist more crises is inevitable, but the food movement also has a unique political opportunity to advance a comprehensive political agenda that centers equity. As Bittman, Pollan, De Schutter, and Salvador put it a few days before Trump's inauguration, "Natural allies are everywhere. . . . It's all connected; the common threads are justice, fairness, and respect. . . . Mature social movements (including those on the right) recognize that it's always a struggle to get what you want." As organizing becomes more intersectional, the interests of subordinated groups help bend the practice of food politics to fight for structural changes in the food system.

One of the ways to channel heightened moments of political organizing is into policy crafting around an agenda that reflects the vision of a social movement.[36] Patricia Allen reasons that the food movement will continue to fail in the food policy realm "unless they can somehow overcome the characteristic inertia of the federal government . . . and somehow overcome or outmaneuver the structures of power and privilege that originally created and continue to maintain these policies."[37] Two promising food movement agendas are a national food policy and a national food strategy. Both would exceed the limited parameters of the Farm Bill, which is too restrictive in its scope to regulate the food system or distribute tax dollars much beyond nutrition assistance and agricultural support.[38]

To advance a national food policy agenda involves developing and then implementing specific recommendations. In 2017, the Johns Hopkins

Center for a Livable Future enumerated comprehensive food and agriculture policy recommendations for the Trump administration and the 115th Congress.[39] These included the jurisdictions of eight federal agencies and focused on food system sustainability and public health. Thinking through a national food policy based on the topic areas alone reveals the complexity of trying to integrate different policy arenas. While not exhaustive, the list is revealing: antibiotics; antitrust law enforcement; aquaculture, fisheries, and seafood; food access and food policy advocacy; food waste; food procurement; food system resilience; food system workers; industrial animal production; and sustainable diets. A national strategy could help cohere these arenas and accomplish broad policy goals. The 2017 report *Blueprint for a National Food Strategy* correctly notes that many laws and policies govern the food system, but there is little integration. Coordination of existing laws and policies would help unify the regulation of the food system. Equitable participation would ensure input from marginalized voices. Transparency in decision-making would foster accountability. Commitment to a long-term process of social change would require concrete plans and flexibility to adapt to new conditions. In brief, this entails "utilizing an organizing authority, incorporating stakeholder and public engagement, enshrining goals in a written document, and ensuring periodic updating."[40]

Over fifteen federal agencies help regulate the food system, so systems thinking and shared policy goals can coordinate the organizing approach taken to current and future food policies. For example, the National Environmental Policy Act is a procedural law passed by Congress that mandates all federal agencies to submit environmental assessments and environmental impact statements for all their proposed actions. While imperfect and contested, it is a concrete example of a law that directs agency actions regardless of who occupies the White House. With a clear target, grassroots organizing can elevate interconnected problems in the food system, lobby Congress, and compel it to call for a coordinated strategy.[41] While an executive order can also direct federal agencies to abide by specific considerations in their daily work, like whether their actions will advance or hinder environmental justice, enforcement fluctuates with administrations, and even when enforcement is implemented, it often lacks coordination. To be effective, the strategy would have legally binding norms and goals that direct federal directives, plans, laws, and policies;

require agencies to reform past policies; and receive adequate funding.[42] The interconnected and compounding crises in the food system, although they are difficult to resolve, demand action.

Scattered throughout these food policy and food strategy reports are references to equity but not to food justice. While the reports hope to inspire the food movement to organize across silos, their focus on food excludes a broader vision. If food movement goals remain split up by interest groups, then these policy and strategy suggestions may replicate the historical limitations of the Farm Bill. The sheer range of problems in the food system compels activists to pick an area of interest and then learn everything about it to shape political outcomes. Of course, across the food movement there is the overarching commitment to feed people and create jobs. Yet, without challenging the ideological sway of racial neoliberalism within the federal government, this value system will corrupt noble endeavors.[43] A food justice national strategy is a possible antidote to advocate with "discursive clarity" around a set of principles to inform all federal programs and policies related to food.[44] This unconventional policy method could generate new institutional momentum to disrupt the revanchist inertia with moral and ethical claims that provide a clear alternative. Because food justice concerns touch every part of the food system and many grassroots social movements have commitments to food justice, there is an opportunity to engage in righteous food politics with populist appeal. Retreating into the local to find solace amid the moral crisis infecting every branch of government is to abdicate responsibility for radical visions and guiding practices. Stepping into the antagonism of democratic politics with the goal of restructuring the rules that govern the food system to conform to food justice goals is to accept the political task of fighting for new hegemonic relations.

What might a food justice national strategy cover as a political tool to shape current and future food policy? Movement convergences such as the 2012 Food + Justice = Democracy conference offer guidance to move forward with some agreed-upon principles.[45] This conference was a significant event marking the maturation of food justice. Organizers tapped into over three hundred activists "by coming together to find the spark of the movement for food justice—an ambitious endeavor seeking to ignite conversations with the purpose of crafting a cohesive public policy agenda for food justice."[46] The diversity of conference attendees suggested the benefits of a broad national mandate that would seek to eliminate inequities in the food system by race, ethnicity, nationality, class, and gender, *and* promote strategies that advance social equity. The conference devised *Principles of Food Justice,* which stated the desire for policy solutions to recognize the interdependence of history and contemporary social problems. This is clearly a prerequisite for any future food policy committed to social justice. Under the principle of "Historical Trauma," the document reads in part, "Acknowledge as fundamental in our consideration of food justice that we cannot deliver food justice without addressing historical trauma and the way it requires an intersectional analysis of our relationship with the land, with each other, with the economy, across cultures, and with our food and other consumption choices."[47] On this basis, a food justice national strategy could mandate federal agencies to devise strategies to address the structural inequalities stemming from colonialism, slavery, discriminatory immigration regimes, and patriarchy, to name only a few sources of historical trauma in the United States.

Drawing on examples from each of my cases, I want to illustrate how crafting food justice policy that focuses on land, labor, urban and rural community development, health, self-determination, and environmental sustainability could guide federal agencies to address historical traumas.[48] Although treated independently in the following sections, a national strategy would entail agency cooperation to solve entangled problems that transcend simple categorization. In many cases, statutes that can advance food justice already exist. Requiring agencies attend to inequities within the food system would focus the federal policy effort on advancing the interests of subordinated groups. Mandating food justice would also direct the state to address many issues that other left-wing social movements have been agitating for a resolution to for many years.

Land

Without land justice, food justice is impossible.[49] In the United States, land inequities manifest in many forms. White settlers' dispossession of land from indigenous people disrupted cultural foodways and the material basis for social reproduction. Black farmers have lost land at an accelerating pace for the last one hundred years due to discriminatory lending policies.[50] Corporate consolidation and concentration in agriculture have led to the expansion of large industrial farms, which has pressured farmers to "get big or get out." Large-scale conventional organic agriculture drives up land values and urbanization envelops farmland, erecting obstacles to land tenure for beginning low-resourced farmers. In cities, there is the intensifying process of gentrification. This contributes to the displacement of low-income communities and communities of color, and drives up the cost of land, raising rents for small food-related business owners and urban farmers.[51] At the same time, gentrification encourages the entrance of more expensive retailers like Whole Foods and boutique bakeries and juice cafés. And these are just some of the problems.[52]

Oakland is undergoing rapid gentrification. For Planting Justice, this has meant shifting food production out of the city into more affordable parts of the East Bay, such as El Sobrante, where the organization runs a five-acre orchard.[53] Instead of challenging private property, its model navigates neoliberal mandates. Building edible landscapes reimagines property by redistributing capital from wealthy and often white people to many low-income, formerly incarcerated black men. While creative, its strategy cannot guarantee a means for poor and working-class people to stay in place. If federal agencies such as the Department of Housing and Urban Development were to increase resources for affordable housing and use regulatory tools to slow housing inflation, gentrification pressures might subside and make urban agriculture a more economically sustainable livelihood.

In San Diego, San Diego Roots emerged out of a campaign to prevent the sale of farmland for development. Lacking the money to buy this land, it turned to educating the public about the importance of local food, hoping to inspire people to keep farming in San Diego's rural areas. Embodying their ideals, San Diego Roots leased farmland. But there have been restrictions and complications of farming along the border, not the least of which is the constant presence of border enforcement agencies and the nonprofit stress of fundraising or monetizing the farm. The neoliberal conditions of working as a nonprofit in a for-profit farming sector complicates the lack of secure land tenure and makes the process of running a farm school precarious. Under a food justice national strategy, the Department of Agriculture could be responsible for reducing barriers to farming for low-resourced groups with fair and affordable loans and policies that mandate preserving farmland, slowing land inflation, and breaking up large farms. Moreover, there is the need for reparations that include debt forgiveness and land and wealth redistribution to descendants of indigenous people and black farmers whose land was stolen. The reason for this is because land dispossession was necessary to advancing white supremacy and as a result, of all private agricultural land, whites own 98 percent of the acres, which is valued at over $1.2 trillion.[54]

Labor

Food justice entails eliminating the exploitation of workers in the food system. The food system runs on the labor of poorly compensated and underprotected women, low-income people, and people of color. Current federal labor laws fail to protect workers, particularly undocumented immigrant farmworkers, who also face an uneven and largely weak set of state-level protections.[55] Therefore, there is a critical need to check the lobbying influence and power of large food corporations with federal agency mandates that eliminate labor exceptions for immigrants, ensure the right to collectively bargain, and provide a livable wage with full access to health care. First and foremost, all food-chain workers require full protection under the National Labor Relations Act and Fair Labor Standards Act.

In Los Angeles, labor exploitation at the intersection of race, ethnicity, citizenship, and class converge. UFCW 770 has fought Walmart for years because its business model is bad for low-income people of color and immigrant communities. Walmart and its contractors have regularly retaliated against workers and eroded grocery retail labor standards. UFCW 770 has also experienced the deterioration of labor protections for meatpacking workers despite record profits and the surging global demand for meat. The Department of Labor, although charged with ensuring fair and safe labor practices, is hamstrung by state laws (e.g., "right to work" laws) and often ignores violations by major corporate actors with disproportionate industry influence.[56] A food justice national strategy would compel the Department of Labor to vigorously prosecute employers for discrimination, expand the most rigorous wage and benefit laws to all food-chain workers, and intervene in workplace practices to protect worker safety (e.g., mandate slowing of the line speed at meatpacking plants). Given the prevalence of undocumented immigrants working in the food system, the Department of Homeland Security must halt deportations and create a pathway to citizenship. The Department of Agriculture could then prioritize helping formerly undocumented immigrant farmworkers become land-owning owner-operators, for instance, through the

Outreach and Assistance for Socially Disadvantaged Farmers and Ranchers and Veteran Farmers and Ranchers Program. From another angle, the Department of Justice might be obliged by a food justice national strategy to carry out far more antitrust investigations against agribusinesses with near monopolies, which would give them the evidence to take law enforcement action. For example, UFCW 770 might benefit from investigations into the beef, pork, and poultry industries if they led to breaking up big companies like JBS, Swift, Tyson, and Cargill. Or if there was a case for monopsony, where a company like Walmart squeezes suppliers for lower prices, an antitrust case could be brought against the company to protect the livelihoods of others in that company's supply chain.

Urban and Rural Community Development

Food and agriculture are key facets in community development.[57] *Development* refers in its broadest sense to building on and improving a community's human, social, physical, financial, environmental, political, and cultural capital. The configuration of capitals reflects the degree and kind of assets and inequities that exist in a place. Capitals condition the opportunities for food justice campaigns. Although food justice is concerned with community well-being and the right to control resources based on communal desires, what constitutes a community varies and reflects power relations.[58] The political salience of using community as a framework to build collective power around some end may be paramount. Ends include the desires of people constituted by a place, by identity based on a shared social position, by a desire or an ideology such as social justice or environmental sustainability, and/or by a common practice, culture, economy, or form of politics.[59]

Honoring the diversity of community demands for the right to their cultural foodways and to determine the shape of their food system pushes back against the monocultural mind-set dominating food and agricultural policy. In each of my cases, activists focused their attention on an issue and used this to improve community well-being. There was never a comprehensive campaign to build an entire food system from farm to table. Such an endeavor requires coordination across a range of stakeholders, which each organization inherently understood. For example, San Diego Roots was part of a major campaign that convinced San

Diego's City Council to pass an ordinance in 2012 allowing residents to have chickens, goats, and bees on their property. Similarly, Planting Justice worked in a coalition early in its history to change urban agriculture laws in Oakland, while UFCW 770 sat on the Los Angeles Food Policy Council, which has successfully led battles to expand local food production and consumption. These are notable outcomes that with broader aims and greater assistance could transform local and regional food systems in line with food justice. Community-led food system development would benefit from mandating that federal funding prioritize advancing equity when giving money. This entails reducing bureaucratic barriers to accessing grants, prioritizing the work of small grassroots organizations in historically marginalized communities, reorganizing budgets to divest from harmful food system practices to reinvest in environmentally and socially just food systems, and committing long-term to projects and places.

Locally based mobilizations are occurring throughout the United States, but communities often have divergent reasons for supporting local food system development, which suggests the process is contested and uneven.[60] Whose perspectives drive the process matters. A food justice national strategy requires procedural justice. Federal priorities would need to align with food sovereignty goals. Communities want an array of local food systems, not all of which reflect typical capitalist property and labor relations.[61] To foster the heterogeneity of community development, each agency with relevant jurisdiction would need to back efforts whose priority is not always economic, but may be social, cultural, or environmental. From a food justice perspective, research into something like beekeeping would measure nonmonetary values and take a community's desire for self-determination seriously. To avoid an urban bias, agencies like the Department of Agriculture could align their Rural Development offices with economic development strategies that build community-controlled food systems *outside* the influence of industrialized and corporately controlled agribusiness. Although more limited, the Economic Development Administration and the Minority Business Development Agency could prioritize food-based community development to improve the economy in urban and rural places suffering from high unemployment and poverty. To address historical traumas, the executive order could charge these agencies with affirmative action strategies that also focus on the noneconomic desires of low-income communities and communities of color.

Health

Given the centrality of food to health, this is one of the most straightforward principles to support. It is also highly contested considering the history of scientific racism, narratives tying health to racialized phenotypes and body types, and the financial influence of corporate agribusiness in flooding low-income communities and communities of color with unhealthy food. The medical industry monetizes treating these same communities for problems that stem from racialized and classed discourses and practices.[62] Simultaneously, there is widespread food insecurity and hunger, which is largely addressed through government charity and corporate benevolence.[63] Taken together, food access and consumption are major arenas for mobilization. Health inequities related to food offer a tangible focal point to navigate the structural drivers behind ethnoracial and class disparities.

A food justice national strategy might force the federal government to take actions internally in the name of equity that it refuses to abide by internationally. In 2014, Terri Robl, the U.S. deputy representative to the UN Economic and Social Council, explained part of the country's position on the right to food: "Overall, we view the right to food as a desirable policy goal; it is our objective to achieve a world where everyone has adequate access to food. *We do not, however, treat the right to food as an enforceable obligation*" (emphasis added).[64] The United States has long ignored its role in global hunger and repeatedly obstructed efforts to hold accountable the trade-distorting policies and practices of its domestic multinational corporate agribusinesses.[65] Therefore, it is unsurprising that the United States is one of only a half dozen UN member states that have refused to ratify the International Covenant on Economic, Social and Cultural Rights, a key treaty upholding the right to food.[66] From a food justice commitment to ending health disparities, this aversion is problematic.

In Los Angeles and Oakland, issues of health and nutrition are prevalent. People lack the means to purchase healthy food. This reflects historical dispossession and discrimination that have marginalized black and Latinx communities by preventing the acquisition of resources that lead to class mobility.[67] UFCW 770 and Planting Justice have sought to address this legacy by advocating for and creating good jobs. There are also dietary health problems that disproportionately harm black and Latinx communities. The physiological aspects are only part of the health equation. Social evaluation and blame pathologize these groups for eating poorly when there are far more white people with the same dietary health problems resulting from the same behavior.[68] The difference is that institutional racism plays a determining role in producing disparities and privileges.

At a minimum, a food justice national strategy would require that the Supplemental Nutrition Assistance Program (SNAP) and the Special Supplemental Nutrition Program for Women, Infants, and Children (WIC) are fully funded, easy to access, and prioritize culturally appropriate, healthy, and sustainable food options. Thinking ahead, the strategy could charge the Department of Health and Human Services with eliminating dietary health disparities. The strategy would dovetail with the Action Plan to Reduce Racial and Ethnic Health Disparities, part of which looks at the social determinants of health and how best to intervene. Additionally, the Federal Collaboration on Health Disparities Research is an important space for food justice scholars and activists to push for a structural analysis of the social determinants of health. These are positive foundations to buttress the development of policies that target poverty, segregation, mass incarceration, and gentrification. A food justice national strategy would also go further than most health interventions, which focus on bringing grocery stores into "food deserts." It would charge agencies like the Department of Agriculture to develop nutrition standards that acknowledge the health problems associated with foods and ingredients pushed by corporate agribusiness (e.g., sugar, corn, soybeans, dairy, and meat). There could also be mandates to eliminate subsidies for unhealthy commodities, ban marketing of junk food, and institute price supports and parity for fruits and vegetables and heritage and cultural crops. To buoy these actions at the community level, the Department of Transportation would need to prioritize its spending in places lacking access to healthy foods to ensure equitable access to public, affordable, and efficient transportation.

Self-Determination

Self-determination has long been a major frame driving food justice activism, which draws on the history of groups like the Black Panther Party.[69] This parallels food movement framing that denounces corporate rule over the food system.[70] Activists, from anarchists calling for a delinking from the political economy of this system, to school teachers advocating for more gardening and culinary arts training to help youth take care of their health, to small-scale organic farmers selling food to local restaurants, share a desire to take back the economy. Unfortunately, such effort often remains individualized. Taking care of oneself (e.g., growing your own food) eclipses collective efforts to build replicable models that chip away at capitalist infrastructure (e.g., credit unions, alternative currencies, and cooperatives). So a food justice approach to self-determination questions models and institutions that foster dependency. The rejoinder is to elevate cultural foodways that corporate agribusinesses conceal by propagating culinary monocultures.[71] Control of the means of production and a voice in all decision-making spaces are therefore prerequisites for community food sovereignty.

As the cases of San Diego Roots and Planting Justice teach, the organizations aspired to take back the economy with both noncommodified and living-wage food work. This was not without complication. While San Diego Roots was more reliant on external foundation and government funding than Planting Justice, they were both still embedded in what critics refer to as the "non-profit industrial complex." The organizations are part of a process that professionalizes social movements, often in ways that demobilize their more radical wings and principles.[72] This often creates divisions within social movements. White and middle-class groups with greater privileges tend to have more resources than people of color and low-income-run groups.[73] In addition to autonomous practices, both organizations built community around noncapitalist principles. One of the challenges, though, was whether to adopt anti-racist principles. San Diego Roots missed many opportunities to foster self-determination around more than just local and organic food by failing to see how race and ethnicity interpolated this process. Planting Justice, conversely, built interracial and cross-class alliances in its prisoner reentry work. Although both organizations have developed socially heterogeneous networks and reached thousands of people through their work, self-determination requires moving beyond the organizational scale.

Perhaps this is counterintuitive, but a food justice national strategy would still have a role to play in fostering community control independent of concentrated power. Because the federal government manages a multitrillion-dollar budget, it should in theory spend its money in line with the desires of the citizenry. Given the demographic heterogeneity of the United States and the long history of oppression of many different social groups, it is necessary to balance diversity with eliminating inequities. For example, a compelling practice of direct democracy is participatory budgeting. Some cities set aside budget money for citizens to determine its use. The Office of Management and Budget could respond to a food justice mandate by encouraging less conventional government spending priorities and coordinating interagency funding directives. Because the priorities of this executive office often dictate the local use of federal money, there is a unique opportunity to compel the federal government to reinforce autonomous yearnings with more participatory input into budgeting. While there is no guarantee this democratic process would allow food justice activists to spend money as they want, it might encourage greater civic participation and alliance building with other groups committed to social justice. A fully funded Healthy Food Financing Initiative, run by the Department of Agriculture, Department of Treasury, and Department of Health and Human Services, would deepen this process if it was refocused to build wealth in underserved communities. One way to foster self-determination would be to prioritize funding worker and community-owned food and agriculture cooperatives. These efforts could also coordinate with the Department of Housing and Urban Development to encourage zoning laws that allow citizens to organize new food networks that transition away from corporately controlled food supply chains (e.g., development of community-based urban agriculture). The resulting food networks would reflect the social priority of equity and set in motion social relations around food determined at a local level.

Environmental Sustainability

An environmentally sustainable foundation is intimately connected to a socially just food system. In the context of air and water pollution, biodiversity collapse, climate change, the use of toxic chemicals, and urban land use conversion, all of which disproportionately harm low-income people and people of color, food justice involves protecting ecosystems and nonhuman nature. This interdependency has motivated an array of food politics. Anti-pesticide activists have fought toxic chemicals in agriculture based on their harm to animals and farmworkers. Climate justice activists see problems like desertification as an issue that both destroys ecosystems and threatens farmers. Water pollution activists link the collapse of fish populations in nitrogen-loaded dead zones like the Gulf of Mexico to the harm this causes to fishers. Because environmental problems in the food system are multifaceted, there are many opportunities to build collective power around policy and regulatory change.

My cases offer a few considerable points. While UFCW 770 dodged the link between environmental problems and its organizing, Planting Justice and San Diego Roots both explicitly articulated why it is important to develop environmentally sustainable alternatives to an industrial food system. The nonprofits used permaculture and organic gardening and farming techniques, which offer alternatives for a climate-just future. On an educational level, Planting Justice and San Diego Roots taught unfamiliar practices to people living in cities. One of the problems is that their reach is limited, a condition shared by most nonprofits.[74] In this context, because labor unions like UFCW 770 represent workers who labor in an environmentally unsustainable food system, they can exacerbate environmental problems and the possibility for building coalitions.[75] If powerful organizations like labor unions do not tackle environmental problems by pressuring the employers of their union members, they are complicit in the harm that falls on their low-income rank and file. Together, the shallow reach of nonprofits and the embeddedness of labor unions in a system that thrives on perverse economic incentives that degrade the environment necessitate federal action.

A food justice national strategy that pushes environmental sustainability from the perspective of equity would likely overlap with Executive Order 12898, Federal Actions to Address Environmental Justice in Minority Populations and Low-Income Populations. But the food system organizes the relationship between human and nonhuman nature in distinct ways, so there is a policy incentive to manage food-related environmental problems. One target could mandate agencies to draft policies and protocols to reduce environmental harm and help the most vulnerable communities become more resilient to environmental problems like climate change. Part of the regulatory system overseen by the Environmental Protection Agency and the Department of Agriculture includes environmental issues like pesticides and natural resource conservation. Few if any policy mechanisms compel these agencies to consider how structural inequalities map onto the environmental protection landscape. For example, the record die-off of bees due to their exposure to the popular class of insecticides called neonicotinoids is framed around the imperative of crop pollination to feed society. This is opposed to focusing on the social inequities associated with the raced, classed, and gendered impacts of the political economy of these insecticides, and the concentrated power of manufacturers like Bayer Crop Science and Syngenta. In brief, a food justice national strategy would enforce and develop environmental statutes to help eliminate environmental inequalities pertaining to food.

· · ·

Before concluding, I want to recognize that there is no policy panacea. Although there is the potential for the state to check the excesses of capital, capital has captured much of the state. Race, class, and gender also stratify this relationship, with powerful groups better positioned to exert their influence. The food justice movement will likely continue to navigate these conditions with only partial victories. Policy prescriptions are therefore incomplete. There will also be new social antagonisms emerging around yet-unforeseen sites of social struggle. This entails remaining open to a diverse field of political action and social change and acknowledging when policy does not equate with a political resolution.

Food justice practices will succumb to the postpolitical logic if they relent in contesting relations of subordination. Activists must keep building grassroots power through confrontational strategies that disrupt the political order and alternative strategies that provide new paths to move beyond the structural limitations of current institutions. Because social inequity is heterogeneous, the oppression-privilege spectrum will produce different intersections of resistance. In some cases, conditions will compel a food politics that leverages the state, while in others, it will mean working outside these confines to produce liberatory alternatives; and in still others, a combination of the two. Making demands on the state can be a radical act in the context of neoliberal capitalism and institutional racism, but deeper problems of political elite intransigence and a lack of political will to enforce laws remain.[76] Politics often impedes policy. A policy may be good, but the politicians and political process erect barriers. To advance a radical democratic politics requires seeing food politics as an agonistic process. Antagonism that disrupts the normal flow of social life with vocalized and public demands that produce discomfort for more powerful groups is always necessary.[77]

Winning something like a national food strategy or policy is only one stage of a dialectical process. Per Grace Lee Boggs, if we take seriously the suggestion that food justice activists are the leaders activists are looking for, then giving power to the state is necessary but insufficient. Communities must create the conditions for food justice wherever they live, work, and play. This will include creating and enforcing laws that advance a food justice agenda. The state is not likely going away anytime soon, so it plays an important role in moving society closer to food justice. But activists need to seize the social space opened when the state welcomes a progressive agenda and devise strategies that ameliorate social inequities outside the parameters of our institutions.[78]

The appeal of food justice is greater than it has ever been. People's longing for a relationship with food not grounded in subordination keeps a flicker of hope alive amid truly daunting odds. Food justice is a robust discursive framework to build alliances across social justice struggles. Creativity abounds in the use of food to address social inequities. And there are countless actions to build more just food networks and markets, confront corporate practices, and create new policies and regulations. Radical food politics is set to keep expanding. If it maintains a commitment to human flourishing, there is a foundation to achieve liberation. Thus the cry for food justice now!

Acknowledgments

Food Justice Now! was in the works for a long time. It is a culmination of conversations, debates, experiences, and reflections that began more than fifteen years ago. While I could say that this has simply been an intellectual journey, it is much more personal than that.

As an undergraduate student at Santa Clara University, I started to develop a set of analytical tools from my sociology and political science majors to understand social justice struggles. I also began to learn what it means to be an activist, an organizer, and a social movement participant. Two campaigns at the intersection of food and human rights stood out. The first focused on organizing students to boycott Taco Bell during the Coalition of Immokalee Workers' nationwide effort to get the company to sign an agreement ensuring farmworkers a penny more for each pound of picked tomatoes. The second pushed the university administration to cancel its contract with Coca-Cola for human rights violations as part of the nationwide United Students Against Sweatshops Killer Coke campaign. These campaigns taught me that progressive victories are possible and that everyone has a role to play in fighting for economic and racial justice. I want to thank some key Santa Clara University professors for helping me to see the inseparable connection between social science and social change. Fr. Paul Fitzgerald, Shawn Ginwright, Jonathan Hunt, Timothy Lukes, Laura Nichols, John Ratliff, and Fr. Mark Ravizza all offered scholarly insights and advice for how to live with conviction in a world of injustice. I also want to acknowledge my friends in the Santa Clara Community Action Program who inspired and challenged me to fight for social change. You know who you are. During my senior year, Chuck Powers, one of my mentors in the Department of Sociology, asked if I considered getting a PhD. He then suggested that I present my thesis paper at the Pacific Sociological Association meeting the fall after graduation. Two years later, I began my graduate school training in the Department of Sociology at the University of Florida.

While in Florida, I received the sociological training needed to conduct the research that grounds this book. In the first semester of graduate school, I enrolled in an environmental justice seminar taught by Brian Mayer. It is here that I grew curious about food and therefore food justice. Brian became my adviser for both my MA, which was my foray into the food justice movement, and my PhD, which helped me deepen my knowledge of food politics and the food movement. Thank you for supporting my intellectual interests and guiding me professionally. In addition, Stephen Perz always allowed my curiosities free range, partially because we share an interdisciplinary view of social science. Thanks to you, I learned the value of hanging out with human geographers. Katrina Schwartz taught me in two environmental politics seminars about the power of the state, despite its limitations, to check the growing influence of neoliberal and postpolitical forces. Given my focus on social movements and qualitative methods, Kendal Broad served as a wonderful guide into the complexities of collective mobilization that aims to change society.

Upon joining the Department of Sociology at Colorado State University, I found remarkable colleagues committed to using their research and teaching to make the world a better place. Special thanks to Michael Carolan, Doug Murray, and Laura Raynolds for directing me to people and places that would expand my research agenda and community engagement. I also appreciate the collegiality and mentorship of Jeni Cross, Peter Hall, Lynn Hempel, Stephanie Malin, KuoRay Mao, Tara Opsal, Lori Peek, and Pete Taylor. This department helps me stay sane amid the pressures of everyday academic life. I am also deeply appreciative for my eclectic writing group at Colorado State University. Sophie Esch, Alexus McLeod, and Dustin Tucker were tireless editors for several chapters of this book and provided accountability at critical writing stages.

Working in the realm of food justice, food movements, and food politics is inspirational. I want to express my gratitude for those scholars who have embraced my work and modeled how to push critical food studies forward. Julian Agyeman, Alison Alkon, Michael K. Goodman, Robert Gottlieb, Margaret Gray, Jill Lindsey Harrison, Alfonso Morales, and Nathan McClintock have been essential to this process. I am also thankful for my colleagues in the Section on Environmental Sociology of the

American Sociological Association and the Geographies of Food and Agriculture Working Group of the American Association of Geographers for being productive spaces to develop many of the ideas that made their way into this book. Shannon Bell, Danny Block, Brett Clark, Kenneth Gould, Jason Konefal, Charles Levkoe, Laura Minkoff-Zern, David Pellow, Kristin Reynolds, Antonio Roman-Alcalá, and Hannah Wittman have all provided professional support at different stages in the research project and writing of this book. In particular, Justin Sean Myers has been an amazing colleague and well of ideas. Thanks for the many conversations, critical brainstorming sessions, and writing quests.

This book would have been impossible without the consistent support and participation of all the social change makers at Planting Justice, San Diego Roots Sustainable Food Project, and United Food and Commercial Workers Local 770. I am forever indebted to you all for your generous participation, passion, and deep understanding of problems in the food system and in society more broadly. Thank you for also demonstrating how we might go about creating a world where there is food justice for everyone. Traveling throughout California felt discombobulating at times, but in Los Angeles, Oakland, and San Diego, I found people who made me feel at home. I am especially appreciative for Annie Lorrie Anderson-Lazo, Andrew Chahrour, Armando Espinoza, Marcelo Felipe Garzo Montalvo, Mannah Gbeh, Nam Le, Mel Lions, Joann Lo, May Nguyen, Matt O'Malley, Lisa Ordonez, Gavin Raders, Renae Santa Cruz, Ron Solano, Mindy Swanson, Jean Tong, Rigo Valdez, and Haleh Zandi.

I express my sincere gratitude to the University of Minnesota Press and my editor, Jason Weidemann, for tirelessly supporting this book. At all stages of the process, I have been in expert hands. Thanks to Ana Bichanich, Emily Hamilton, Melody Negron, Laura Westlund, and the rest of the production and marketing teams for fine-tuning my manuscript and strategizing how to reach a wide audience. Your advice and expertise have been exceptional. I am grateful, as well, to the two anonymous reviewers for their thoughtful feedback and suggestions. Obviously, any errors or omissions are my own.

In closing, my family has always been a source of sustenance. I want to honor my late grandmother, Charlotte Bratlien, for loving me through food and teaching me that all people deserve dignity and respect, as well as my late grandfather, Frank Sbicca, for your generosity of spirit and open-mindedness. Without my parents, John and Janice Sbicca, encouraging me from a young age to read everything I could get my hands on, I would not be here. Despite our differences, you also imparted the value of political participation. My wife, Jennifer Sbicca, is an endless source of support, love, and affection. I am forever grateful for your joyous presence and adventurous spirit and for bringing our newest treasure, Enzo, into the world. I love you.

Approach and Data

I have always been interested in how people collectively navigate their social worlds in the context of uneven power relations as well as how power manifests and is contested. This curiosity pushed me in this study to investigate dialectically the perceptions and actions of many different activists and organizations. I use ethnography, case study, and historical comparative methods of analysis. Triangulating these methodological approaches helps me explain the relationships between the social struggles identified in this book and the processual idea and practice of food justice. While people know and can express their views on something like food justice, these thoughts do not emerge in a vacuum. They manifest into action in relation to the material conditions of social life.

Karl Marx's famous dictum, in *The Eighteenth Brumaire of Louis Bonaparte*, that people make history but not under conditions of their own choosing, is especially apt. Marx was interested in why the French revolution of 1848 took a dictatorial form when fifty years prior the first French revolution hinted that the country was bound for a more democratic and equal society. He arrived at answers through a dialectical historical materialist method. The method is based in the understanding that groups fight for their interests by navigating present conditions shaped by the past. Social conditions are interconnected materially and ideologically, but will inevitably change because of the human capacity to know this, which reinforces the perennial possibility for social change. As Frederick Engels wrote in *Socialism: Utopian and Scientific*, "Dialectics . . . comprehends things and their representations, ideas, in their essential connection, concatenation, motion, origin and ending."[1] The dialectical method suggests the processual nature of society, its openness to contestation, and the utopian horizon of better futures.

To operationalize this dialectical approach, I designed the study and plan for the book with key considerations around my case selection. First, the organizations have an explicit commitment to food and equity (e.g., economic, health, social, political). Given the increasing significance of equity concerns in the food movement, my organizations mirror a major universe of cases. Second, all my cases are enmeshed in distinct social problems—in this case, the prison industrial complex, immigration, and labor conditions. Third, the organizations have clear goals and a distinct population they serve, represent, or cooperatively struggle for social change with. Having such organizational structure afforded me a way to draw broader conclusions about organizational efficacy and location within a larger set of social conditions. Fourth, my cases offer a diverse racial and ethnic makeup to center voices often marginalized within the food movement and to compare them with more dominant voices. Fifth, the cases are all located in major metropolitan areas with sizable urban agriculture movements and close to agriculturally productive rural areas. Although California is distinct, it is the most populated state in the United States, with major metropolitan areas that contain path-blazing food activism and many kinds of food politics common elsewhere. Moreover, given the themes I cover in chapter 5, *collective power, diversity,* and *solidarity,* I am attentive to the value of cases reflecting the complexities of large and socially and economically diverse populations. Sixth, the cases speak to explicit forms of food politics. Given my focus on the dialectical development of food politics committed to food justice, my cases each help to unearth a range of power relations. Last, I focus on cases never researched in systematic detail. It is important to shed light on the operation and political context of groups who lack much public attention outside of their immediate community to learn more about the contours of contemporary food politics.

With these considerations in mind, I chose Planting Justice, San Diego Roots Sustainable Food Project (San Diego Roots), and United Food and Commercial Workers Local 770 (UFCW 770) as my cases. I then split seven months of fieldwork roughly between the three organizations, each in a different city. In Oakland beginning in June 2012, I interned with Planting Justice, assisting the organization with administrative office duties, such as developing a database and internal personnel and programmatic evaluation materials, and installing edible landscapes at people's homes. Additionally, because I was on the board of directors during fieldwork, I also attended board meetings and functions. A little more than two months later, I interned with San Diego Roots on its six-acre farm, Wild Willow Farm. I prepared compost; formed rows;

planted seeds; managed the nursery; watered plants; pulled weeds; harvested crops; fed the chickens; prepared CSA baskets, teas, and herbal tinctures; and attended weekly sustainable farming workshops. For the last two and a half months, in Los Angeles, I interned with UFCW 770 in its Organizing Department. I assisted with administrative office duties such as developing maps and surveys; called strategic community partners to participate in various demonstrations; helped prepare for meetings with community activists and business owners; visited food processing, distribution, and grocery workplaces; and joined union-sponsored or union-supported protests. Then over a three-year period through 2015, I maintained informal communication with key informants within each organization and made occasional visits to learn about any changes.

During my time in the field, I was especially attentive to the hopes and pressures faced by each organization. Given that each organization is made up of people who hold perceptions that inform their behavior, I uncovered major similarities and differences by collecting in-depth semi-structured interviews with staff, volunteers, participants, and important community allies and supporters. The research depended on an initial seventy interviews. I conducted sixty-four in person and six over the phone. The breakdown was twenty-five interviews with Planting Justice, twenty-six with San Diego Roots, and nineteen with UFCW 770. My interview sample included a cross section of each organization's participants based on their roles and responsibilities. In the cases of Planting Justice and San Diego Roots, I interviewed over 90 percent of current active participants. In the case of UFCW 770, I primarily interviewed organizers, union representatives, shop stewards, and key union leaders. The interviews were conducted one time with each participant, ran between one and two hours, and were digitally recorded and then transcribed. I then completed a second intensive phase of interviewing in the summer of 2015 to learn more about the experiences of formerly incarcerated people working with Planting Justice. During this time, I conducted ten phone interviews, primarily with formerly incarcerated staff but also with key community partners involved in restorative justice work.

I was interested not only in organizational issues but also in how these organizations, as proxies, helped me detect structural conditions that shape their work and the social movements of which they are part. By considering what people think about conjunctures in the food system and elsewhere, I tracked the discursive and interpretive patterns people use to navigate their food politics. Conversely, by unpacking some of the histori-cal and sociological conditions that inform the realm of political prac-tices, I read these food politics against a broader set of social forces. This iterative process reveals the importance of reading activists' views of the present against their practices as they relate to the structuring of race and class inequities. Disentangling these relationships helped me identify social contradictions, like the fact that the interpretation of the exploita-tion of immigrant labor within San Diego conditions views on volunteer labor practices at San Diego Roots. Tracing these dialectical relations helped me to determine possible ideological and strategic shifts—in this case, to eliminate ethnoracial and labor exploitation in agriculture.

To gain a complete sense of the experiences and perspectives that inform activism within each organization as well as how the lessons por-tend for the food politics of the food movement, I deliberately interviewed people from many different backgrounds. As a native Californian who has lived in Southern California and the San Francisco Bay Area, I am very familiar with the geographic differences and demographic diversity of the state. It was important to me to deliberately try to reflect this diversity in my research. Except in the case of San Diego Roots, most of the people I spoke with were people of color. While I worked with UFCW 770, my interviewees were primarily Latinx and Asian, and when I worked with Planting Justice, my interviewees were mostly black and Latinx, and with Planting Justice there was also a sizable white minority. I did not collect deliberately much information on class, but education served as a rough proxy. Most of the people I interviewed had earned a college degree or completed some college. Except in the case of Planting Justice, I spoke with an almost even number of men and women. Given my interest in speaking with many formerly incarcerated men who were working for Planting Justice, men skewed the distribution in that case.

Throughout the research process and writing of this book, I also collected and analyzed digital and physical texts. These enrich the dia-lectical method and conjunctural analysis used in this book because they provide broader sociological explanations for how food justice represents a front for expanding the politics of social struggle. First, while working with each organization, I amassed internal documents, posters, leaflets, financial records, personnel information, promotional materials, and reports. These physical materials offer clues into how organizations per-ceive themselves and their work. They also provide important information on internal processes and the outcomes of various decision-making processes. Second, I collected digital materials on each organization. This includes YouTube videos, Facebook postings, Google Groups, listservs, and blogs. Some materials are organizational products, while others come from friends, critics, dispassionate observers, or other sources of social media. This leads to my third textual source, digital news media. All the issues and organizations in this study received different forms of news coverage. I first searched for these materials through various databases such as LexisNexis and Access World News to collect national and local newspaper coverage on each organization. I also used these databases to search for specific sectors within which each organization works. These searches included the relevant cities and the types of activism taking place. Fourth, I sought reports by nonprofits; foundations; policy institutes; and local, state, and federal agencies on matters of relevance to this study. These reports are essential as sources of information to cross-check statements made in interviews or in the field. Relatedly, I build on and synthesize the academic and activist work of writers who focus on the social movements I cover in the book. Bringing these works into conversation with my other texts and data offers yet another archival feedback into a dialectical narrative charting the expansive possibilities of food justice.

I undertake research not just to understand the world, but to change it. Paolo Freire suggests, "Solidarity requires that one enter into the situation of those with whom one is solidary; it is a radical posture."[2] Because solidarity aims to get at the root of the problem, this raises a series of questions. What does it mean to act in solidarity? What are the obligations scholars have toward the movements they work in and study? What is the difference between "speaking for" and "speaking with" the food movements we study? How do scholars make useful critiques without just being critical? How can we orient our scholarship to support policy changes that help favorably restructure the conditions under which food movements work?

My book offers one approach to answering these questions, perhaps even practicing food justice from the vantage of a professor who straddles the world of social movements.[3] I found through this study that researching grassroots organizations placed me in a position where I might be viewed as an exploiter extracting "data" to surmise some "fact" or "finding." My approach to dealing with this power dynamic was to engage reciprocally with the organizations that center my cases. Ethnographic methods put me into close and ongoing interaction with the protagonists of the research, so I felt the need to find concrete ways to act in solidarity. I remained flexible in the early stages of each case study to learn about the goals and needs that organizations and their social movement networks prioritized. Instead of having fully formed questions about particular aspects of how food politics were understood and practiced, I remained open to some of the questions organizations asked about their own activism. This sensitized me to their daily hopes and pressures. Additionally, I expressed my solidarity through the reciprocal act of sweat equity. Each organization put some of my skill sets to work to address its immediate needs. These organizations operated on thin budgets and faced an array of daunting problems. Knowing that researchers who fail to "pull their weight" can be a burden, I offered my labor in myriad ways and made sure to ask questions in interviews that facilitated a reflexive deepening of their work.[4]

With this research of reciprocity in mind, I portray food politics in their unique, yet incomplete, conjunctures. I connect how people come to know and act in regard to food politically to new available avenues for the food movement to further food justice. The process of giving entails offering new lenses for social movements to view themselves and their social change targets. When I offer critiques, they are in the spirit of writing as but one part of the contestation between competing interests that drive the dialectical process. I share the perspective of the anarchist and political theorist Murray Bookchin, who proposed, "Only a dialectic that combines searching critique with social creativity can disassemble the best materials from our shattered world and bring them to the service of remaking a new one."[5] Racist, xenophobic, capitalist, and neoliberal ideologies help reproduce conjunctures that social movements confront in Oakland, San Diego, Los Angeles, and more broadly throughout the United States. I break down how these ideologies manifest materially as inequities and chronicle how this inspires reimagining food justice. My hope is that a critical engagement with the challenges and prospects of revolutionizing food politics to center food justice is generative of food movement mobilizations capable of advancing human flourishing.

Notes

Introduction

1. Although not always explicitly, many people who identify as food justice organizers are engaged in a Freirean form of praxis, which means *"reflection* and *action* directed at the structures to be transformed" (Freire 2000, 126).

2. The research entailed seven months of ethnographic fieldwork, eighty interviews, countless informal follow-up conversations, and hundreds of documentary sources. See "Appendix: Approach and Data" for further details.

3. I use *oppression* to reference those relations of ruling wherein groups experience subordination based on their economic class, ethnicity, race, gender, sexuality, ability, or other identity. In most instances, I am using this in the broad sense of both the experience of exploitation as a worker and domination based on a socially constructed identity.

4. I use *Latinx* because it is a more inclusive term. Also, when referring to men and women it avoids the masculine default, *Latino.*

5. Although many industrial unions were dominated by white men, there are prominent examples of multiracial labor organizing in the fields of California, the United Farm Workers chief among them.

6. Hislop (2015) paints a nuanced picture of the food justice movement but still shows that the major concern of those he surveyed across the United States and Canada is the issue of food security. Social justice was often expressed as a concern, but this did not necessarily translate into food politics that addressed social inequalities. That said, there is a recent shift, perhaps pushed by the election of Donald Trump. The most promising example of thinking beyond the food movement and across an array of interrelated problems is the national HEAL (Health, Environment, Agriculture, and Labor) Food Alliance.

7. Although similar arguments have been made to "get beyond food," that is, investigate the underlying inequalities that create problems in the food system (e.g., Guthman 2008a; Sbicca 2012; Passidomo 2014; Reynolds 2015; Broad 2016), there has been far less attention to *how* to make this happen and the possible *mechanisms* that inhibit or facilitate food justice activism from taking place. This

gap, and the question of what it means to engage in movement building in both prefigurative and confrontational ways, is the political analysis that drives much of this book.

8. Hurley 1995; Bullard 2000; Sze 2007.

9. Gottlieb and Joshi 2010, 6.

10. Alkon and Agyeman 2011, 5.

11. Alkon and Agyeman 2011, 5.

12. Guthman 2008b; McMichael 2009.

13. Cadieux and Slocum 2015, 13.

14. Hislop 2015; Reynolds and Cohen 2016.

15. Meyer and Whittier 1994.

16. Garzo Montalvo and Zandi 2011.

17. Here I am building on Laclau and Mouffe's (2014) discussion of the difference between relations of subordination and relations of oppression. The former are relations "in which an agent is subjected to the decisions of another," while the latter consist of "those relations of subordination which have transformed themselves into sites of antagonisms" (137–38).

18. Gramsci 1971, 178.

19. Gramsci 1971, 178.

20. Gramsci 1971, 178.

21. Hill 1972.

22. Bohstedt 2010.

23. LaDuke 2005.

24. Poppendieck 1999.

25. Kotz 1969.

26. Wright Edelman 2017.

27. Heynen 2009.

28. Wagner-Pacifici 1994.

29. The relationship between food security and food justice is often muddled. Yet many scholars and activists argue that food justice is the justice-oriented version of food security. This linear representation obfuscates the more important historical point that the antecedents to contemporary food justice are those movements, organizing, and activism that connect social justice considerations to food, regardless of terminology.

30. To access the digital archive of this magazine, visit the Farmworker Movement Documentation Project at University of California at San Diego, https://libraries.ucsd.edu/farmworkermovement/archives/#foodjustice.

31. Jessie Smith Noyes Foundation, n.d.

32. foodjustice.wikispaces.com 2008.

33. Bové and Dufour 2002; McMichael 2009.

34. Probyn 2000.

35. Meyer and Tarrow 1998. When used throughout this book, *social forces* refers to the constellation of particular combinations of discourses, symbols, norms, practices, organizational forms, and institutions that influence and are also the target of group behavior. They reflect a hegemony forged in some time and place that is nevertheless temporary and open to contestation and change.

36. Sitrin and Azzellini 2014; Castells 2015; della Porta 2015.

37. Engels 1940; Lenin 2002; Lukács 1971.

38. See, for instance, the work of Bhaskar (2008) on critical realism and Emirbayer (1997) and Donati (2010) on relational sociology to get a sense of the reverberations of dialectical thinking.

39. Boggs and Boggs 2008; Fraser 2013.

40. Marable 1983; Mies 1986.

41. For an explication of the importance of racial formation theory to understanding food justice as a racial project that confronts neoconservatism and neoliberalism, see Sbicca and Myers (2017).

42. Lefebvre 2009, 99; Laclau and Mouffe 2014.

43. Norrie 2010.

44. Boggs and Boggs 2008, 128.

45. Bevington and Dixon 2005; Khasnabish and Haiven 2014.

46. Burawoy 2005, 2008; Wright 2010.

47. Marx 1976b.

48. Žižek 1999; Rancière 2006.

49. Brenner and Theodore 2002; Harvey 2005.

50. Goldberg 2009; Lentin and Titley 2011; Bonilla-Silva 2013.

51. Bourdieu 1999.

52. Fukuyama 2006.

53. Mills 2000.

54. Laclau and Mouffe 2014.

55. Žižek 1999, 204.

56. Boggs and Boggs 2008.

57. Collins 2002.

58. Boggs 2011, 76.

59. See, for instance, books on solving problems in the food system by Pollan (2008), Winne (2010), and Hesterman (2012).

60. Schlosberg 2007; Agyeman 2013.

1. Inequality and Resistance

1. Allen 2008, 158.

2. Bourdieu 1999; Brenner and Theodore 2002; Harvey 2005; Wacquant 2009.

3. Omi and Winant 2015.

4. Bonilla-Silva 2013.

5. Bonilla-Silva 2013.

6. Saez and Zucman 2016.

7. Detention Watch Network 2015.

8. Hagler 2015.

9. Piven and Cloward 1979.

10. Calhoun 1993.

11. Laclau and Mouffe 2014, 137.

12. Piven and Cloward 1979.

13. Carson 1962; Gottlieb 2005; Taylor 2009.

14. McAdam and Snow 2010, 1.

15. Allen 2004.

16. Dimitri and Oberholtzer 2009; Cockrall-King 2012; Center for a Livable Future 2015; Low et al. 2015.

17. Martinez et al. 2010; Guthman 2011; Johnston and Baumann 2015; Low et al. 2015.

18. Myers and Sbicca 2015, 18.

19. Myers and Sbicca 2015, 19.

20. Allen 2004; Guthman 2004.

21. Wright 2010, 20.

22. In California, where there are many powerful social justice movements, there is high social movement spillover. This insight by social movement scholars focuses on the diffusion of activists, frames, organizations, strategies, and tactics. Large metropolitan areas with dense social movement networks offer particularly interesting cases to investigate how the food movement conceives of and practices food politics.

23. Sinclair 1906, 126.

24. Jayaraman 2013.

25. Food Chain Workers Alliance 2012.

26. Liu and Apollon 2011.

27. National Safety Council 2017.

28. Eisenhauer 2001; Short, Guthman, and Raskin 2007; Alkon and Norgaard 2009.

29. Sobal 2008.

30. Guthman 2011.

31. Nestle 2013.

32. McClintock 2011.

33. Carolan 2011.

34. Bookchin 1990, 24, 45–46.

35. Szasz 2007; Park and Pellow 2011.

36. Gottlieb and Joshi 2010.

37. Carolan 2011; Sage 2011.

38. Beyond Pesticides (http://www.beyondpesticides.org/) and other advocacy organizations have compiled, analyzed, and determined trends across the scientific research where federal and state governments and industry have avoided chronicling the harms associated with agricultural dependency on pesticides.

39. Harrison 2011.

40. Marx 1976a; Foster, Clark, and York 2010.

41. Foster 1999.

42. Worster 2004.

43. Gregory 1991.

44. The Northeast Sustainable Agriculture Working Group 2015.

45. Meyer and Whittier 1994.

46. Belasco 2014.

47. Goodwyn 1978.

48. Ali 2010.

49. Postel 2007.

50. Goodwyn 1978.

51. Ali 2010.

52. Hunt 2003.

53. Gerteis 2007.

54. Postel 2007.

55. Hild 2007.

56. Goodwyn 1978.

57. Smil 2001.

58. Commoner 1971.

59. Carson 1962, 64.

60. Brulle 2000; Gottlieb 2005.

61. Obach 2015.

62. Belasco 2014.

63. Guthman 2004.

64. Getz, Brown, and Shreck 2008.

65. Allen and Kovach 2000; Jaffee and Howard 2010.

66. Allen et al. 2003.

67. Oran and Kim 2013.

68. LeVaux 2013. The French dairy giant then purchased WhiteWave for $12.5 billion in 2017 to form DanoneWave.

69. Howard 2016.

70. Howard 2016.

71. Allen and Kovach 2000.

72. Guthman 2004.

73. Gray 2014; Sbicca 2015a.

74. McWilliams 1939; McWilliams 1999; Murray 1982.

75. Food Chain Workers Alliance 2012.

76. Ganz 2009.

77. London and Anderson 1970.

78. Ganz 2009.

79. Mitchell 1996.

80. Hall 2001.

81. Mitchell 1996.

82. Ganz 2009.

83. Ganz 2009.

84. Mitchell 2012.

85. Pulido 1996.

86. Walker 2004.

87. The AFL-CIO formed in 1955 and is the largest federation of unions in the United States.

88. Martin 2003; Rodman et al. 2016.

89. Joseph 2006.

90. Ture and Hamilton 1992.

91. Self 2005.

92. Abu-Lughod 2007.

93. Bloom and Martin 2013.

94. For a full list of Black Panther Party Community programs, see https://web.stanford.edu/group/blackpanthers/programs.shtml.

95. Heynen 2009.

96. Alkon 2012; Sbicca 2012; Broad 2016.

97. The Black Panther Intercommunal News Service, July 8, 1972.

98. Mares and Peña 2010; McCutcheon 2011.

99. Kropotkin 1943.

100. Van Deburg 1992.

101. Churchill and Vander Wall 2002.

102. Major 1971, 300.

103. Taylor 2013.

104. Gramsci 1971, 185.

105. Wright 2010.

106. Guthman 2004.

107. Mitchell 1996; Ganz 2009.

108. Wright 2010, 25.

109. Churchill and Vander Wall 2002; Austin 2008.

110. Guthman 2008a; Bradley and Herrera 2016.

111. Walker 2004, 302.

112. Mitchell 1996; Ganz 2009.

113. Kelley 2002, ix.
114. Guthman 2008b.
115. Taylor 1989.

2. Opposing the Carceral State

1. The number of formerly incarcerated people working with Planting Justice is accurate as of April 2016.
2. This is accurate as of April 2016.
3. Söderback, Söderström, and Schälander 2004; Pudup 2008; Jiler 2006; McKay 2011.
4. Oshinsky 1996; Solomon et al. 2004.
5. McKay 2011; Gilbert 2012; Sbicca 2016.
6. Mandela 1994, 476.
7. Gilmore 2007, 247.
8. Civil Eats 2016.
9. Wacquant 2009; Carson 2014; Cadieux and Slocum 2015.
10. Pager 2007; Alexander 2012; Feagin 2014.
11. See, for instance, Herbert 1997; van Hoven Sibley 2008; Hipp et al. 2010.
12. Starr, Fernandez, and Scholl 2011.
13. Gilmore 2007; Pager 2007; Wacquant 2009.
14. Duxbury 2012; BondGraham and Winston 2015.
15. See California Department of Justice (2014) for further details. The ratio of violent versus property crimes in 2014 was roughly 3:17. Official statistics kept by the California Department of Justice do not include drug crimes, only drug arrests.
16. Open Budget Oakland n.d.
17. BondGraham and Winston 2013.
18. Armaline, Sanchez, and Correia 2014.
19. Woods 2006.
20. Matier 2014.
21. BondGraham and Winston 2012.
22. BondGraham and Winston 2014.
23. Hyatt 2014a.
24. Hyatt 2014b. For a summary of the so-called Riders scandal, which cost Oakland $11 million, see Monmaney (2000).
25. KTVU 2011.
26. Artz 2015a.
27. Bloom and Martin 2013.
28. Artz 2015b.
29. Jones 2012.

30. Gammon 2012.

31. Wakefield and Uggen 2010.

32. Glaze and Kaeble 2014.

33. Petersilia 2003; Travis 2005; Goff et al. 2007; Pager 2007.

34. Mollison 1988, ix.

35. Permaculture design and certification, which are growing in popularity among urban agriculturalists, usually requires taking an expensive course. The apprentice model is generally a for-profit model running a person anywhere from about $500 to upward of $2,000 depending on the length of the course and requirements for on-site learning. For a decolonizing approach to permaculture, see Watson (2016).

36. Alkon 2012.

37. To offer everyone on staff a position on the board requires that at least 50 percent of the board be financially disinterested.

38. The board has varied in size, from the low to upper twenties. As of winter 2018, it sat at twenty-one people. The board consists of people traditionally ignored: immigrants, people of color, and young people. Given the corporate culture of many nonprofits, there is an assumption that to join a board requires that you are a bigwig in your respective professional area.

39. As of spring 2016, there was an expectation that board members contribute four volunteer hours a month, regularly attend board of directors meetings, join at least one committee, and become a monthly sustainer at a minimum of five dollars a month. Board members remind each other of these commitments, which most meet or exceed, but when people are busy or face extenuating circumstances, there is respect for life's demands.

40. Light in Prison 2015.

41. Shabazz 2015.

42. Shabazz 2015.

43. Cacho 2012.

44. New York Times Editorial Board 2013.

45. Light in Prison n.d.

46. Zakaria 2012.

47. Irwin 2004.

48. Petersilia 2008; Pew Center on the States 2011. According to a report by the California Department of Corrections and Rehabilitation (2014), the recidivism rate for former prisoners tracked over a three-year period has fluctuated between 67 and 61 percent for people released between 2002 and 2009. However, the recidivism rate for those released since 2010 has declined, perhaps due to the Assembly Bill 109.

49. Bell 2016a.

50. Glaze and Kaeble 2014.

NOTES TO CHAPTER 2 · **209**

51. Shabazz 2015.
52. Petersilia 2003.
53. Bell 2016b.
54. Pager 2007; Russell-Brown 2009.
55. Petersilia 2003.
56. Cacho 2012.
57. Bradley and Herrera 2016; Cadieux and Slocum 2015.
58. These budget statistics are true as of April 2016. The budget is now likely different because Planting Justice acquired the entire Rolling River Nursery catalog and now runs a large nursery on its farm in El Sobrante.
59. Planting Justice n.d.
60. Alexander 2012, 186.
61. Zehr 1990; Wright 1996; Marshall 1999.
62. Johnstone 2013.
63. Walgrave 2013.
64. Opsal 2012; LeBel et al. 2015.
65. White and Graham 2015, 3.
66. Graham and White 2015; Hynes 1996; Pudup 2008.
67. Kaplan 1995; Saldivar-Tanaka and Krasny 2004; Söderback, Söderström, Elisabeth Schälander 2004.
68. Hayes-Conroy and Martin 2010.
69. Deane 2016a.
70. See, for instance, Bradley and Galt (2014) on the work of Dig Deep Farms & Produce.
71. Gibson-Graham 1996; Wright 2010; Omi and Winant 2015.
72. Opsal 2012.
73. Lebel, Richie, and Maruna 2015.
74. Pathways to Resilience includes The Green Life, Earthseed Consulting, Planting Justice, Wildheart Gardens, Impact Hub Oakland, United Roots, and Sustainability Economies Law Center.
75. Pathways to Resilience n.d.
76. Thomas and Starhawk n.d. As of April 2017, there were 1,060 signatories.
77. Pellow 2014.
78. One of the leaders of the Pathways to Resilience program helped start the Black Permaculture Network. Its solidarity statement links racial, economic, food, and environmental justice struggles: http://blackpermaculturenetwork.org/solidarity-statement/.
79. Maruna 2011.
80. Planting Justice 2014.
81. Uggen 1999; Maruna 2001.
82. Deane 2016.

83. See, for instance, Baker (2004), who talks about "food citizenship."
84. Levkoe 2006.
85. Uggen, Manza, and Behrens 2004.
86. Incarcerated Workers Organizing Committee 2016; Vongkiatkajorn 2016.
87. Bell 2016a.
88. Levin 2015.
89. Levin 2015.
90. Gottlieb and Joshi 2010; Sbicca 2012, 2014; Cadieux and Slocum 2015; Hislop 2015.
91. See the collection of comments from leaders of color about Black Lives Matter movement (Civil Eats 2016).
92. Guthman 2011.

3. Taking Back the Economy

1. Walker 2004.
2. Harrison 2011.
3. Mitchell 1996; Arcury and Quandt 2007.
4. Pachirat 2011.
5. Cummins and Murphy 2013; Food Chain Workers Alliance 2015.
6. Galt 2013; McClintock 2014; Sbicca 2015b; Sbicca 2015a; Ekers et al. 2016.
7. Jayaraman 2013.
8. Walker 2004.
9. Walmart captures about 25 percent of the food retail market share. Statista n.d.
10. Knupfer 2013; Obach 2015.
11. Complete California food cooperative statistics are hard to come by. At a national level, there is a growth in worker-run cooperatives (Palmer 2015). I exclude agricultural cooperatives from my discussion because they tend to operate within the confines of the conventional food system (Deller et al. 2009).
12. Guthman 2004; Harrison 2011; Holmes 2013; Jayaraman 2013; Gray 2014.
13. Holt-Giménez 2017.
14. Sbicca 2015a.
15. Guthman 2008b; Harrison 2011.
16. Myers and Sbicca 2015.
17. Lefebvre 1991; Massey 1994.
18. San Diego Roots Sustainable Food Project n.d.
19. Hoppe 2014.
20. Hoppe 2014. Seventy to 80 percent of small family farm labor is carried out by the operator and spouse, while almost 70 percent of family farms have a negative operating profit margin.

21. Guthman 2004; Walker 2004.

22. Galt 2013; Ekers et al. 2016; Weiler, Otero, and Wittman 2016.

23. Despite a thriving $30 million sector—there are more registered organic farms in San Diego County than in any county in the United States, producing over 125 different crops, although most acreage is dedicated to citrus—San Diego's food movement tends to overlook the concerns of farmworkers. Two major reports and assessments of San Diego's conventional and alternative food systems overlook how the political economy of migrant farmworkers impacts their future sustainability (Ellsworth and Feenstra 2010; San Diego Food System Working Group 2011). Such reports smooth over the racialized agricultural political economy and immigration regime: most farmworkers speak Spanish and come from Mexico, many of whom are likely undocumented (Aguirre International 2005; Nabhan et al. 2012). There is also heavy reliance on this labor: as of 2007, the number of paid farmworkers (21,114) doubled that of growers (Ellsworth and Feenstra 2010).

24. Hale et al. 2011. Taylor and Lovell 2014.

25. According to 2013 990-EZ tax returns, San Diego Roots received $99,365 in contributions, gifts, grants, and similar donations and made $70,619 from farm school tuition, produce sales, and other fee-for-service work. The organization's long-term goal is to increase its programs' revenue generation. For information on 2014, see http://www.sandiegoroots.org/report-2014/2014-ye-report.html# financial.

26. The farm ran a surplus in 2013–15.

27. The Luiseño called Palomar Mountain "Paauw."

28. Ekers et al. 2016.

29. San Diego Roots estimates that it reached twenty-five hundred people at Wild Willow Farm in 2013.

30. Gibson-Graham 2006a, xii.

31. Dailey 2010.

32. EricVideo 2010.

33. Sbicca 2015b; Ekers et al. 2016.

34. Goodman and Redclift 2002; Fitzgerald 2003.

35. Cadieux and Slocum 2015.

36. At the time of my fieldwork, the internship was being transformed into a farm school requiring tuition. As of April of 2017, these courses cost anywhere from $400 to $1,400, depending on the course length and time commitment. According to San Diego Roots tax documents between 2012 and 2016, the tuition made the organization less reliant on grants.

37. McClintock (2014) has made similar observations about urban agriculture.

38. Marsden and Franklin 2013; Levkoe and Wakefield 2014.

39. Sbicca 2014.

40. Mares and Alkon 2011.

41. In *A Postcapitalist Politics,* Gibson-Graham argue that their deconstructive project of dethroning the centrality of capitalism requires "reading for difference rather than dominance" (2006b, xxxi–xxxii).

42. Slocum and Cadieux 2015.

43. See, for example, Mitchell 1996; Guthman 2004; Walker 2004.

44. Title VII of the Civil Rights Act of 1964 prohibits employment discrimination based on race, color, religion, sex, or national origin.

45. This history is reconstructed from an internally circulated history drafted in 1989 by the former president of UFCW 770, Ricardo F. Icaza.

46. Union Facts n.d.

47. Milkman 2006.

48. Tomassetti, Tilly, and Zipperer 2012.

49. Mordechay 2011; Flaming and Burns 2012; Los Angeles County Economic Development Corporation 2012; Los Angeles 2020 Commission 2013; Bergman 2014; Mordechay 2014; Economic Roundtable 2015.

50. Robinson 1983.

51. Marable 1983.

52. Young 2000, 123.

53. Young 2000, 146.

54. The makeup of the executive office reflects the leadership as of March 2018.

55. The makeup of the field representatives reflects the leadership as of March 2018.

56. Gray 2014.

57. Gray 2014.

58. Guthman 2004; Alkon and McCullen 2011; Sbicca 2015a.

59. Aronowitz 2014.

60. Guthman 2011.

61. Schneider 2015.

62. Carolan 2011; Nestle 2013.

63. Food Chain Workers Alliance 2012.

64. The Walmart 1%. The endnote accompanying these numbers reads, "Sam Walton's dependents include his children Alice, Rob, and Jim, as well as Christy, who is the widow of his late son John. This calculation is based on share ownership data from Walmart's 2014 filings and Walmart's declared FY 2015 dividend of $1.92 per share."

65. National Employment Law Project (2012). High-wage and mid-wage jobs account for 79 percent of all lost jobs during the Great Recession, while 58 percent of the recovery growth is in lower-wage jobs. Two of the ten lower-wage jobs with the biggest recovery growth are food-chain workers, who also happen to be

the lowest-paid workers. Corporate profit margins are at an all-time high, while wages as a percent of the economy are at an all-time low.

66. Schnaiberg 1980; Obach 2004; Mayer 2008.

67. See Howard (2016) for a robust discussion of corporate concentration throughout the food system.

68. Bassford et al. 2010.

69. This narrative is largely confirmed by the work of historian Nelson Lichtenstein (2009).

70. Coleman-Jensen et al. 2012.

71. California Food Policy Advocates 2014.

72. Food Chain Workers Alliance and Solidarity Research Cooperative 2016.

73. Food Chain Workers Alliance and Solidarity Research Cooperative 2016.

74. Los Angeles Food Policy Council 2013.

75. Los Angeles Food Policy Council 2013.

76. Guzick 1984, 422.

77. Sbicca 2017.

78. The Service Employees International Union has built on United Food and Commercial Workers' efforts with their support for the fast food worker–led Fight for $15 movement. However, United Food and Commercial Workers seems to be changing its tactical approach to Walmart because the energy generated by its strikes and OUR Walmart organizing has not produced the level of desired changes. For some insightful commentary, see Moberg (2015) and Olney (2015).

79. Moberg 2015.

80. Olney 2015.

81. Wattenhofer 2016. Walmart leaving Los Angeles's Chinatown was part of a nationwide closure of Neighborhood Markets, which have faced stiff opposition and also proven incapable of competing in urban, and more liberal, markets.

82. Eisenhauer (2001) explains the process of supermarket redlining and its effects on public health.

83. Xu 2014.

84. Hassanein 2003; Lyson 2004; Levkoe 2006.

85. Los Angeles Food Policy Council n.d.

86. Since March of 2018 there are coalitions or governments in Austin, Chicago, Cincinnati, Colorado (along the Front Range), Madison, New York, Oakland, Twin Cities (Minneapolis/St. Paul), and San Francisco that have established or are looking to establish a Good Food Purchasing Program.

87. Delwiche et al. 2014.

88. Heynen 2010; Barnard 2016.

4. Immigration Food Fights

1. Food Chain Workers Alliance 2012; Nicholls 2013; Terriquez 2015.

2. "Social boundaries are objectified forms of social differences manifested in unequal access to and unequal distribution of resources (material and non-material) and social opportunities" (Lamont and Molnár 2002, 168).

3. Public Policy Institute of California n.d.

4. Wilson and Lee 2013.

5. Food Chain Workers Alliance 2012; Food Chain Workers Alliance and Solidarity Research Cooperative 2016.

6. Food Chain Workers Alliance 2012; Food Chain Workers Alliance and Solidarity Research Cooperative 2016.

7. Knobloch 1996.

8. Gates 2014.

9. For a full discussion of the idea of imported colonialism, see Ngai (2014).

10. Guthman 2004; Slocum 2007; Alkon and McCullen 2011.

11. Holmes 2013.

12. Berlin 2000; Churchill 2002; Du Bois 1935 [1992]; Grinde and Johansen 1995; Jaimes 1992; Marable 1983

13. Harrison and Lloyd 2012; Ribas 2016.

14. As the eminent sociologist and social movement scholar Charles Tilly (2005) has shown, interpersonal transactions are the "stuff" that produces social inequality and maintains social boundaries. That is, there is an ongoing relational process that we can dissect in order to understand the (re)formation of collective identities. The corollary for noncitizens is that social boundaries can also be political boundaries that undermine democratic inclusion and participation. Some of the most innovative spaces, then, for political mobilization are those that bridge citizenship boundaries, which expand the scope of social movement mobilization and tactics. Developing new narratives of "us" and "them" is imperative to breaching social boundaries.

15. One need look no further than the internship and apprenticeship list housed by A National Sustainable Agriculture Assistance Program to get a sense of how typical nonwage exchange is to the spread of organic farming: https://attra.ncat.org/attra-pub/internships/.

16. Chavez 2013.

17. Harrison and Lloyd 2013; Sbicca 2015a; Holmes 2013.

18. Massey, Durand, and Malone 2002; Fitting 2011; Massey and Pren 2012.

19. McMillan 2016.

20. Guthman 2004.

21. Carolan 2011.

22. Fisher and Gottlieb 2014; Reynolds 2015; Sbicca 2015b.

23. Trioni 2012; Meissner et al. 2013.

24. There are about ninety-three thousand uniformed military personnel in the San Diego metropolitan area, which is one of the highest concentrations of military personnel in the United States. There are also seven military bases in San Diego County. San Diego also has a very large defense industry, which includes Northrop Grumman, Parsons, Cubic, Raytheon, General Dynamics NASSCO, General Atomics, Lockheed Martin, and Boeing. For more details, see Kyle (2012) and San Diego Military Advisory Council (2014).

25. Mayhew 2003, 306.

26. Nienstedt 2003.

27. Davis, Miller, and Mayhew 2003.

28. Chavez 2013; Nevins 2002.

29. San Diego Immigrant Rights Consortium, Justice Overcoming Boundaries of San Diego County, and American Civil Liberties Union of San Diego & Imperial Counties (2007).

30. Such conditions are well documented (e.g., a documentary exposé called *The Invisible Mexicans of Deer Canyon* by John Carlos Frey).

31. Martinez and Núñez-Alvarez 2009.

32. San Diego Immigrant Rights Consortium, Justice Overcoming Boundaries of San Diego County, and American Civil Liberties Union of San Diego & Imperial Counties 2007.

33. Health and Human Services Agency 2011. In line with most San Diegans' geographical imagination, I cut statistics for Coronado from the South Bay and added them to Central San Diego.

34. Meissner et al. 2013.

35. Pastor et al. 2012.

36. Jayaraman 2014.

37. Pachirat 2011; Ribas 2016.

38. Artz 2012; Kandel 2006.

39. Barboza 2001; Gee and Bunge 2017.

40. One of the ongoing tensions is that there is a belief among some in the business community that the labor movement is only interested in increasing its membership and dues. Adding fuel to this line of reasoning was the recent, albeit ultimately futile, attempt by the Los Angeles Federation of Labor to put in an exemption to the $15 minimum wage increase for unionized employers. Business opponents thought this would encourage more businesses to allow for collective bargaining to avoid the minimum wage law (Jamison, Zahniser, and Alpert Reyes 2015).

41. Pastor et al. 2012.

42. Castles and Davidson 2000; Chavez 2013.

43. Milkman 2006.

44. Milkman 2000.

45. Ganz 2009.

46. Watts 2002.

47. Milkman 2000; Rosenfeld and Kleykamp 2009; Ness 2010.

48. Sipchen 1997.

49. Watts 2002.

50. Icaza 1994.

51. Pastor 2015.

52. Snow, Zurcher, and Ekland-Olson 1980; Van Dyke 2003.

53. Aronowitz 2014. Even after the AFL-CIO Executive Council passed a resolution in 2000 calling for the repeal of employment eligibility verification required under the Immigration Reform and Control Act, a position it once supported, a number of UFCW locals opposed the changes. However, along with many in the labor movement who recognized the importance of immigrants to the movement's future, UFCW 770 had independently adopted this position.

54. Cleeland 1999; Usheroff 2014.

55. United Food and Commercial Workers 2015.

56. City News Service 2016.

57. United Food and Commercial Workers 2016.

58. United Food and Commercial Workers Local 770 2015; Vasquez 2015.

59. See, for example, the work of Milkman (2006) on immigrant labor organizing in Los Angeles and Bacon (2008) on the conditions that produce the need to organize immigrant labor pools.

60. Bacon 2009.

61. City of Vernon n.d.

62. Compa 2004. Meatpacking is a dangerous job. According to the U.S. Bureau of Labor Statistics, more than one in ten workers experience illness or injury, which is double the rate for all manufacturing.

63. Scholars and organizers that produce citizen science have documented the discrimination that immigrants and workers of color experience when it comes to promotions. See, for instance, Pachirat (2011); Food Chain Workers Alliance (2012); Ribas (2015).

64. These worker centers never came to fruition.

65. McDonnell 2009.

66. Bacon 2009.

67. A new union rep came in after the mass firing in hopes that he would build a new relationship with the workforce. According to this rep, he does not know much about the mass firing and maintains that the union supported the fired workers as much as possible. Yet there are unions such as UNITE HERE that successfully win clauses in collective bargaining agreements that prevent the use of E-verify and I-9 that might prevent immigrants from getting jobs (Lee 2015).

68. General Brotherhood of Workers n.d.
69. Catron 2013; Kazin 2013; Sarlin 2013.
70. These eight million workers make up 5 percent of the labor force (Krogstad and Passel 2015).
71. United Food and Commercial Workers 2013.
72. Lind 2016.
73. Lazare 2016; Mascaro 2016.
74. Lazare 2016.
75. Washington Post Staff 2015.
76. I reconstruct Salvador's story from my interview with him in 2012 and his testimony in a video posted to Facebook and YouTube (Planting Justice 2016b).
77. Spener 2009.

5. Radicalizing Food Politics

1. Pollan 2010; Allen 2012.
2. Myers and Sbicca 2015.
3. Flammang 2009.
4. I have critiqued the food focus of food justice practice in greater detail elsewhere (Sbicca 2016a).
5. Mouffe 2000.
6. Broad 2016; Alkon and Guthman 2017.
7. Rancière 2010, 54.
8. May 2008.
9. Boggs 2011, 76.
10. Rancière 2001.
11. Rancière 2001.
12. Guthman 2008b; Mares and Alkon 2011; McClintock 2014. Harrison (2011) offers an incisive analysis of the food movement in relation to using the regulatory power of the state to monitor and reduce the toxic outcomes associated with pesticide drift.
13. Omi and Winant 2014.
14. Laclau and Mouffe 2014, 118.
15. Sbicca and Myers 2017.
16. Laclau and Mouffe 2014, 128.
17. Tattersall 2010.
18. Fine 2006.
19. Gabriel 2006, 2008.
20. Fine 2006.
21. UFCW was part of CTW when I was conducting initial fieldwork. However, after eight years, they left in 2013 to rejoin the American Federation of Labor

and Congress of Industrial Organizations (AFL-CIO). This period with CTW was a time of increased labor organizing and confrontational labor politics.

22. Baker 1985.

23. Greenwalt 1985.

24. Sbicca 2017.

25. Cho et al. 2012.

26. Warehouse Workers United and Cornelio 2011.

27. The coalition Good Jobs L.A. consists of workers in Service Employees International Union, the Brotherhood Crusade, Coalition for Humane Immigrant Rights of Los Angeles, Community Coalition, Consejo de Federaciones Mexicanas en Norteamérica, and the Korean Resource Center.

28. Lo and Jacobson 2011. Interestingly, UFCW 770, WWU, and OUR Walmart are all part of the Food Chain Workers Alliance. They represent some of the major organizations working together to fight for economic justice in the food system.

29. Lopez 2014.

30. Tarrow 2011, 9.

31. Gottlieb and Joshi 2010, 233.

32. Domhoff 2005.

33. Tarrow 2011, 9.

34. Burke 2015.

35. Insight Garden Program n.d.(a).

36. Insight Garden Program n.d.(b).

37. Planting Justice 2016a.

38. Douglass 2016, 288.

39. Alexander 2012.

40. Douglass 2016, 288–89.

41. See chapter 2, note 48.

42. Deane 2015.

43. Deane 2015.

44. This is the counterfactual point also made by Schurman and Munro (2010) regarding the global anti-biotechnology movement. Even though the movement has not won every battle, were they not to have engaged in confrontational politics and fought to eliminate, label, and otherwise slow down biotechnology, there would be a much greater market presence of genetically modified organisms. I have also made a similar point in an article about the significance of the confrontational politics used by UFCW 770 and its food justice allies in Los Angeles (Sbicca 2017).

45. Garzo Montalvo 2015, 126.

46. Garzo Montalvo 2015, 127–128.

47. Slocum 2007; Guthman 2008a; Alkon and McCullen 2011.

48. Iverson 2007.

49. Reynolds 2015.

50. Bonilla-Silva 2013.

51. An edited volume on food justice by Alkon and Agyeman (2011) offers many ways in which people of color use their communities' assets to strive for racial and economic justice.

52. In the educational context, see Yosso (2005).

53. Morier (2015). In case I will be misinterpreted, I think that social welfare programs are necessary to maintain an adequate standard of living for all. However, without major restructuring of the economy that eliminates the need for social welfare programs, there cannot be true economic justice and racial justice.

54. Castells 1983.

55. Gelderloos 2013, 31.

56. Gelderloos 2013, 31.

57. Reger, Myers, and Einwohner 2008.

58. White 2017.

59. Araiza 2014.

60. Dorceta Taylor (2000) has convincingly demonstrated that a commitment to social justice helps bring differently situated interests and movements, say, regarding class, gender, and race, to fight for environmental justice. There are similar processes taking place across left urban social movements (Harvey 1996), particularly with regard to the framing of problems and solutions (Snow et al. 1986).

61. Sbicca 2012.

62. Liwanag 2013.

63. For an example of the political and social importance of Mexican and Central American cultural foodways, see Mares and Peña (2010).

64. Boggs 2010.

65. For more details on the history and consequences of NAFTA on Mexican farmers and subsequent migration patterns to the United States, see Martin (2005) and Fernández-Kelly and Massey (2007).

66. Boggs 2010.

67. Freire 2000, 49–50.

68. Freire 2000, 49–50.

69. Nevins 2002; Chavez 2013.

70. Nienstedt 2003.

71. Jacobs 1980; Hames-Garcia 2004; Davis 2005; CR10 Publications Collective 2008; Berger 2014a; Berger 2014b; Pellow 2014.

72. Sbicca 2016; Sbicca and Myers 2017.

73. Deane 2016b.

74. Sbicca 2012.

75. Slocum and Cadieux 2015.

76. Minkoff-Zern 2012; Aptekar 2015.

77. Laclau and Mouffe 2014, 168.

78. Laclau and Mouffe 2014, 168.

79. Cairns and Johnston (2015) offer a compelling intersectional analysis focused on food and femininity that speaks to the social embeddedness of race, class, gender, and sexuality within the realm of cooking, shopping for food, and working in alternative food initiatives.

Conclusion

1. As Hislop (2015) has shown in his study of the food justice movement in the United States, there are many different articulations and actions that people take under the banner of food justice.

2. Gramsci 1971, 276.

3. Boggs and Boggs 2008, 208.

4. The Movement for Black Lives n.d.

5. Climate Justice Alliance n.d.

6. Dream Defenders n.d.

7. Day of Dinners 2017.

8. Johnston, Biro, and MacKendrick 2009.

9. Guthman 2004; Born and Purcell 2006.

10. Hinrichs and Allen 2008.

11. Anguelovski 2015a, 2015b.

12. Boggs and Boggs 2008: xxxiv–xxxv.

13. Gottlieb 2001, 231.

14. Allen 2004. There was little money made available for "community food projects" during this five-year period (up to $1,000,000 the first year and up to $2,500,000 the remaining four years). Also, this money went to "private non-profits," which carry out valuable work but avoid solving the problems perpetrated by the rest of the Farm Bill that they are reacting to. Discursively, however, "community food security" changed how some people understand food system problems and solutions and practically made money available to expand the grassroots reach of the food movement.

15. Winders 2009.

16. Allen 2004.

17. Regardless of whether one views this system in terms of a supply chain, a network of some sort, or a system of intersecting systems (hydrological, economic, social, etc.), there is a sophisticated degree of interdependency between many moving parts that brings food to our tables.

18. Klein 2017.

19. Bittman et al. 2014.

20. For a brief overview of this Twitter chat, see https://storify.com/ucsusa /national-food-policy-tweetchat. You can also go to Twitter and put in the hashtag #NFPTalk and read through the conversation, which took place on December 3, 2014.

21. WKKF (WK_Kellogg_Fdn) 2014.

22. Ghaziani 2008.

23. Mouffe 2000; Laclau and Mouffe 2014.

24. Concerned Scientists (UCSUSA) 2014.

25. Bittman 2014; Pollan 2014.

26. Rodriguez (5RO5) 2014c; Rodriguez (5RO5) 2014c. The Growing Food and Justice for All Initiative, which grew out of the work of Will Allen and Growing Power in Milwaukee, Wisconsin, started hosting The Gathering in 2008 to highlight the assets and needs of low-income communities and communities of color and to build solidarity across social difference.

27. Rodriguez (5RO5) 2014b.

28. Nowhere is this patchwork approach more obvious than in the guise of food policy councils. Recent reviews of food policy councils (e.g., Harper et al. 2009; Scherb, Frattarolli, and Pollack 2012; Chen, Clayton, and Palmer 2015) suggest that there is important work taking place at a city and sometimes statewide level, but that it varies dramatically from place to place. This partially reflects different needs in different places, but also it shows a lack of attention to some major areas of concern such as labor practices.

29. Mooney, Tanaka, and Ciciurkaite 2014.

30. Klein 2017.

31. For text of the speech, see the online encyclopedia kept by Stanford University: kingencyclopedia.stanford.edu.

32. Beyond the Moment 2017.

33. Lake Research Partners and Bellwether Research and Consulting 2015.

34. There was also a letter opposing Puzder that a coalition consisting of Corporate Accountability International, Food Chain Workers Alliance, Friends of the Earth, and Real Food Media drafted and sent out to the food movement. Over one hundred food and farm organizations signed this letter before it was sent to every senator.

35. O'Keefe and Marte 2017.

36. McAdam 1999.

37. Allen 2004, 187.

38. Johnson and Monke 2014; Lilliston 2014.

39. Johns Hopkins Center for a Livable Future 2017.

40. Center for Agriculture and Food Systems at Vermont Law School and Harvard Law School Food Law and Policy Clinic 2017.

222 · NOTES TO CONCLUSION

41. Center for Agriculture and Food Systems at Vermont Law School and Harvard Law School Food Law and Policy Clinic 2017.

42. Center for Agriculture and Food Systems at Vermont Law School and Harvard Law School Food Law and Policy Clinic 2017.

43. For example, see Harrison 2017 on the failure of federal agencies to implement environmental justice.

44. Allen 2004.

45. Institute for Agriculture and Trade Policy 2012b.

46. Institute for Agriculture and Trade Policy 2012a.

47. Institute for Agriculture and Trade Policy 2012b.

48. I derive these policy categories from the *Principles of Food Justice* as well as from other food justice and food movement convergences, including The Gathering conferences and the national food policy Twitter chat. They also reflect policy arenas that intersect with other social justice movements.

49. Kerssen and Brent 2017.

50. Penniman 2017.

51. Havens and Roman Alcalá 2016.

52. McClintock 2018.

53. Planting Justice was able to raise $104,000 to build a nursery and aquaponics farm on a marginal piece of land next to the 880 freeway in deep east Oakland. Although Planting Justice will still work the site, as of March 2018, this land is in the process of being turned over to the Sogorea Tè Land Trust to decolonize land by officially recognizing Ohlone ancestral claims.

54. Gilbert, Wood, and Sharp 2002.

55. Rodman et al. 2016.

56. Howard 2016.

57. Pothukuchi and Kaufman 1999; Lyson 2004; Carolan 2011; Green and Haines 2015.

58. Collins 2010.

59. This is a nonexhaustive list of what might constitute a community.

60. Low et al. 2015.

61. Kurtz 2015.

62. Guthman 2011; Hatch 2016.

63. Poppendieck 1999; Fisher 2017.

64. Robl 2014.

65. Holt-Giménez and Patel 2009.

66. To understand the spirit of this treaty, the food-related article reads in part, "The States Parties to the present Covenant, recognizing the fundamental right of everyone to be free from hunger, shall take, individually and through international co-operation, the measures, including specific programmes, which are needed. . . . (b) Taking into account the problems of both food-importing and

food-exporting countries, to ensure an equitable distribution of world food supplies in relation to need."

67. McClintock 2011; Sbicca 2017.

68. Guthman 2011.

69. Sbicca 2012; Bradley and Herrera 2016; Broad 2016.

70. Goodman, DuPuis, and Goodman 2012.

71. White 2011.

72. Incite! Women of Color against Violence 2007.

73. Reynolds 2015.

74. Incite! Women of Color against Violence 2007.

75. Sbicca 2015b.

76. Pulido, Kohl, and Cotton 2016.

77. Piven and Cloward 1979.

78. Per the work of Gibson-Graham (2006), this might include solidarity economies in the guise of cooperative enterprises, noncapitalist forms of land control and use, noncommodified forms of labor, and free schools, all of which could help prefigure more just social relations around food.

Appendix

1. Engels 1998, 48.

2. Freire 2000, 49.

3. For insight from other food scholars who have grappled with this question as well, see Reynolds and Cohen (2016) and Levkoe et al. (2016).

4. I offer more details of my research approach in Sbicca 2015c.

5. Bookchin 1990, 170–71.

Bibliography

Abu-Lughod, Janet L. 2007. *Race, Space, and Riots in Chicago, New York, and Los Angeles*. New York: Oxford University Press.

Aguirre International. 2005. *The California Farm Labor Force: Overview and Trends from the National Agricultural Workers Survey*. Burlingame, Calif.: Aguirre International.

Agyeman, Julian. 2013. *Introducing Just Sustainabilities: Policy, Planning, and Practice*. London: Zed Books.

Alexander, Michelle. 2012. *The New Jim Crow: Mass Incarceration in the Age of Colorblindness*. New York: New Press.

Ali, Omar H. 2010. *In the Lion's Mouth: Black Populism in the New South, 1886–1900*. Jackson: University Press of Mississippi.

Alkon, Alison Hope. 2012. *Black, White, and Green: Farmers Markets, Race, and the Green Economy*. Athens: University of Georgia Press.

Alkon, Alison Hope, and Julian Agyeman. 2011. *Cultivating Food Justice: Race, Class, and Sustainability*. Cambridge, Mass.: MIT Press.

Alkon, Alison Hope, and Julie Guthman. 2017. *The New Food Activism: Opposition, Cooperation, and Collective Action*. Berkeley: University of California Press.

Alkon, Alison Hope, and Christie Grace McCullen. 2011. "Whiteness and Farmers Markets: Performances, Perpetuations . . . Contestations?" *Antipode* 43 (4): 937–59.

Alkon, Alison Hope, and Kari Marie Norgaard. 2009. "Breaking the Food Chains: An Investigation of Food Justice Activism." *Sociological Inquiry* 79 (3): 289–305.

Allen, Patricia. 2004. *Together at the Table: Sustainability and Sustenance in the American Agrifood System*. University Park: Pennsylvania State University Press.

Allen, Patricia. 2008. "Mining for Justice in the Food System: Perceptions, Practices, and Possibilities." *Agriculture and Human Values* 25 (2): 157–61.

Allen, Patricia, Margaret FitzSimmons, Michael Goodman, and Keith Warner. 2003. "Shifting Plates in the Agrifood Landscape: The Tectonics of Alternative Agrifood Initiatives in California." *Journal of Rural Studies* 19 (1): 61–75.

Allen, Patricia, and Martin Kovach. 2000. "The Capitalist Composition of Organic: The Potential of Markets in Fulfilling the Promise of Organic Agriculture." *Agriculture and Human Values* 17 (3): 221–32.

Allen, Will. 2012. *The Good Food Revolution: Growing Healthy Food, People, and Communities.* New York: Gotham Books.

Anguelovski, Isabelle. 2015a. "Alternative Food Provision Conflicts in Cities: Contesting Food Privilege, Injustice, and Whiteness in Jamaica Plain, Boston." *Geoforum* 58: 184–94.

Anguelovski, Isabelle. 2015b. "Healthy Food Stores, Greenlining and Food Gentrification: Contesting New Forms of Privilege, Displacement and Locally Unwanted Land Uses in Racially Mixed Neighborhoods." *International Journal of Urban and Regional Research* 39 (6): 1209–30.

Aptekar, Sofya. 2015. "Visions of Public Space: Reproducing and Resisting Social Hierarchies in a Community Garden." *Sociological Forum* 30 (1): 209–27.

Araiza, Lauren. 2014. *To March for Others: The Black Freedom Struggle and the United Farm Workers.* Philadelphia: University of Pennsylvania Press.

Arcury, Thomas A., and Sara A. Quandt. 2007. "Delivery of Health Services to Migrant and Seasonal Farmworkers." *Annual Review of Public Health* 28: 345–63.

Armaline, William T., Claudio G. Vera Sanchez, and Mark Correia. 2014. " 'The Biggest Gang in Oakland': Re-Thinking Police Legitimacy." *Contemporary Justice Review* 17 (3): 375–99.

Aronowitz, Stanley. 2014. *The Death and Life of American Labor: Toward a New Worker's Movement.* New York: Verso.

Artz, Georgeanne M. 2012. "Immigration and Meatpacking in the Midwest." *Choices* 27 (2). http://choicesmagazine.org/.

Artz, Matthew. 2015a. "Oakland Faces $28 Million Budget Shortfall." *Contra Costa Times,* February. http://www.contracostatimes.com/.

Artz, Matthew. 2015b. "Settlement Reached in Occupy Oakland Mass Arrest." *Mercury News,* January 13. https://www.mercurynews.com.

Austin, Curtis J. 2008. *Up against the Wall: Violence in the Making and Unmaking of the Black Panther Party.* Fayetteville: University of Arkansas Press.

Bacon, David. 2008. *Illegal People: How Globalization Creates Migration and Criminalizes Immigrants.* Boston: Beacon Press.

Bacon, David. 2009. "Criminals because We Worked." *Truthout,* June 20. http://truth-out.org/.

Baker, Bob. 1985. "Tentative Market Pact Falls Apart: Butchers Reject Offer; Teamsters Strongly Approve It." *Los Angeles Times,* December 27. http://articles.latimes.com/1985-12-27/news/mn-25417_1_meat-cutter.

Baker, Lauren E. 2004. "Tending Cultural Landscapes and Food Citizenship in Toronto's Community Gardens." *Geographical Review* 94 (3): 305–25.

Barboza, David. 2001. "Meatpackers' Profits Hinge on Pool of Immigrant Labor." *New York Times,* December 21. http://www.nytimes.com/2001/12/21 /us/meatpackers-profits-hinge-on-pool-of-immigrant-labor.html.

Barnard, Alex. 2016. *Freegans: Diving into the Wealth of Food Waste in America.* Minneapolis: University of Minnesota Press.

Bassford, Nicky, Lark Galloway-Gilliam, Gwendolyn Flynn, and CHC Food Resource Development Workgroup. 2010. *Food Desert to Food Oasis: Promoting Grocery Store Development in South Los Angeles.* Los Angeles: Community Health Councils.

Belasco, Warren J. 2014. *Appetite for Change: How the Counterculture Took On the Food Industry.* 2nd ed. Ithaca, N.Y.: Cornell University Press.

Bell, Maurice. 2016a. "Call to Action (Statement in Solidarity with the National Prison Strike 2016)." Planting Justice, Oakland, Calif. June 13. http://plant ingjustice.org/blog/call-to-action-statement-in-solidarity-with-the-national -prison-strike-2016.

Bell, Maurice. 2016b. Response to "Why Are Federal Prisoners Disproportionately People of Color? How Does That Affect Discussions around Reforms?" by Nazgol Ghandnoosh. https://medium.com/.

Berger, Dan. 2014a. *Captive Nation: Black Prison Organizing in the Civil Rights Era.* Chapel Hill: University of North Carolina Press.

Berger, Dan. 2014b. *The Struggle Within: Prisons, Political Prisoners, and Mass Movements in the United States.* Oakland, Calif.: PM Press.

Bergman, Ben. 2014. "Los Angeles Job Growth Falling behind Other Cities, Study Says." *Southern California Public Radio,* September 11, 2014. http:// www.scpr.org/.

Berlin, Ira. 2000. *Many Thousands Gone: The First Two Centuries of Slavery in North America.* Cambridge, Mass.: Harvard University Press.

Bevington, Douglas, and Chris Dixon. 2005. "Movement-Relevant Theory: Rethinking Social Movement Scholarship and Activism." *Social Movement Studies* 4 (3): 185–208.

Beyond the Moment. 2017. "FAQ." https://beyondthemoment.org/faq/.

Bhaskar, Roy. 2008. *Dialectic: The Pulse of Freedom.* New York: Routledge.

Bittman, Mark (bittman). 2014. "A6. I see it as part of the same struggle. You can't make big changes in food w/o making big changes in many other things. #NFPTALK." Twitter, December 3, 20:33 UTC.

Bittman, Mark, Michael Pollan, Olivier De Schutter, and Ricardo Salvador. 2017. "Food and More: Expanding the Movement for the Trump Era." *Civil Eats* (blog). http://civileats.com/.

Bittman, Mark, Michael Pollan, Ricardo Salvador, and Olivier De Schutter. 2014. "How a National Food Policy Could Save Millions of American Lives." *Washington Post,* November 7.

The Black Panther Intercommunal News Service. July 8, 1972. https:// ceimlarchives4blackpanther.wordpress.com/.

Bloom, Joshua, and Waldo E. Martin Jr. 2013. *Black against Empire: The History and Politics of the Black Panther Party.* Berkeley: University of California Press.

Boggs, Grace Lee. 2010. "Thinking Dialectically about Solidarity." *MROnline,* December 20. https://mronline.org/2010/12/20/thinking-dialectically-about -solidarity/.

Boggs, Grace Lee. 2011. *The Next American Revolution: Sustainable Activism for the Twenty-First Century.* Berkeley: University of California Press.

Boggs, James, and Grace Lee Boggs. 2008. *Revolution and Evolution in the Twentieth Century.* New York: Monthly Review Press.

Bohstedt, John. 2010. *The Politics of Provisions: Food Riots, Moral Economy, and Market Transition in England, c. 1550–1850.* Burlington, Vt.: Ashgate.

BondGraham, Darwin, and Ali Winston. 2012. "The High Costs of Outsourcing Police." *East Bay Express,* August 8. https://www.eastbayexpress.com/oakland /the-high-costs-of-outsourcing-policeandnbsp/Content?oid=3306199.

BondGraham, Darwin, and Ali Winston. 2013. "Throwing More Money at Police." *East Bay Express,* May 29. https://www.eastbayexpress.com/oak land/throwing-more-money-at-police/Content?oid=3560590.

BondGraham, Darwin, and Ali Winston. 2014. "Oakland Cops Think City Is Too Liberal." *East Bay Express,* January 29. https://www.eastbayexpress .com/oakland/oakland-cops-think-city-is-too-liberal/Content?oid=3823283.

BondGraham, Darwin, and Ali Winston. 2015. "OPD Still Appears to Be Tar- geting Blacks." *East Bay Express,* February 4. http://www.eastbayexpress .com/oakland/opd-still-appears-to-be-targeting-blacks/Content?oid=4185368.

Bonilla-Silva, Eduardo. 2013. *Racism without Racists: Color-Blind Racism and the Persistence of Racial Inequality in the United States.* 4th ed. New York: Rowman & Littlefield.

Bookchin, Murray. 1990. *Remaking Society.* New York: Black Rose Books.

Born, Branden, and Mark Purcell. 2006. "Avoiding the Local Trap Scale and Food Systems in Planning Research." *Journal of Planning Education and Research* 26 (2): 195–207.

Bourdieu, Pierre. 1999. *Acts of Resistance: Against the Tyranny of the Market.* New York: New Press.

Bové, José, and François Dufour. 2002. *The World Is Not for Sale: Farmers against Junk Food.* New York: Verso.

Bradley, Katharine, and Ryan E. Galt. 2014. "Practicing Food Justice at Dig Deep Farms & Produce, East Bay Area, California: Self-Determination as a Guiding Value and Intersections with Foodie Logics." *Local Environment* 19 (2): 172–86.

Bradley, Katharine, and Hank Herrera. 2016. "Decolonizing Food Justice: Naming, Resisting, and Researching Colonizing Forces in the Movement." *Antipode* 48 (1): 97–114.

Brenner, Neil, and Nik Theodore. 2002. "Cities and the Geographies of 'Actually Existing Neoliberalism.'" *Antipode* 34 (3): 349–79.

Broad, Garrett. 2016. *More Than Just Food: Food Justice and Community Change.* Berkeley: University of California Press.

Brulle, Robert J. 2000. *Agency, Democracy, and Nature: The US Environmental Movement from a Critical Theory Perspective.* Cambridge, Mass.: MIT Press.

Bullard, Robert. 2014. "State of the Environmental Justice Executive Order after 20 Years." Dr. Robert Bullard: Father of Environmental Justice (website), January 1. http://drrobertbullard.com/2014/01/01/state-of-the-environmental-justice-executive-order-after-20-years-3/.

Bullard, Robert D. 2000. *Dumping in Dixie: Race, Class, and Environmental Quality.* Boulder, Colo.: Westview Press.

Bulwa, Demian. 2010. "NAACP Focuses on Officer-Involved Shootings." *SF Gate,* December 17. https://www.sfgate.com/bayarea/article/NAACP-focuses-on-officer-involved-shootings-2453109.php.

Burawoy, Michael. 2005. "American Sociological Association Presidential Address: For Public Sociology." *British Journal of Sociology* 56 (2): 259–94.

Burawoy, Michael. 2008. "Open Letter to C. Wright Mills." *Antipode* 40 (3): 365–75.

Burke, Sarah. 2015. "Growing a Better System." *East Bay Express,* April 15. https://www.eastbayexpress.com/oakland/growing-a-better-system/Content?oid=4247622.

Cacho, Lisa Marie. 2012. *Social Death: Racialized Rightlessness and the Criminalization of the Unprotected.* New York: New York University Press.

Cadieux, Kirsten Valentine, and Rachel Slocum. 2015. "What Does It Mean to Do Food Justice?" *Journal of Political Ecology* 22: 1–26.

Cairns, Kate, and Josée Johnston. 2015. *Food and Femininity.* New York: Bloomsbury Academic.

Calhoun, Craig. 1993. "'New Social Movements' of the Early Nineteenth Century." *Social Science History* 17 (3): 385–427.

California Department of Corrections and Rehabilitation. 2014. *2013 Outcome Evaluation Report.* Sacramento, Calif.: Office of Research.

California Department of Justice. 2014. *Crime in California 2014.* Sacramento, Calif.: California Justice Information Services Division, Bureau of Criminal Information and Analysis, Criminal Justice Statistics Center.

California Food Policy Advocates. 2014. *Nutrition & Food Insecurity Profiles.* July 30, 2014 Update. http://cfpa.net/county-profiles.

Carolan, Michael. 2011. *The Real Cost of Cheap Food.* New York: Earthscan.

Carson, E. Ann. 2014. *Prisoners in 2013.* Washington, D.C.: U.S. Department of Justice, Office of Justice Programs, Bureau of Justice Statistics.

Carson, Rachel. 1962. *Silent Spring.* Boston: Houghton Mifflin.

Castells, Manuel. 1983. *The City and the Grassroots: A Cross-Cultural Theory of Urban Social Movements.* Berkeley: University of California Press.

Castells, Manuel. 2015. *Networks of Outrage and Hope: Social Movements in the Internet Age.* 2nd ed. Cambridge: Polity.

Castles, Stephen, and Alastair Davidson. 2000. *Citizenship and Migration: Globalization and the Politics of Belonging.* New York: Routledge.

Catron, Peter. 2013. "Immigrant Unionization through the Great Recession." *American Sociological Review* 78 (2): 315–32.

Center for Agriculture and Food Systems at Vermont Law School and Harvard Law School Food Law and Policy Clinic. 2017. *Blueprint for a National Food Strategy.* Burlington, Vt.

Center for a Livable Future. 2015. *Food Policy Councils in North America: 2015 Trends.* Baltimore: John Hopkins University Press.

Chavez, Leo. 2013. *The Latino Threat: Constructing Immigrants, Citizens, and the Nation.* 2nd ed. Stanford, Calif.: Stanford University Press.

Chen, Wei-ting, Megan L. Clayton, and Anne Palmer. 2015. *Community Food Security in the United States: A Survey of the Scientific Literature.* Baltimore: Johns Hopkins Center for a Livable Future.

Cho, Eunice Hyunhye, Anastasia Christman, Maurice Emsellem, Catherine K. Ruckelshaus, and Rebecca Smith. 2012. *Chain of Greed: How Walmart's Domestic Outsourcing Produces Everyday Low Wages and Poor Working Conditions for Warehouse Workers.* New York: National Employment Law Project.

Churchill, Ward. 2002. *Struggle for the Land: Native North American Resistance to Genocide, Ecocide, and Colonization.* San Francisco: City Lights Books.

Churchill, Ward, and Jim Vander Wall. 2002. *Agents of Repression: The FBI's Secret Wars against the Black Panther Party and the American Indian Movement.* Cambridge, Mass.: South End Press.

City News Service. 2016. "El Super Ordered to Pay Workers as Labor Dispute Continues." *Long Beach Press-Telegram,* April 8. https://www.presstelegram.com/2016/04/08/el-super-ordered-to-pay-workers-as-labor-dispute-continues/.

City of Vernon. n.d. "Vernon Means Business." Accessed February 2, 2016. http://www.cityofvernon.org/business.

Civil Eats. 2016. "Leaders of Color Discuss Structural Racism and White Privilege in the Food System." *Civil Eats* (blog). http://civileats.com/.

Cleeland, Nancy. 1999. "Nonunion-Market Trend Attacked." *Los Angeles Times,* September 29. http://articles.latimes.com/1999/sep/29/business/fi-15204.

Climate Justice Alliance. n.d. "Who is CJA?" http://www.ourpowercampaign.org/cja.

Cockrall-King, Jennifer. 2012. *Food and the City: Urban Agriculture and the New Food Revolution.* Amherst, N.Y.: Prometheus Books.

Coleman-Jensen, Alisha, Mark Nord, Margaret Andrews, and Steven Carlson. 2012. *Household Food Security in the United States in 2011.* ER R-141, U.S. Department of Agriculture, Economic Research Service.

Collins, Patricia Hill. 2002. *Black Feminist Thought: Knowledge, Consciousness, and the Politics of Empowerment.* 2nd ed. New York: Routledge.

Collins, Patricia Hill. 2010. "The New Politics of Community." *American Sociological Review* 75 (1): 7–30.

Commoner, Barry. 1971. *The Closing Circle: Nature, Man, and Technology.* New York: Knopf.

Compa, Lance A. 2004. *Blood, Sweat, and Fear: Workers' Rights in US Meat and Poultry Plants.* New York: Human Rights Watch.

Concerned Scientists (UCSUSA). 2014. "Q6: From Wendy in Boulder, CO: Do you see a national food policy as our best mechanism for addressing issues of equity? How? #NFPtalk." Twitter, December 3, 20:30 UTC.

CR10 Publications Collective. 2008. *Abolition Now! Ten Years of Strategy and Struggle against the Prison Industrial Complex.* Oakland, Calif.: AK Press.

Cummins, Ronnie, and Dave Murphy. 2013. "Exposed: How Whole Foods and the Biggest Organic Foods Distributor Are Screwing Workers." *Alternet,* January 31. https://www.alternet.org/food/exposed-how-whole-foods-and-biggest-organic-foods-distributor-are-screwing-workers.

Dailey, Keli. 2010. "Ups and Downs on the Farm Scene." *San Diego Union-Tribune,* October 13. http://www.sandiegouniontribune.com/sdut-ups-and-downs-farm-scene-2010oct13-story.html.

Davis, Angela Y. 2005. *Abolition Democracy: Beyond Empire, Prisons, and Torture.* New York: Seven Stories Press.

Davis, Mike, Jim Miller, and Kelly Mayhew. 2003. *Under the Perfect Sun: The San Diego Tourists Never See.* New York: New Press.

Day of Dinners. 2017. *Host Guidebook.* Project of Dream Defenders. Toolkit adapted from guides written by Women's March and The People's Supper.

Deane, Nicole. 2015. "We Don't Need Another Jail—Part 1." Planting Justice, Oakland, Calif. November 17. http://plantingjustice.org/blog/we-dont-need-another-jail-part-i.

Deane, Nicole. 2016a. "Changing California's 65% Recidivism Rate Is 100% Possible." Planting Justice, Oakland, Calif. March 8. http://plantingjustice.org/blog/changing-california.

Deane, Nicole. 2016b. "Planting Justice." *Ignited Magazine,* April 29. https://ignitedmag.wordpress.com/2016/04/29/planting-justice/.

Della Porta, Donatella. 2015. *Social Movements in Times of Austerity: Bringing Capitalism Back into Protest Analysis.* Cambridge: Polity.

Deller, Steven, Ann Hoyt, Brent Hueth, and Reka Sundaram-Stukel. 2009. *Research on the Economic Impact of Cooperatives.* Madison: University of Wisconsin Center for Cooperatives.

Delwiche, Alexa, Colleen McKinney, Lindsey Day Farnsworth, Samuel Pratsch, and Martin Mailkey. 2014. *The Good Food Purchasing Pledge: A Case Study Evaluation & Year One Progress Update.* Los Angeles: Los Angeles Food Policy Council.

Detention Watch Network. 2015. *Banking on Detention: Local Lockup Quotas & the Immigrant Dragnet.* Washington, D.C.: Detention Watch Network.

Dimitri, Carolyn, and Lydia Oberholtzer. 2009. "Marketing US Organic Foods: Recent Trends from Farms to Consumers." *Economic Information Bulletin* 58. Washington, D.C.: United States Department of Agriculture.

Domhoff, William. 2005. "Basics of Studying Power." https://www2.ucsc.edu /whorulesamerica/methods/studying_power.html.

Donati, Pierpaolo. 2010. *Relational Sociology: A New Paradigm for the Social Sciences.* New York: Routledge.

Douglass, Frederick. 2016. *The Portable Frederick Douglass.* New York: Penguin Books.

Dream Defenders. n.d. "About." Accessed June 27, 2017. http://www.dream defenders.org/about.

Du Bois, W. E. B. [1935] 1992. *Black Reconstruction in America, 1860–1880.* New York: Free Press.

Duxbury, Micky. 2012. "Lessening the Impact of Incarceration on Oakland—An Overview." *Oakland Local,* June 26. http://www.csus.edu/calst /Journalism%20Awards/Latest%20Journalism%20Award%20entries/Print -Special%20Enterprise/Mickey%20Duxbury/Impact%20of%20Incarceration %20on%20Oakland_Series%20of%205.pdf.

Economic Roundtable. 2015. *Los Angeles Rising: A City That Works for Everyone.* Los Angeles: UCLA Labor Center; UCLA Institute for Research on Labor and Employment.

Eisenhauer, Elizabeth. 2001. "In Poor Health: Supermarket Redlining and Urban Nutrition." *GeoJournal* 53 (2): 125–33.

Ekers, Michael, Charles Z. Levkoe, Samuel Walker, and Bryan Dale. 2016. "Will Work for Food: Agricultural Interns, Apprentices, Volunteers, and the Agrarian Question." *Agriculture and Human Values* 33 (3): 705–20.

Ellsworth, Susan, and Gail Feenstra. 2010. *Assessing the San Diego County Food System: Indicators for a More Food Secure Future.* Davis, Calif.: Sustainable Agriculture Research and Education Program, and Agricultural Sustainability Institute.

Emirbayer, Mustafa. 1997. "Manifesto for a Relational Sociology." *American Journal of Sociology* 103 (2): 281–317.

Engels, Friedrich. 1940. *Dialectics of Nature*. New York: International Publishers.

Engels, Friedrich. 1998. *Socialism: Utopian and Scientific*. New York: International Publishers.

EricVideo. 2010. "La Milpa Organica Farm Last Days Part II." *YouTube*, September 22. https://www.youtube.com/watch?v=Wvzux754JVM.

Feagin, Joe R. 2014. *Racist America: Roots, Current Realities, and Future Reparations*. New York: Routledge.

Fernández-Kelly, Patricia, and Douglas S. Massey. 2007. "Borders for Whom? The Role of NAFTA in Mexico-US Migration." *ANNALS of the American Academy of Political and Social Science* 610 (1): 98–118.

Fine, Janice Ruth. 2006. *Worker Centers: Organizing Communities at the Edge of the Dream*. Ithaca, N.Y.: Cornell University Press.

Fisher, Andrew. 2017. *Big Hunger: The Unholy Alliance between Corporate America and Anti-hunger Groups*. Cambridge, Mass.: MIT Press.

Fisher, Andy, and Robert Gottlieb. 2014. "Who Benefits When Walmart Funds the Food Movement?" *Civil Eats* (blog). http://civileats.com/.

Fitting, Elizabeth. 2011. *The Struggle for Maize: Campesinos, Workers, and Transgenic Corn in the Mexican Countryside*. Durham, N.C.: Duke University Press.

Fitzgerald, Deborah Kay. 2003. *Every Farm a Factory: The Industrial Ideal in American Agriculture*. New Haven, Conn.: Yale University Press.

Flaming, Daniel, and Patrick Burns. 2012. *Getting to Work: Unemployment and Economic Recovery in Los Angeles*. Los Angeles: Economic Roundtable.

Flammang, Janet A. 2009. *The Taste for Civilization: Food, Politics, and Civil Society*. Urbana: University of Illinois Press.

Food Chain Workers Alliance. 2012. *The Hands That Feed Us: Challenges and Opportunities for Workers along the Food Chain*. Los Angeles.

Food Chain Workers Alliance. 2015. *Walmart at the Crossroads: The Environmental and Labor Impact of Its Food Supply Chain*. Los Angeles.

Food Chain Workers Alliance and Solidarity Research Cooperative. 2016. *No Piece of the Pie: U.S. Food Workers in 2016*. Los Angeles: Food Chain Workers Alliance.

foodjustice.wikispaces.com. 2008. "Food Justice Manifesto Updated October 2008." http://web.archive.org/web/20101009135242/http://foodjustice.wiki spaces.com/Food+Justice+Manifesto+Updated+october+2008.

Foster, John Bellamy. 1999. "Marx's Theory of Metabolic Rift: Classical Foundations for Environmental Sociology." *American Journal of Sociology* 105 (2): 366–405.

Foster, John Bellamy, Brett Clark, and Richard York. 2010. *The Ecological Rift: Capitalism's War on the Earth*. New York: Monthly Review Press.

Fraser, Nancy. 2013. *Fortunes of Feminism: From State-Managed Capitalism to Neoliberal Crisis.* London: Verso.

Freire, Paulo. 2000. *Pedagogy of the Oppressed.* 30th Anniversary Edition. New York: Bloomsbury Academic.

Fukuyama, Francis. 2006. *The End of History and the Last Man.* New York: Free Press.

Gabriel, Jackie. 2006. "Organizing *The Jungle:* Industrial Restructuring and Immigrant Unionization in the American Meatpacking Industry." *Journal of Labor and Society* 9 (3): 337–59.

Gabriel, Jackie. 2008. "Si, Se Puede: Organizing Latino Immigrant Workers in South Omaha's Meatpacking Industry." *Journal of Labor Research* 29 (1): 68–87.

Galt, Ryan E. 2013. "The Moral Economy Is a Double-Edged Sword: Explaining Farmers' Earnings and Self-Exploitation in Community-Supported Agriculture." *Economic Geography* 89 (4): 341–65.

Gammon, Robert. 2012. "School Closures Drive Oakland School Board Races." *East Bay Express,* October 24. https://www.eastbayexpress.com/oakland/school-closures-drive-oakland-school-board-races/Content?oid=3372036.

Ganz, Marshall. 2009. *Why David Sometimes Wins: Leadership, Organization, and Strategy in the California Farm Worker Movement.* New York: Oxford University Press.

Garzo Montalvo, M. F., and Zandi, H. 2011. "The Modern/Colonial Food System in a Paradigm of War." Planting Justice, Oakland, Calif. http://plantingjustice.org/resources/food-justice-research/the-moderncolonial-food-system-in-a-paradigm-of-war/.

Garzo Montalvo, Marcelo Felipe. 2015. "To the American Food Justice Movements: A Critique That Is Also an Offering." *Journal of Agriculture, Food Systems, and Community Development* 5 (4): 125–29.

Gates, Henry Louis, Jr. 2014. "How Many Slaves Landed in the US?" *The Root,* January 6. https://www.theroot.com/how-many-slaves-landed-in-the-us-1790873989.

Gee, Kelsey, and Jacob Bunge. 2017. "Tighter Refugee Rules Seen Squeezing Meat Companies." *Wall Street Journal,* January 28. https://www.wsj.com/articles/tighter-refugee-rules-seen-squeezing-meat-companies-1485617876.

Gelderloos, Peter. 2013. *The Failure of Nonviolence: From the Arab Spring to Occupy.* Seattle, Wash.: Left Bank Books.

General Brotherhood of Workers. n.d. Accessed April 7, 2017. http://www.generalbrotherhoodofworkers.org/.

Gerteis, Joseph. 2007. *Class and the Color Line: Interracial Class Coalition in the Knights of Labor and the Populist Movement.* Durham, N.C.: Duke University Press.

Getz, Christy, Sandy Brown, and Aimee Shreck. 2008. "Class Politics and Agricultural Exceptionalism in California's Organic Agriculture Movement." *Politics & Society* 36 (4): 478–507.

Ghaziani, Amin. 2008. *The Dividends of Dissent: How Conflict and Culture Work in Lesbian and Gay Marches on Washington.* Chicago: University of Chicago Press.

Gibson-Graham, J. K. 2006a. *The End of Capitalism (As We Knew It): A Feminist Critique of Political Economy.* Minneapolis: University of Minnesota Press.

Gibson-Graham, J. K. 2006b. *A Postcapitalist Politics.* Minneapolis: University of Minnesota Press.

Gilbert, Emily. 2012. "Five Urban Garden Programs That Are Reaching Inmates and At-Risk Populations." World Watch Institute. http://blogs.worldwatch.org/.

Gilbert, Jess, Spencer D. Sharp, and Gwen Sharp. 2002. "Who Owns the Land? Agricultural Land Ownership by Race/Ethnicity." *Rural America* 17 (2): 55–62.

Gilmore, Ruth Wilson. 2007. *Golden Gulag: Prisons, Surplus, Crisis, and Opposition in Globalizing California.* Berkeley: University of California Press.

Glaze, Lauren E. and Danielle Kaeble. 2014. "Correctional Populations in the United States, 2013." Washington D.C.: U.S. Department of Justice, Office of Justice Programs, Bureau of Justice Statistics.

Goff, Ashley, Emmeline Rose, Suzanna Rose, and David Purves. 2007. "Does PTSD Occur in Sentenced Prison Populations? A Systematic Literature Review." *Criminal Behaviour and Mental Health* 17 (3): 152–62.

Goldberg, David Theo. 2009. *The Threat of Race: Reflections on Racial Neoliberalism.* Malden, Mass.: Blackwell.

Goodman, David, E. Melanie DuPuis, and Michael K. Goodman. 2012. *Alternative Food Networks: Knowledge, Practice, and Politics.* New York: Routledge.

Goodman, David, and Michael Redclift. 2002. *Refashioning Nature: Food, Ecology and Culture.* New York: Routledge.

Goodwyn, Lawrence. 1978. *The Populist Moment: A Short History of the Agrarian Revolt in America.* New York: Oxford University Press.

Gottlieb, Robert. 2001. *Environmentalism Unbound: Exploring New Pathways for Change.* Cambridge, Mass.: MIT Press.

Gottlieb, Robert. 2005. *Forcing the Spring: The Transformation of the American Environmental Movement.* Washington, D.C.: Island Press.

Gottlieb, Robert, and Anupama Joshi. 2010. *Food Justice.* Cambridge, Mass.: MIT Press.

Graham, Hannah, and Rob White. 2015. *Innovative Justice.* New York: Routledge.

Gramsci, Antonio. 1971. *Selections from the Prison Notebooks.* New York: International Publishers.

Gray, Margaret. 2014. *Labor and the Locavore: The Making of a Comprehensive Food Ethic.* Berkeley: University of California Press.

Green, Gary Paul, and Anna Haines. 2015. *Asset Building and Community Development.* 4th ed. Thousand Oaks, Calif.: Sage.

Greenwalt, Frank. 1985. "Meat Cutters End Strike—Union Members OK 3-Year Pact on 2nd Vote." *Daily News of Los Angeles,* December 30.

Gregory, James Noble. 1991. *American Exodus: The Dust Bowl Migration and Okie Culture in California.* New York: Oxford University Press.

Grinde, Donald A., and Bruce Elliott Johansen. 1995. *Ecocide of Native America: Environmental Destruction of Indian lands and Peoples.* San Francisco: Clear Light Books.

Guthman, Julie. 2004. *Agrarian Dreams: The Paradox of Organic Farming in California.* Berkeley: University of California Press.

Guthman, Julie. 2008a. "'If They Only Knew': Colorblindness and Universalism in California Alternative Food Institutions." *The Professional Geographer* 60 (3): 387–97.

Guthman, Julie. 2008b. "Neoliberalism and the Making of Food Politics in California." *Geoforum* 39 (3): 1171–83.

Guthman, Julie. 2011. *Weighing In: Obesity, Food Justice, and the Limits of Capitalism.* Berkeley: University of California Press.

Guzick, William J. 1984. "Employer Neutrality Agreements: Union Organizing under a Nonadversarial Model of Labor Relations." *Industrial Relations Law Journal* 6 (4): 421–80.

Hagler, Jamal. 2015. "8 Facts You Should Know about the Criminal Justice System and People of Color." Center for American Progress. https://www.americanprogress.org/.

Hale, James, Corrine Knapp, Lisa Bardwell, Michael Buchenau, Julie Marshall, Fahriye Sancar, and Jill S. Litt. 2011. "Connecting Food Environments and Health through the Relational Nature of Aesthetics: Gaining Insight through the Community Gardening Experience." *Social Science & Medicine* 72 (11): 1853–63.

Hall, Greg. 2001. *Harvest Wobblies: The Industrial Workers of the World and Agricultural Laborers in the American West, 1905–1930.* Corvallis: Oregon State University Press.

Hames-Garcia, Michael Roy. 2004. *Fugitive Thought: Prison Movements, Race, and the Meaning of Justice.* Minneapolis: University of Minnesota Press.

Harper, Alethea, Annie Shattuck, Eric Holt-Giménez, Alison Alkon, and Frances Lambrick. 2009. *Food Policy Councils: Lessons Learned.* Oakland, Calif.: Food First, Institute for Food and Development Policy.

Harrison, Jill Lindsey. 2011. *Pesticide Drift and the Pursuit of Environmental Justice.* Cambridge, Mass.: MIT Press.

Harrison, Jill Lindsey. 2017. "'We Do Ecology, not Sociology': Interactions among Bureaucrats and the Undermining of Regulatory Agencies' Environmental Justice Efforts." *Environmental Sociology* 3 (3): 197–212.

Harrison, Jill Lindsey, and Sarah E. Lloyd. 2012. "Illegality at Work: Deportability and the Productive New Era of Immigration Enforcement." *Antipode* 44 (2): 365–85.

Harrison, Jill Lindsey, and Sarah E. Lloyd. 2013. "New Jobs, New Workers, and New Inequalities: Explaining Employers' Roles in Occupational Segregation by Nativity and Race." *Social Problems* 60 (3): 281–301.

Harvey, David. 1996. *Justice, Nature and the Geography of Difference.* Oxford: Blackwell.

Harvey, David. 2005. *A Brief History of Neoliberalism.* Oxford: Oxford University Press.

Hassanein, Neva. 2003. "Practicing Food Democracy: A Pragmatic Politics of Transformation." *Journal of Rural Studies* 19 (1): 77–86.

Hatch, Anthony Ryan. 2016. *Blood Sugar: Racial Pharmacology and Food Justice in Black America.* Minneapolis: University of Minnesota Press.

Havens, Erin, and Antonio Roman Alcalá. 2016. *Land for Food Justice? AB 551 and Structural Change.* Land and Sovereignty Policy Brief #8, Summer 2016. Oakland, Calif.: Food First/Institute for Food and Development Policy.

Hayes-Conroy, Allison, and Deborah G. Martin. 2010. "Mobilising Bodies: Visceral Identification in the Slow Food movement." *Transactions of the Institute of British Geographers* 35 (2): 269–81.

Health and Human Services Agency. 2011. *San Diego County Demographics Profile by Region and Subregional Area.* County of San Diego, HHSA, Public Health Services, Community Health Statistics Unit.

Herbert, Steven Kelly. 1997. *Policing Space: Territoriality and the Los Angeles Police Department.* Minneapolis: University of Minnesota Press.

Hesterman, Oran B. 2012. *Fair Food: Growing a Healthy, Sustainable Food System for All.* New York: PublicAffairs.

Heynen, Nik. 2009. "Bending the Bars of Empire from Every Ghetto for Survival: The Black Panther Party's Radical Antihunger Politics of Social Reproduction and Scale." *Annals of the Association of American Geographers* 99 (2): 406–22.

Heynen, Nik. 2010. "Cooking up Non-violent Civil-Disobedient Direct Action for the Hungry: 'Food Not Bombs' and the Resurgence of Radical Democracy in the US." *Urban Studies* 47 (6): 1225–40.

Hild, Matthew. 2007. *Greenbackers, Knights of Labor, and Populists: Farmer-Labor Insurgency in the Late-Nineteenth-Century South.* Athens: University of Georgia Press.

Hill, Christopher. 1972. *The World Turned Upside Down: Radical Ideas during the English Revolution.* London: Temple Smith.

Hinrichs, C. Clare, and Patricia Allen. 2008. "Selective Patronage and Social Justice: Local Food Consumer Campaigns in Historical Context." *Journal of Agricultural and Environmental Ethics* 21 (4): 329–52.

Hipp, John R., Joan Petersilia, and Susan Turner. 2010. "Parolee Recidivism in California: The Effect of Neighborhood Context and Social Service Agency Characteristics." *Criminology* 48 (4): 947–79.

Hislop, Rasheed Salaam. 2015. "Reaping Equity: A Survey of Food Justice Organizations in the USA." MSc Thesis, University of California, Davis. Ann Arbor, Mich.: ProQuest LLC.

Holmes, Seth. 2013. *Fresh Fruit, Broken Bodies: Migrant Farmworkers in the United States.* Berkeley: University of California Press.

Holt-Giménez, Eric. 2017. *A Foodie's Guide to Capitalism: Understanding the Political Economy of What We Eat.* New York: Monthly Review Press.

Holt-Giménez, Eric, and Raj Patel. 2009. *Food Rebellions: Crisis and the Hunger for Justice.* Oakland, Calif.: Food First Books.

Hoppe, Robert A. 2014. *Structure and Finances of U.S. Farms: Family Farm Report, 2014 Edition.* Washington, D.C.: United States Department of Agriculture, Economic Research Service.

Howard, Philip. 2016. *Concentration and Power in the Food System: Who Controls What We Eat?* New York: Bloomsbury.

Hunt, James L. 2003. *Marion Butler and American Populism.* Chapel Hill: University of North Carolina Press.

Hurley, Andrew. 1995. *Environmental Inequalities: Class, Race, and Industrial Pollution in Gary, Indiana, 1945–1980.* Chapel Hill: University of North Carolina Press.

Hyatt, Abraham. 2014a. "Oakland's Most Decorated Officers Responsible for High Number of Brutality Lawsuits, Shootings." *SF Gate,* April 7. https://blog.sfgate.com/inoakland/2014/04/07/oaklands-most-decorated-officers-responsible-for-high-number-of-brutality-lawsuits-shootings/.

Hyatt, Abraham. 2014b. "Oakland Spent $74 Million Settling 417 Police Brutality Lawsuits." *SF Gate,* April 14. https://blog.sfgate.com/inoakland/2014/04/14/oakland-spent-74-million-settling-417-police-brutality-lawsuits-oakland-police-beat/.

Hynes, H. Patricia. 1996. *A Patch of Eden: America's Inner City Gardens.* White Water Junction, Vt.: Chelsea Green.

Icaza, Ricardo F. 1994. "Controversy over Prop. 187." *Los Angeles Times,* November 2.

Incarcerated Workers Organizing Committee. 2016. "Announcement of Nationally Coordinated Prisoner Workstoppage for Sept 9, 2016." https://iwoc.noblogs.org/.

Incite! Women of Color against Violence. 2007. *The Revolution Will Not Be Funded: Beyond the Non-profit Industrial Complex.* Cambridge, Mass.: South End Press.

Insight Garden Program. n.d.(a). "About Us." Berkeley, Calif. Accessed December 5, 2015. http://insightgardenprogram.org/about-us/.

Insight Garden Program. n.d.(b). "Meet Some of Our Graduates." Berkeley, Calif. Accessed December 5, 2015. http://insightgardenprogram.org/testimonials/.

Institute for Agriculture and Trade Policy. 2012a. "Moving Ahead on Food Justice." http://www.iatp.org/.

Institute for Agriculture and Trade Policy. 2012b. *Principles of Food Justice.* http://www.iatp.org/.

Irwin, John. 2004. *The Warehouse Prison: Disposal of the New Dangerous Class.* New York: Oxford University Press.

Iverson, Susan VanDeventer. 2007. "Camouflaging Power and Privilege: A Critical Race Analysis of University Diversity Policies." *Educational Administration Quarterly* 43 (5): 586–611.

Jacobs, James B. 1980. "The Prisoners' Rights Movement and Its Impacts, 1960–80." *Crime and Justice* 2: 429–70.

Jaffee, Daniel, and Philip H. Howard. 2010. "Corporate Cooptation of Organic and Fair Trade Standards." *Agriculture and Human Values* 27 (4): 387–99.

Jaimes, M. Annette. 1992. *The State of Native America: Genocide, Colonization, and Resistance.* Boston: South End Press.

Jamison, Peter, David Zahniser, and Emily Alpert Reyes. 2015. "L.A. Labor Leaders Seek Minimum Wage Exemption for Firms with Union Workers." *Los Angeles Times,* May 27. http://www.latimes.com/local/lanow/la-me-ln-los-angeles-minimum-wage-unions-20150526-story.html.

Jayaraman, Saru. 2013. *Behind the Kitchen Door.* Ithaca, N.Y.: Cornell University Press.

Jayaraman, Saru. 2014. *Shelved: How Wages and Working Conditions for California's Food Retail Workers Have Declined as the Industry Has Thrived.* Food Labor Research Center, University of California, Berkeley.

Jessie Smith Noyes Foundation. n.d. "Food Justice Manifesto." Accessed April 21, 2016. http://www.noyes.org/.

Jiler, James. 2006. *Doing Time in the Garden: Life Lessons through Prison Horticulture.* Oakland, Calif.: New Village.

Johns Hopkins Center for a Livable Future. 2017. *Food and Agriculture Policy Recommendations.* Baltimore, Md.

Johnson, Renée, and Jim Monke. 2014. *What Is the Farm Bill?* Washington, D.C.: Congressional Research Service.

Johnston, Josée, and Shyon Baumann. 2015. *Foodies: Democracy and Distinction in the Gourmet Foodscape.* 2nd ed. New York: Routledge.

Johnston, Josée, Andrew Biro, and Norah MacKendrick. 2009. "Lost in the Supermarket: The Corporate-Organic Foodscape and the Struggle for Food Democracy." *Antipode* 41 (3): 509–32.

Johnstone, Gerry. 2013. *Restorative Justice: Ideas, Values, Debates.* New York: Routledge.

Jones, Carolyn. 2012. "Oakland Begins $28 Million in Budget Cuts." *SF Gate,* January 26, 2012. https://www.sfgate.com/politics/article/Oakland-begins -28-million-in-budget-cuts-2710971.php.

Joseph, Peniel E. 2006. "Introduction: Toward a Historiography of the Black Power Movement." In *The Black Power Movement: Rethinking the Civil Rights-Black Power Era,* edited by P. Joseph, 1–26. New York: Routledge.

Kandel, William. 2006. "Meat-Processing Firms Attract Hispanic Workers to Rural America." *Amber Waves* 4 (3): 10–15.

Kaplan, Stephen. 1995. "The Restorative Benefits of Nature: Toward an Integrative Framework." *Journal of Environmental Psychology* 15 (3): 169–82.

Kazin, Michael. 2013. "How Labor Learned to Love Immigration." *New Republic,* May 13. https://newrepublic.com/article/113203/labor-and-immigration -how-unions-got-board-immigration-reform.

Kelley, Robin D. G. 2002. *Freedom Dreams: The Black Radical Imagination.* Boston: Beacon Press.

Kerssen, Tanya M., and Zoe Brent. 2017. "Grounding the US Food Movement: Bringing Land into Food Justice." In *The New Food Activism: Opposition, Cooperation and Collective Action,* edited by Alison Hope Alkon and Julie Guthman, 284–315. Berkeley: University of California Press.

Khasnabish, Alex, and Max Haiven. 2014. *The Radical Imagination: Social Movement Research in the Age of Austerity.* London: Zed Books.

Klein, Naomi. 2017. *No Is Not Enough: Resisting Trump's Shock Politics and Winning the World We Need.* Chicago: Haymarket Books.

Knobloch, Frieda. 1996. *The Culture of Wilderness: Agriculture as Colonization in the American West.* Chapel Hill: University of North Carolina Press.

Knupfer, Anne Meis. 2013. *Food Co-ops in America: Communities, Consumption, and Economic Democracy.* Ithaca, N.Y.: Cornell University Press.

Kotz, Nick. 1969. *Let Them Eat Promises.* New York: Doubleday.

Krogstad, Jens Manuel, and Jeffrey S. Passel. 2015. "5 Facts about Illegal Immigration in the U.S." Pew Research Center. http://www.pewresearch.org/.

Kropotkin, Peter. 1943. *The State: Its Historic Role.* London: Freedom Press.

KTVU. 2011. "Oakland Paying Out Extraordinary Police Abuse Settlements." http://www.ktvu.com/.

Kurtz, Hilda E. 2015. "Scaling Food Sovereignty: Biopolitics and the Struggle for Local Control of Farm Food in Rural Maine." *Annals of the Association of American Geographers* 105 (4): 859–73.

Kyle, Keegan. 2012. "Counting Military Jobs in San Diego: Fact Check." *Voice of San Diego,* August 7. https://www.voiceofsandiego.org/topics/news /counting-military-jobs-in-san-diego-fact-check.

Laclau, Ernesto, and Chantal Mouffe. 2014. *Hegemony and Socialist Strategy: Towards a Radical Democratic Politics.* New York: Verso.

LaDuke, Winona. 2005. *Recovering the Sacred: The Power of Naming and Claiming.* Cambridge, Mass.: South End Press.

Lake Research Partners and Bellwether Research and Consulting. 2015. "Food Policy Research Findings." Washington, D.C.: Lake Research Partners.

Lamont, Michèle, and Virág Molnár. 2002. "The Study of Boundaries in the Social Sciences." *Annual Review of Sociology* 28 (1): 167–95.

Lazare, Sarah. 2016. "Children Caught in Sweep as Feds Begin Mass Deportations." *Common Dreams.* http://www.commondreams.org/.

LeBel, Thomas P., Matt Richie, and Shadd Maruna. 2015. "Helping Others as a Response to Reconcile a Criminal Past: The Role of the Wounded Healer in Prisoner Reentry Programs." *Criminal Justice and Behavior* 42 (1): 108–20.

Lee, Esther Yu-Hsi. 2015. "Labor Unions Move to Protect Immigrants, Regardless of Legal Status." *Think Progress,* March 26. https://thinkprogress.org/labor-unions-move-to-protect-immigrants-regardless-of-legal-status-11576ac69da2/.

Lefebvre, Henri. 1991. *The Production of Space.* Malden, MA: Blackwell.

Lefebvre, Henri. 2009. *Dialectical Materialism.* Minneapolis: University of Minnesota Press.

Lenin, V. I. 2002. *Materialism and Empirio-Criticism: Critical Comments on a Reactionary Philosophy.* Honolulu, Hawaii: University Press of the Pacific.

Lentin, Alana, and Gavin Titley. 2011. *The Crises of Multiculturalism: Racism in a Neoliberal Age.* London: Zed Books.

LeVaux, Ari. 2013. "Carmel Valley-Born Earthbound Farm Sells to Massive WhiteWave Foods." *Monterey County Weekly,* December 12. http://www.montereycountyweekly.com/archives/2013/1212/carmel-valley-born-earthbound-farm-sells-to-massive-whitewave-foods/article_9dd92a3e-62ba-11e3-a977-0019bb30f31a.html.

Levin, Sam. 2015. "County to Spend More Money on Jails, Not Services." *East Bay Express,* January 28. http://www.eastbayexpress.com/oakland/county-to-spend-more-money-on-jails-not-services/Content?oid=4178787.

Levkoe, Charles Z. 2006. "Learning Democracy through Food Justice Movements." *Agriculture and Human Values* 23 (1): 89–98.

Levkoe, Charles Z., Nathan McClintock, Laura-Anne Minkoff-Zern, Amy K. Coplen, Jennifer Gaddis, Joann Lo, Felipe Tendick-Matesanz, and Anelyse M. Weiler. 2016. "Forging Links between Food Chain Labor Activists and Academics." *Journal of Agriculture, Food Systems, and Community Development* 6 (2): 129–42.

Levkoe, Charles Z., and Sarah Wakefield. 2014. "Understanding Contemporary Networks of Environmental and Social Change: Complex Assemblages within Canada's 'Food Movement.'" *Environmental Politics* 23 (2): 302–20.

Lichtenstein, Nelson. 2009. *The Retail Revolution: How Wal-Mart Created a Brave New World of Business.* New York: Picador.

Light in Prison. 2015. "True Life Story of the Men Returning Home Success-fully from San Quentin State Prison." *YouTube.* https://www.youtube.com/watch?v=x6AiepeiYME.

Light in Prison. n.d. "San Quentin State Prison (SQ)." Accessed February 13, 2016. https://lightinprison.org/.

Lilliston, Ben. 2014. "We Deserve More Than This Bad Farm Bill." Washington, D.C.: Institute for Agriculture and Trade Policy. http://www.iatp.org/.

Lind, Dara. 2016. "The Nationwide Immigration Raids Targeting Central American Families, Explained." *Vox.* https://www.vox.com/2015/12/28/10673452/deportation-central-american-immigrant-families.

Liu, Yen, Yvonne Yen, and Dominique Apollon. 2011. *The Color of Food.* Oakland, Calif.: Applied Research Center.

Liwanag, Mark. 2013. "On Planting Firmly—San Diego Roots Sustainable Food Project Documentary." *YouTube.* Accessed April 23, 2014. https://www.youtube.com/watch?v=Z3rbNwEjTIw.

Lo, Joann, and Ariel Jacobson. 2011. "Human Rights from Field to Fork: Improving Labor Conditions for Food-Sector Workers by Organizing across Boundaries." *Race/Ethnicity: Multidisciplinary Global Contexts* 5 (1): 61–82.

London, Joan, and Henry Pope Anderson. 1970. *So Shall Ye Reap.* New York: Crowell.

Lopez, Ricardo. 2014. "Workers Reach $21-Million Settlement against Wal-Mart, Warehouses." *Los Angeles Times,* May 14. http://www.latimes.com/business/la-fi-wal-mart-warehouse-workers-20140515-story.html.

Los Angeles County Economic Development Corporation. 2012. "LAEDC Urges the Los Angeles City Council to Phase-out Gross Receipts Business Tax." Press release, April 25. https://laedc.org/wp-content/uploads/2012/04/LAEDCStatement_BTAC.pdf.

Los Angeles Food Policy Council. 2013. *Los Angeles Food System Snapshot.* http://goodfoodla.org/.

Los Angeles Food Policy Council. n.d. "Objectives: Good Food for All Goals." http://goodfoodla.org/objectives/good-food-for-all-goals/.

Los Angeles 2020 Commission. 2013. *A Time for Truth.* Los Angeles.

Low, Sarah A., Aaron Adalja, Elizabeth Beaulieu, Nigel Key, Steve Martinez, Alex Melton, Agnes Perez, Katherine Ralston, Hayden Stewart, Shellye Suttles, Stephen Vogel, and Becca B. R. Jablonski. 2015. "Trends in U.S. Local and Regional Food Systems." Washington, D.C.: United States Department of Agriculture.

Lukács, Georg. 1971. *History and Class Consciousness.* Cambridge, Mass.: MIT Press.

Lyson, Thomas. 2004. *Civic Agriculture: Reconnecting Farm, Family and Community.* Lebanon, N.H.: University Press of New England.

Major, Reginald. 1971. *A Panther Is a Black Cat.* New York: William Morrow.

Mandela, Nelson. 1994. *Long Walk to Freedom.* Boston: Little, Brown.

Marable, Manning. 1983. *How Capitalism Underdeveloped Black America: Problems in Race, Political Economy, and Society.* Cambridge, Mass.: South End Press.

Mares, Teresa M., and Devon G. Peña. 2010. "Urban Agriculture in the Making of Insurgent Spaces in Los Angeles and Seattle." In *Insurgent Public Space: Guerrilla Urbanism and the Remaking of Contemporary Cities,* edited by Jeffrey Hou, 241–54. New York: Routledge.

Mares, Teresa Marie, and Alison Hope Alkon. 2011. "Mapping the Food Movement: Addressing Inequality and Neoliberalism." *Environment and Society* 2 (1): 68–86.

Marsden, Terry, and Alex Franklin. 2013. "Replacing Neoliberalism: Theoretical Implications of the Rise of Local Food Movements." *Local Environment* 18 (5): 636–41.

Marshall, Tony F. 1999. *Restorative Justice: An Overview.* London: Home Office.

Martin, Philip. 2003. *Promise Unfulfilled: Unions, Immigration, and the Farm Workers.* Ithaca, N.Y.: Cornell University Press.

Martin, Philip. 2005. "Mexico-US Migration." In *NAFTA Revisited: Achievements and Challenges,* edited by Gary Clyde Hufbauer and Jeffrey J. Schott, 441–66. Washington, D.C.: Institute for International Economics.

Martinez, Konane M., and Anna Hoff Arcela Núñez-Alvarez. 2009. *Coming Out of the Dark: Emergency Preparedness Plan for Farmworkers in San Diego County.* National Latino Research Center, California State University San Marcos.

Martinez, Steve, Michael Hand, Michelle Da Pra, Susan Pollack, Katherine Ralston, Travis Smith, Stephen Vogel, Shellye Clark, Luanne Lohr, Sarah Low, and Constance Newman. 2010. *Local Food Systems: Concepts, Impacts, and Issues.* Economic Research Report 97. Washington, D.C.: United States Department of Agriculture, Economic Research Service.

Maruna, Shadd. 2001. *Making Good: How Ex-Convicts Reform and Rebuild Their Lives.* Washington, D.C.: American Psychological Association.

Maruna, Shadd. 2011. "Reentry as a Rite of Passage." *Punishment & Society* 13 (1): 3–28.

Marx, Karl. 1976a. *Capital,* vol. 1. New York: Vintage.

Marx, Karl. 1976b. *Theses on Feuerbach (Thesis XI).* New York: International Publishers.

Mascaro, Lisa. 2016. "Deportations Revive Rift between Obama and Fellow Democrats." *Los Angeles Times,* January 9. http://www.latimes.com/nation/la-na-obama-deportations-20160108-story.html.

Massey, Doreen. 1994. *Space, Place and Gender.* Cambridge: Polity.

Massey, Douglas S., Jorge Durand, and Nolan J. Malone. 2002. *Beyond Smoke and Mirrors: Mexican Immigration in an Era of Economic Integration*. New York: Russell Sage Foundation.

Massey, Douglas S., and Karen A. Pren. 2012. "Unintended Consequences of US immigration Policy: Explaining the Post-1965 Surge from Latin America." *Population and Development Review* 38 (1): 1–29.

Matier, Phil. 2014. "KPIX 5 Poll: Oakland Residents Say Not Enough Officers but Oppose Higher Parcel Taxes for Police." *CBS SF Bay Area*. http://sanfrancisco.cbslocal.com/2014/05/07/kpix-5-poll-oakland-residents-say-not-enough-officers-but-oppose-higher-parcel-taxes-for-police/.

May, Todd. 2008. *The Political Thought of Jacques Rancière: Creating Equality*. Edinburgh, Scotland: Edinburgh University Press.

Mayer, Brian. 2008. *Blue-Green Coalitions: Fighting for Safe Workplaces and Healthy Communities*. Ithaca, N.Y.: Cornell University Press.

Mayhew, Kelley. 2003. "Life in Vacationland: The 'Other' San Diego." In *Under the Perfect Sun: The San Diego Tourists Never See*, edited by Mike Davis, Kelley Mayhew, and Jim Miller, 271–360. New York: New Press.

McAdam, Doug. 1999. *Political Process and the Development of Black Insurgency, 1930–1970*. 2nd ed. Chicago: University of Chicago Press.

McAdam, Doug, and David A. Snow. 2010. "Social Movements." In *Readings on Social Movements*, edited by Doug McAdam and David A. Snow, 1–8. New York: Oxford University Press.

McClintock, Nathan. 2011. "From Industrial Garden to Food Desert: Demarcated Devaluation in the Flatlands of Oakland, California." In *Cultivating Food Justice, Race, Class, and Sustainability*, edited by Alison Alkon Hope and Julian Agyeman, 89–120. Cambridge, Mass.: MIT Press.

McClintock, Nathan. 2014. "Radical, Reformist, and Garden-Variety Neoliberal: Coming to Terms with Urban Agriculture's Contradictions." *Local Environment* 19 (2): 147–71.

McClintock, Nathan. 2018. "Cultivating (a) Sustainability Capital: Urban Agriculture, Eco-Gentrification, and the Uneven Valorization of Social Reproduction." *Annals of the American Association of Geographers* 108 (2): 579–90.

McCutcheon, Priscilla. 2011. "Community Food Security: For Us, by Us: The Nation of Islam and the Pan African Orthodox Christian Church." In *Cultivating Food Justice: Race, Class, and Sustainability*, edited by Alison Alkon Hope and Julian Agyeman, 177–96. Cambridge, Mass.: MIT Press.

McDonnell, Patrick J. 2009. "Computer 'Raid' in Vernon Leaves Factory Workers Devastated." *Los Angeles Times*, June 12. http://articles.latimes.com/2009/jun/12/local/me-desktop-raid12.

McKay, George. 2011. *Radical Gardening: Politics, Idealism, and Rebellion in the Garden*. London: Frances Lincoln.

McMichael, Philip. 2009. "A Food Regime Genealogy." *Journal of Peasant Studies* 36 (1): 139–69.

McMillan, Tracie. 2016. "Can We Afford to Pay U.S. Farmworkers More?" *National Geographic,* March 31. http://theplate.nationalgeographic.com/2016/03/31/can-we-afford-to-pay-u-s-farmworkers-more/.

McWilliams, Carey. 1939. *Factories in the Field: The Story of Migratory Field Labor in California.* New York: Praeger.

McWilliams, Carey. 1999. *California: The Great Exception.* Berkeley: University of California Press.

Meissner, Doris, Donald M. Kerwin, Muzaffar Chishti, and Claire Bergeron. 2013. *Immigration Enforcement in the United States: The Rise of a Formidable Machinery.* Washington, D.C.: Migration Policy Institute.

Meyer, David S., and Sidney Tarrow. 1998. "A Movement Society: Contentious Politics for a New Century." In *The Social Movement Society: Contentious Politics for a New Century,* edited by David S. Meyer and Sidney G. Tarrow, 1–28, London: Rowman and Littlefield.

Meyer, David S., and Nancy Whittier. 1994. "Social Movement Spillover." *Social Problems* 41 (2): 277–98.

Mies, Maria. 1986. *Patriarchy and Accumulation on a World Scale: Women in the International Division of Labour.* London: Zed Books.

Milkman, Ruth. 2000. *Organizing Immigrants: The Challenge for Unions in Contemporary California.* Ithaca, N.Y.: Cornell University Press.

Milkman, Ruth. 2006. *LA Story: Immigrant Workers and the Future of the US Labor Movement.* New York: Russell Sage Foundation.

Mills, C. Wright. 2000. *The Sociological Imagination.* New York: Oxford University Press.

Minkoff-Zern, Laura-Anne. 2012. "Pushing the Boundaries of Indigeneity and Agricultural Knowledge: Oaxacan Immigrant Gardening in California." *Agriculture and Human Values* 29 (3): 381–92.

Mitchell, Don. 1996. *The Lie of the Land: Migrant Workers and the California Landscape.* Minneapolis: University of Minnesota Press.

Mitchell, Don. 2012. *They Saved the Crops: Labor, Landscape, and the Struggle over Industrial Farming in Bracero-era California.* Athens: University of Georgia Press.

Moberg, David. 2015. "The Union behind the Biggest Campaign against Walmart in History May Be Throwing In the Towel. Why?" *In These Times,* August 11. http://inthesetimes.com/article/18271/which-way-our-walmart.

Mollison, Bill. 1988. *Permaculture: A Designer's Manual.* Sisters Creek, Tasmania: Tagari Publication.

Monmaney, Terence. 2000. "Rampart-Like Scandal Rocks Oakland Justice System, Politics." *Los Angeles Times,* December 11. http://articles.latimes.com/2000/dec/11/news/mn-64091.

Mooney, Patrick H., Keiko Tanaka, and Gabriele Ciciurkaite. 2014. "Food Policy Council Movement in North America: A Convergence of Alternative Local Agrifood Interests?" In *Alternative Agrifood Movements: Patterns of Convergence and Divergence,* edited by Douglas H. Constance, Marie-Christine Renard, and Marta G. Rivera-Ferre, 229–55. Research in Rural Sociology and Development, vol. 21. Bingley, U.K.: Emerald Group.

Mordechay, Kfir. 2011. *FragmentedEconomy, StratifiedSociety, and the ShatteredDream.* Civil Rights Project/Proyecto Derechos Civile.

Mordechay, Kfir. 2014. *Vast Changes and an Uneasy Future: Racial and Regional Inequality in Southern California.* Civil Rights Project/Proyecto Derechos Civile.

Morier, Douglas. 2015. *Rising Food Insecurity in Los Angeles County.* Social Determinants of Health, Issue 3. Los Angeles County Department of Public Health.

Mouffe, Chantal. 2000. *The Democratic Paradox.* New York: Verso.

The Movement for Black Lives. n.d. "Platform." Accessed June 27, 2017. https://policy.m4bl.org/platform/.

Murray, Douglas L. 1982. "The Abolition of El Cortito, the Short-Handled Hoe: A Case Study in Social Conflict and State Policy in California Agriculture." *Social Problems* 30 (1): 26–39.

Myers, Justin Sean, and Joshua Sbicca. 2015. "Bridging Good Food and Good Jobs: From Secession to Confrontation within Alternative Food Movement Politics." *Geoforum* 61: 17–26.

Nabhan, Gary, Maribel Alvarez, Jeffrey Banister, and Regina Fitzsimmons. 2012. *Hungry for Change: Borderlands Food and Water in the Balance.* The Southwest Center's Kellogg Program in Sustainable Food Systems, Tucson, Ariz.

National Employment Law Project. 2012. *The Low-Wage Recovery and Growing Inequality.* New York. http://nelp.3cdn.net/.

National Safety Council. 2017. *Injury Facts®, 2017 Edition.* Itasca, Ill.

Negra, Diane. 2002. "Ethnic Food Fetishism, Whiteness, and Nostalgia in Recent Film and Television." *Velvet Light Trap* 50: 62–76.

Ness, Immanuel. 2010. *Immigrants, Unions, and the New U.S. Labor Market.* Philadelphia: Temple University Press.

Nestle, Marion. 2013. *Food Politics: How the Food Industry Influences Nutrition and Health.* Berkeley: University of California Press.

Nevins, Joseph. 2002. *Operation Gatekeeper: The Rise of the "Illegal Alien" and the Making of the U.S.-Mexico Boundary.* New York: Routledge.

New York Times Editorial Board. 2013. "California's Continuing Prison Crisis." *New York Times,* August 10. http://www.nytimes.com/2013/08/11/opinion/sunday/californias-continuing-prison-crisis.html.

Ngai, Mae M. 2014. *Impossible Subjects: Illegal Aliens and the Making of Modern America*. Princeton, NJ: Princeton University Press.

Nicholls, Walter. 2013. *The DREAMers: How the Undocumented Youth Movement Transformed the Immigrant Rights Debate*. Stanford, Calif.: Stanford University Press.

Nienstedt, John. 2003. "Cross-Border Perceptions." San Diego: KPBS/Competitive Edge Research Poll.

Norrie, Alan. 2010. *Dialectic and Difference: Dialectical Critical Realism and the Grounds of Justice*. New York: Routledge.

The Northeast Sustainable Agriculture Working Group. 2015. "News Release." June 10. http://nesawg.org/.

Obach, Brian Keith. 2004. *Labor and the Environmental Movement: The Quest for Common Ground*. Cambridge, Mass.: MIT Press.

Obach, Brian Keith. 2015. *Organic Struggle: The Movement for Sustainable Agriculture in the United States*. Cambridge, Mass.: MIT Press.

O'Keefe, Ed, and Jonnelle Marte. 2017. "Andrew Puzder Withdraws Labor Nomination, Throwing White House into More Turmoil." *Washington Post*, February 15. https://www.washingtonpost.com/powerpost/now-6-republicans -are-on-the-fence-about-andrew-puzder/2017/02/15/e34cada6-f38b-11e6-8d72 -263470bf0401_story.html?utm_term=.9107e883c238.

Olney, Peter. 2015. "Where Did the OUR Walmart Campaign Go Wrong?" *In These Times*, December 14. http://inthesetimes.com/working/entry/18692 /our-walmart-union-ufcw-black-friday.

Omi, Michael, and Howard Winant. 2014. *Racial Formation in the United States*. 3rd ed. New York: Routledge.

Open Budget Oakland. n.d. "City of Oakland, Adopted Budget 2013–15." Accessed December 11, 2015. http://openbudgetoakland.org/.

Opsal, Tara. 2012. "'Livin' on the Straights': Identity, Desistance, and Work among Women Post-Incarceration." *Sociological Inquiry* 82 (3): 378–403.

Oran, Olivia, and Soyoung Kim. 2013. "Organic Salad Producer Earthbound Farm Prepped for Sale—Sources." Reuters, May 6. https://www.reuters.com /article/earthbound-sale/organic-salad-producer-earthbound-farm-prepped -for-sale-sources-idUSL2N0DK1JX20130506.

Oshinsky, David. M. 1996. *Worse Than Slavery: Parchman Farm and the Ordeal of Jim Crow Justice*. New York: Free Press.

Pachirat, Timothy. 2011. *Every Twelve Seconds: Industrialized Slaughter and the Politics of Sight*. New Haven, Conn.: Yale University Press.

Pager, Devah. 2007. *Marked: Race, Crime, and Finding Work in an Era of Mass Incarceration*. Chicago: University of Chicago Press.

Palmer, Tim. 2015. *US Worker Cooperatives: A State of the Sector*. San Francisco: Democracy at Work Institute.

Park, Lisa Sun-Hee, and David N. Pellow. 2011. *The Slums of Aspen: Immigrants vs. the Environment in America's Eden.* New York: New York University Press.

Passidomo, Catarina. 2014. "Whose Right to (Farm) the City? Race and Food Justice Activism in Post-Katrina New Orleans." *Agriculture and Human Values* 31 (3): 385–96.

Pastor, Manuel. 2015. "How Immigrant Activists Changed L.A." *Dissent,* Winter. https://www.dissentmagazine.org/article/how-immigrant-activists-changed -los-angeles.

Pastor, Manuel, Rhonda Ortiz, Vanessa Carter, Justin Scoggins, and Anthony Perez. 2012. *California Immigrant Integration Scorecard.* Los Angeles: University of Southern California, Center for the Study of Immigrant Integration.

Pathways to Resilience. n.d. Accessed November 23, 2015. http://pathways2 resilience.org/.

Pellow, David Naguib. 2014. *Total Liberation: The Power and Promise of Animal Rights and the Radical Earth Movement.* Minneapolis: University of Minnesota Press.

Penniman, Leah. 2017. "4 Not-So-Easy Ways to Dismantle Racism in the Food System." *YES! Magazine,* April 27. http://www.yesmagazine.org/people -power/4-not-so-easy-ways-to-dismantle-racism-in-the-food-system-20170427.

Petersilia, Joan. 2003. *When Prisoners Come Home: Parole and Prisoner Reentry.* New York: Oxford University Press.

Petersilia, Joan. 2008. "California's Correctional Paradox of Excess and Deprivation." *Crime and Justice* 37 (1): 207–78.

Pew Center on the States. 2011. *State of Recidivism: The Revolving Door of America's Prisons.* Washington, D.C.: Pew Charitable Trusts.

Piven, Frances Fox, and Richard A. Cloward. 1979. *Poor People's Movements: Why They Succeed, How They Fail.* New York: Random House.

Planting Justice. 2014. "Pathways 2 Resilience Rights of Passage Ceremony." http://www.plantingjustice.org/.

Planting Justice. 2016a. "Brothers Out Doing Well." *YouTube.* https://www.you tube.com/watch?v=qDIAFcCUeiU.

Planting Justice. 2016b. "Join Planting Justice to Stand against Deportations." *YouTube.* https://www.youtube.com/watch?v=7T2iZky3PC4.

Planting Justice. n.d. "Grass Roots Canvass Program." Accessed April 13, 2017. http://www.plantingjustice.org/canvass/.

Pollan, Michael. 2008. *In Defense of Food: An Eater's Manifesto.* New York: Penguin.

Pollan, Michael. 2010. "The Food Movement, Rising." *New York Review of Books,* June 10. http://www.nybooks.com/articles/2010/06/10/food-movement -rising/.

Pollan, Michael (michaelpollan). 2014. "Q6 a food policy that make healthy calories more competitive with junk calories contributes mightily to equity. #NFPTalk." Twitter, December 3, 20:35 UTC.

Poppendieck, Janet. 1999. *Sweet Charity? Emergency Food and the End of Entitlement.* New York: Penguin.

Postel, Charles. 2007. *The Populist Vision.* New York: Oxford University Press.

Pothukuchi, Kameshwari, and Jerome L. Kaufman. 1999. "Placing the Food System on the Urban Agenda: The Role of Municipal Institutions in Food Systems Planning." *Agriculture and Human Values* 16 (2): 213–24.

Probyn, Elspeth. 2000. *Carnal Appetites: FoodSexIdentities.* London: Routledge.

Public Policy Institute of California. n.d. "Just the FACTS: Immigrants in California." Accessed March 28, 2017. http://www.ppic.org/.

Pudup, Mary Beth. 2008. "It Takes a Garden: Cultivating Citizen-Subjects in Organized Garden Projects." *Geoforum* 39 (3): 1228–40.

Pulido, Laura. 1996. *Environmentalism and Economic Justice: Two Chicano Struggles in the Southwest.* Tucson: University of Arizona Press.

Pulido, Laura, Ellen Kohl, and Nicole-Marie Cotton. 2016. "State Regulation and Environmental Justice: The Need for Strategy Reassessment." *Capitalism Nature Socialism* 27 (2): 12–31.

Rancière, Jacques. 2001. "Ten Theses on Politics." *Theory & Event* 5 (3).

Rancière, Jacques. 2006. *Hatred of Democracy.* London: Verso.

Rancière, Jacques. 2010. *Dissensus: On Politics and Aesthetics.* London: Continuum.

Reger, Jo, Daniel J. Myers, and Rachel L. Einwohner. 2008. *Identity Work in Social Movements.* Minneapolis: University of Minnesota Press.

Reynolds, Kristin. 2015. "Disparity Despite Diversity: Social Injustice in New York City's Urban Agriculture System." *Antipode* 47 (1): 240–59.

Reynolds, Kristin, and Nevin Cohen. 2016. *Beyond the Kale: Urban Agriculture and Social Justice Activism in New York City.* Athens: University of Georgia Press.

Ribas, Vanesa. 2016. *On the Line: Slaughterhouse Lives and the Making of the New South.* Berkeley: University of California Press.

Robinson, Cedric J. 1983. *Black Marxism: The Making of the Black Radical Tradition.* Chapel Hill: University of North Carolina Press.

Robl, Teri. 2014. "Explanation of Position on Agenda Item 68(b), L.42: Right to Food." United States Mission to the United Nations. http://usun.state.gov/.

Rodman, Sarah O., Colleen L. Barry, Megan L. Clayton, Shannon Frattaroli, Roni A. Neff, and Lainie Rutkow. 2016. "Agricultural Exceptionalism at the State Level: Characterization of Wage and Hour Laws for U.S. Farmworkers." *Journal of Agriculture, Food Systems, and Community Development* 6 (2): 89–110.

Rodriguez, Rodrigo (5RO5). 2014a. "If we don't address the structural racism in the "food movement" then a national food policy is nothing more than rhetoric #NFPtalk." Twitter, December 3, 20:32 UTC.

Rodriguez, Rodrigo (5RO5). 2014b. "I've yet to hear anything about migrant farm workers or land and resource removal in Black, Brown and Indigenous communities #NFPtalk." Twitter, December 3, 20:23 UTC.

Rodriguez, Rodrigo (5RO5). 2014c. "People of color farmers and communities are consistently marginalized in food and farming spaces where their voice is important #NFPtalk." Twitter, December 3, 20:34 UTC.

Rosenfeld, Jake, and Meredith Kleykamp. 2009. "Hispanics and Organized Labor in the United States, 1973 to 2007." *American Sociological Review* 74 (6): 916–37.

Russell-Brown, Katheryn. 2009. *The Color of Crime: Racial Hoaxes, White Fear, Black Protectionism, Police Harassment, and Other Macroaggressions.* 2nd ed. New York: New York University Press.

Saez, Emmanuel, and Gabriel Zucman. 2016. "Wealth Inequality in the United States since 1913: Evidence from Capitalized Income Tax Data." *Quarterly Journal of Economics* 131 (2): 519–78.

Sage, Colin. 2011. *Environment and Food.* New York: Routledge.

Saldivar-Tanaka, Laura, and Marianne E. Krasny. 2004. "Culturing Community Development, Neighborhood Open Space, and Civic Agriculture: The Case of Latino Community Gardens in New York City." *Agriculture and Human Values* 21 (4): 399–412.

San Diego Food System Working Group. 2011. *Final Recommendations of the San Diego Urban-Rural Roundtable: Presented to Supervisor Ron Roberts, County of San Diego, Mayor Jerry Sanders, City of San Diego.* San Francisco: Roots of Change.

San Diego Immigrant Rights Consortium, Justice Overcoming Boundaries of San Diego County, and American Civil Liberties Union of San Diego & Imperial Counties. 2007. *Firestorm: Treatment of Vulnerable Populations during the San Diego Fires.*

San Diego Military Advisory Council. 2014. *7th Annual San Diego Military Economic Impact Study.* San Diego.

San Diego Roots Sustainable Food Project. n.d. "Index." Accessed April 25, 2017. http://www.sandiegoroots.org/index.php.

Sarlin, Benjy. 2013. "How Unions Went from Border Hawks to Immigration Doves." *Talking Points Memo,* January 14. https://talkingpointsmemo.com /dc/how-unions-went-from-border-hawks-to-immigration-doves.

Sbicca, Joshua. 2012. "Growing Food Justice by Planting an Anti-Oppression Foundation: Opportunities and Obstacles for a Budding Social Movement." *Agriculture and Human Values* 29 (4): 455–66.

Sbicca, Joshua. 2014. "The Need to Feed: Urban Metabolic Struggles of Actually Existing Radical Projects." *Critical Sociology* 40 (6): 817–34.

Sbicca, Joshua. 2015a. "Farming While Confronting the Other: The Production and Maintenance of Boundaries in the Borderlands." *Journal of Rural Studies* 39: 1–10.

Sbicca, Joshua. 2015b. "Food Labor, Economic Inequality and the Imperfect Politics of Process in the Alternative Food Movement." *Agriculture and Human Values* 32 (4): 675–87.

Sbicca, Joshua. 2015c. "Solidarity and Sweat Equity: For Reciprocal Food Justice Research." *Journal of Agriculture, Food Systems, and Community Development* 5 (4): 1–5.

Sbicca, Joshua. 2016. "These Bars Can't Hold Us Back: Plowing Incarcerated Geographies with Restorative Food Justice." *Antipode* 48 (5): 1359–79.

Sbicca, Joshua. 2017. "Resetting the Good Food Table: Labor and Food Justice Alliances in Los Angeles." In *The New Food Activism: Opposition, Cooperation and Collective Action*, edited by Alison Hope Alkon and Julie Guthman, 107–32. Berkeley: University of California Press.

Sbicca, Joshua, and Justin Sean Myers. 2017. "Food Justice Racial Projects: Fighting Racial Neoliberalism from the Bay to the Big Apple." *Environmental Sociology* 3 (1): 30–41.

Scherb, Allyson, Anne Palmer, Shannon Frattarolli, and Keshia Pollack. 2012. "Exploring Food System Policy: A Survey of Food Policy Councils in the United States." *Journal of Agriculture, Food Systems and Community Development* 2 (4): 3–14.

Schlosberg, David. 2007. *Defining Environmental Justice: Theories, Movements, and Nature*. New York: Oxford University Press.

Schnaiberg, Allan. 1980. *Environment: From Surplus to Scarcity*. New York: Oxford University Press.

Schneider, Mike. 2015. "Grocery Chains Leave Food Deserts Barren, AP Analysis Finds." Associated Press, December 7. https://apnews.com/8bfc99c7c99 646008acf25e674e378cf.

Schurman, Rachel, and William A. Munro. 2010. *Fighting for the Future of Food: Activists versus Agribusiness in the Struggle over Biotechnology*. Minneapolis: University of Minnesota Press.

Self, Robert O. 2005. *American Babylon: Race and the Struggle for Postwar Oakland*. Princeton, N.J.: Princeton University Press.

Shabazz, Rashad. 2015. *Spatializing Blackness: Architectures of Confinement and Black Masculinity in Chicago*. Urbana: University of Illinois Press.

Short, Anne, Julie Guthman, and Samuel Raskin. 2007. "Food Deserts, Oases, or Mirages? Small Markets and Community Food Security in the San Francisco Bay Area." *Journal of Planning Education and Research* 26 (3): 352–64.

Sinclair, Upton. 1906. *The Jungle*. New York: Doubleday, Jabber.

Sipchen, Bob. 1997. "Labor of Love." *Los Angeles Times,* March 9. http://articles .latimes.com/1997-03-09/news/ls-36265_1_labor-movement.

Sitrin, Marina, and Dario Azzellini. 2014. *They Can't Represent Us! Reinventing Democracy from Greece to Occupy*. London: Verso.

Slocum, Rachel. 2007. "Whiteness, Space and Alternative Food Practice." *Geoforum* 38 (3): 520–33.

Slocum, Rachel, and Kirsten Valentine Cadieux. 2015. "Notes on the Practice of Food Justice in the US: Understanding and Confronting Trauma and Inequity." *Journal of Political Ecology* 22: 27–52.

Smil, Vaclav. 2001. *Enriching the Earth: Fritz Haber, Carl Bosch, and the Transformation of World Food Production*. Cambridge, Mass.: MIT Press.

Snow, David A., E. Burke Rochford Jr., Steven K. Worden, and Robert D. Benford. 1986. "Frame Alignment Processes, Micromobilization, and Movement Participation." *American Sociological Review* 51 (4): 464–81.

Snow, David A., Louis A. Zurcher Jr., and Sheldon Ekland-Olson. 1980. "Social Networks and Social Movements: A Microstructural Approach to Differential Recruitment." *American Sociological Review* 45 (5): 787–801.

Sobal, Jeffery. 2008. "Sociological Analysis of the Stigmatisation of Obesity." In *A Sociology of Food and Nutrition: Introducing the Social Appetite,* edited by J. Germov and L. William, 381–400. 3rd ed. Melbourne: Oxford University Press.

Söderback, Ingrid, Marianne Söderström, and Elisabeth Schälander. 2004. "Horticultural Therapy: The 'Healing Garden' and Gardening in Rehabilitation Measures at Danderyd Hospital Rehabilitation Clinic, Sweden." *Pediatric Rehabilitation* 7 (4): 245–60.

Solomon, Amy L., Kelly Dedel Johnson, Jeremy Travis, and Elizabeth C. McBride. 2004. *From Prison to Work: The Employment Dimensions of Prisoner Reentry*. Washington, D.C.: Urban Institute Press.

Spener, David. 2009. *Clandestine Crossings: Migrants and Coyotes on the Texas-Mexico Border*. Ithaca, N.Y.: Cornell University Press.

Starr, Amory, Luis A. Fernandez, and Christian Scholl. 2011. *Shutting Down the Streets: Political Violence and Social Control in the Global Era*. New York: New York University Press.

Statista. n.d. "Market Share of the Leading Grocery Retailers in the United States in 2014." Accessed June 8, 2016. http://www.statista.com/.

Szasz, Andrew. 2007. *Shopping Our Way to Safety: How We Changed from Protecting the Environment to Protecting Ourselves*. Minneapolis: University of Minnesota Press.

Sze, Julie. 2007. *Noxious New York: The Racial Politics of Urban Health and Environmental Justice*. Cambridge, Mass.: MIT Press.

Tarrow, Sidney. 2011. *Power in Movement: Social Movements and Contentious Politics.* 3rd ed. New York: Cambridge University Press.

Tattersall, Amanda. 2010. *Power in Coalition: Strategies for Strong Unions and Social Change.* Ithaca, N.Y.: Cornell University Press.

Taylor, Dorceta E. 2000. "The Rise of the Environmental Justice Paradigm: Injustice Framing and the Social Construction of Environmental Discourses." *American Behavioral Scientist* 43 (4): 508–80.

Taylor, Dorceta E. 2009. *The Environment and the People in American Cities, 1600s–1900s: Disorder, Inequality, and Social Change.* Durham, N.C.: Duke University Press.

Taylor, G. Flint. 2013. "How the FBI Conspired to Destroy the Black Panther Party." *In These Times,* December 4. http://inthesetimes.com/article/15949/how_the_fbi_conspired_to_destroy_the_black_panther_party.

Taylor, John R., and Sarah Taylor Lovell. 2014. "Urban Home Food Gardens in the Global North: Research Traditions and Future Directions." *Agriculture and Human Values* 31 (2): 285–305.

Taylor, Verta. 1989. "Social Movement Continuity: The Women's Movement in Abeyance." *American Sociological Review* 54 (5): 761–75.

Terriquez, Veronica. 2015. "Intersectional Mobilization, Social Movement Spillover, and Queer Youth Leadership in the Immigrant Rights Movement." *Social Problems* 62 (3): 343–62.

Thomas, Pandora, and Starhawk. n.d. *Solidarity Statement from the Permaculture Community.* Black Permaculture Network. Accessed April 14, 2017. http://blackpermaculturenetwork.org/solidarity-statement/.

Tilly, Charles. 2005. *Identities, Boundaries, and Social Ties.* Boulder, Colo.: Paradigm.

Tomassetti, Julia, Chris Tilly, and Ben Zipperer. 2012. *The State of the Unions in 2012: A Profile of Union Membership in Los Angeles, California, and the Nation.* Los Angeles: UCLA Institute for Research on Labor and Employment.

Travis, Jeremy. 2005. *But They All Come Back: Facing the Challenges of Prisoner Reentry.* Washington, D.C.: Urban Institute Press.

Trioni, Gino. 2012. "Navy Awards $377M in IDIQs for Surveillance Tech R&D." *GovConWire,* February 9. http://www.govconwire.com/2012/02/navy-awards-377m-in-idiqs-for-surveillance-tech-rd/.

Ture, Kwame, and Charles V. Hamilton. 1992. *Black Power: The Politics of Liberation in America.* New York: Vintage Books.

Uggen, Christopher. 1999. "Ex-Offenders and the Conformist Alternative: A Job Quality Model of Work and Crime." *Social Problems* 46 (1): 127–151.

Uggen, Christopher, Jeff Manza, and Angela Behrens. 2004. "'Less Than the Average Citizen': Stigma, Role Transition and the Civic Reintegration of

Convicted Felons." In *After Crime and Punishment: Pathways to Offender Reintegration,* edited by Shadd Maruna and Russ Immarigeon, 261–93. Devon, U.K.: Willan.

Union Facts. n.d. "United Food & Commercial Workers, Local 770." Accessed April 26, 2017. https://www.unionfacts.com/.

United Food and Commercial Workers. 2013. "UFCW Activists Arrested at Massive Immigration March." http://www.ufcw.org/2013/10/09/ufcw-activists -arrested-at-massive-immigration-march/.

United Food and Commercial Workers. 2015. "UFCW Members at El Super Strike in Protest against the Company's Unfair Labor Practices." http:// forlocals.ufcw.org/2015/12/01/ufcw-members-at-el-super-strike-in-protest -against-the-companys-unfair-labor-practices/.

United Food and Commercial Workers. 2016. "El Super Reports 5th Consecutive Quarter with a Decline in Customer Traffic since Start of Union Initiated Consumer Boycott." http://www.ufcw.org/2016/05/03/el-super-sales-decline-for -the-5th-consecutive-quarter-since-start-of-ufcw-initiated-consumer-boycott/.

United Food and Commercial Workers Local 770. 2015. "Complaints against Multinational Supermarket Chain a Test of Labor Protections in International Trade Agreements." Press release, November 12. https://www.commondreams .org/newswire/2015/11/12/complaints-against-multinational-supermarket -chain-test-labor-protections.

Usheroff, Marni. 2014. "Ethnic Stores Are 'New Frontier' in Grocery-Labor Battles." *Orange County Register,* February 7. https://www.ocregister.com /2014/02/07/ethnic-stores-are-new-frontier-in-grocery-labor-battles/.

Van Deburg, William L. 1992. *New Day in Babylon: The Black Power Movement and American Culture, 1965–1975.* Chicago: University of Chicago Press.

Van Dyke, Nella. 2003. "Crossing Movement Boundaries: Factors That Facilitate Coalition Protest by American College Students, 1930–1990." *Social Problems* 50 (2): 226–50.

Van Hoven, Bettina, and David Sibley. 2008. "'Just Duck': The Role of Vision in the Production of Prison Spaces." *Environment and Planning. D, Society and Space* 26 (6): 1001–17.

Vasquez, Maria. 2015. "'No One Has Ever Tried This Before': Mexican, U.S. Workers Bring Employer Charges under NAFTA." *In These Times,* December 9. http://inthesetimes.com/working/entry/18661/no_one_has_ever_tried_this _before_mexican_u.s._workers_bring_employer_charg.

Vongkiatkajorn, Kanyakrit. 2016. "Inmates Are Kicking Off a Nationwide Prison Strike Today." *Mother Jones,* September 9. https://www.mother jones.com/politics/2016/09/national-prison-strike-inmates/.

Wacquant, Loïc. 2009. *Punishing the Poor: The Neoliberal Government of Social Insecurity.* Durham, N.C.: Duke University Press.

Wagner-Pacifici, Robin. 1994. *Discourse and Destruction: The City of Philadelphia versus MOVE.* Chicago: University of Chicago Press.

Wakefield, Sara, and Christopher Uggen. 2010. "Incarceration and Stratification." *Annual Review of Sociology* 36: 387–406.

Walgrave, Lode. 2013. *Restorative Justice, Self-interest and Responsible Citizenship.* New York: Routledge.

Walker, Richard. 2004. *The Conquest of Bread: 150 Years of California Agribusiness.* New York: New Press.

The Walmart 1%. n.d. "The Walton Family: America's New Robber Barons." Accessed December 15, 2015. http://walmart1percent.org/how-rich-are-the -waltons/.

Warehouse Workers United and Deogracia Cornelio. 2011. *Shattered Dreams and Broken Bodies: A Brief Review of the Inland Empire Warehouse Industry.* Los Angeles.

Washington Post Staff. 2015. "Full Text: Donald Trump Announces a Presidential Bid." *Washington Post,* June 16. https://www.washingtonpost.com/news /post-politics/wp/2015/06/16/full-text-donald-trump-announces-a-presidential -bid/?utm_term=.a5c53c740b0b.

Watson, Jesse. 2016. "Decolonizing Permaculture." *Resilience,* February 19. http://www.resilience.org/stories/2016-02-19/decolonizing-permaculture/.

Wattenhofer, Jeff. 2016. "Chinatown's Much-Hated Walmart Closing after Just Two Years." *Los Angeles Curbed,* January 19. https://la.curbed.com /2016/1/19/10845470/chinatowns-controversial-walmart-neighborhood-market -is-no-more.

Watts, Julie R. 2002. *Immigration Policy and the Challenge of Globalization.* Ithaca, N.Y.: Cornell University Press.

Weiler, Anelyse M., Gerardo Otero, and Hannah Wittman. 2016. "Rock Stars and Bad Apples: Moral Economies of Alternative Food Networks and Precarious Farm Work Regimes." *Antipode* 48 (4): 1140–62.

White, Monica M. 2011. "D-Town Farm: African American Resistance to Food Insecurity and the Transformation of Detroit." *Environmental Practice* 13 (4): 406–17.

White, Monica M. 2017. "'A Pig and a Garden': Fannie Lou Hamer and the Freedom Farms Cooperative." Food and Foodways 25 (1): 20–39.

White, Rob, and Hannah Graham. 2015. "Greening Justice: Examining the Interfaces of Criminal, Social and Ecological Justice." *British Journal of Criminology* 55 (5): 845–65.

Wilson, Christopher E., and Erik Lee. 2013. *The State of the Border Report: A Comprehensive Analysis of the U.S.-Mexico Border.* Washington, D.C.: Mexico Institute at Woodrow Wilson International Center for Scholars.

Winders, Bill. 2009. *The Politics of Food Supply: U.S. Agricultural Policy in the World Economy.* New Haven, Conn.: Yale University Press.

Winne, Mark. 2010. *Food Rebels, Guerrilla Gardeners, and Smart-Cookin' Mamas: Fighting Back in an Age of Industrial Agriculture*. Boston: Beacon Press.

WKKF (WK_Kellogg_Fdn). 2014. "MT @foodchainworker: #NFPtalk for 1st time food mvm't is working as 1: health, environment, agriculture & labor for a real food revolution." Twitter, December 3, 20:25 UTC.

Woods, Tryon. 2006. *Focus: Oakland Policing Survey*. People United for a Better Oakland (PUEBLO). Oakland, Calif.

Worster, Donald. 2004. *Dust Bowl: The Southern Plains in the 1930s*. New York: Oxford University Press.

Wright, Erik Olin. 2010. *Envisioning Real Utopias*. London: Verso.

Wright, Martin. 1996. *Justice for Victims and Offenders: A Restorative Response to Crime*. 2nd ed. Winchester, U.K.: Waterside Press.

Wright Edelman, Marian. 2017. "'Why America May Go to Hell' Still Holds Water 50 Years Later." *Pittsburgh Courier*, April 17. https://newpittsburghcou rieronline.com/2017/04/17/why-america-may-go-to-hell-still-holds-water-50 -years-later/.

Xu, Wan. 2014. "South LA Residents Shop for Employment at Juanita Tate Marketplace." *Intersections South LA*, April 23. http://intersectionssouthla.org /story/south-la-residents-shop-for-employment-at-juanita-tate-marketplace/.

Yosso, Tara J. 2005. "Whose Culture Has Capital? A Critical Race Theory Discussion of Community Cultural Wealth." *Race Ethnicity and Education* 8 (1): 69–91.

Young, Iris Marion. 2000. *Inclusion and Democracy*. Oxford: Oxford University Press.

Zakaria, Fareed. 2012. "Zakaria: Incarceration Nation." *CNN*, March 22. http:// globalpublicsquare.blogs.cnn.com/2012/03/22/ zakaria-incarceration-nation/.

Zehr, Howard. 1990. *Changing Lenses: A New Focus for Criminal Justice*. Scottdale, Pa.: Herald Press.

Žižek, Slavoj. 1999. *The Ticklish Subject: The Absent Centre of Political Ontology*. London: Verso.

Index

Page numbers in italic refer to figures.

262 · INDEX

JOSHUA SBICCA is assistant professor of sociology at Colorado State University.

9 781517 904012